# Samuel Johnson
# AMONG THE
# MODERNISTS

EDITED BY **ANTHONY W. LEE**

# Samuel Johnson
# AMONG THE MODERNISTS

EDITED BY **ANTHONY W. LEE**

CLEMSON UNIVERSITY PRESS

First Edition, 2019
Paperback Edition, 2022

ISBN: 978-1-942954-66-8 (print)
ISBN: 978-1-80207-028-6 (paperback)
eISBN: 978-1-942954-67-5 (e-book)

Published by Clemson University Press
in association with Liverpool University Press

For information about Clemson University Press,
please visit our website at www.clemson.edu/press.

Library of Congress Cataloging-in-Publication Data
Names: Lee, Anthony W., editor.
Title: Samuel Johnson among the modernists / edited by Anthony W. Lee.
Description: First edition. | Clemson, SC : Clemson University Press, [2019]
| Includes bibliographical references and index.
Identifiers: LCCN 2018047988 (print) | LCCN 2018059059 (ebook) |
ISBN 9781942954675 (e-book) | ISBN 9781942954668 (print)
Subjects: LCSH: Johnson, Samuel, 1709-1784--Criticism and interpretation. |
Modernism (Literature)--History and criticism.
Classification: LCC PR3537.M57 (ebook) | LCC PR3537.M57 S26 2019 (print) |
DDC 828/.609--dc23
LC record available at https://lccn.loc.gov/2018047988

Typeset in Minion Pro by Carnegie Book Production.

# Contents

Acknowledgments     vii

Short Titles     ix

Abbreviations     xi

Introduction: Modernity Johnson?     1
     *Anthony W. Lee*

1   Johnson, T. S. Eliot, and the City     21
     *Melvyn New*

2   "Saint Samuel of Fleet Street": Johnson and Woolf     41
     *Anthony W. Lee*

3   "Intellectually 'Fuori del Mondo'": Pound's Johnson     69
     *Joe Moffett*

4   The Antinomies of Progress: Johnson, Conrad, Joyce     85
     *Clement Hawes*

5   Johnson Goes to War     115
     *Jack Lynch*

6   Samuel Beckett and Samuel Johnson: Like-minded Masters of
Life's Limitations     133
     *Thomas M. Curley*

7   The "Plexed Artistry" of Nabokov and Johnson          165
        *Carrie D. Shanafelt*

8   Johnson and Borges: Some Reflections                  189
        *Greg Clingham*

9   Ernest Borneman's *Tomorrow Is Now* (1959): Thoughts about
    a Lost Novel, with Glances toward Samuel Johnson and other
    Modernists                                            213
        *Robert G. Walker*

Notes                                                     239

Contributors                                              279

Index                                                     283

# Acknowledgments

The seeds of this volume were planted during a visit to the booksellers' venue at the 2017 NEMLA conference in Baltimore, where I met John Morgenstern, Director and Executive Editor of the Clemson University Press. I mentioned a "Samuel Johnson and Cultural Capital" panel I had organized for an EC/ASECS meeting later that year. As we talked, my ideas about the session began to evolve toward a more specific focus, that of Johnson and Modernism. John was immediately enthusiastic about the possibility of expanding my notion into a book. I am grateful for this initial enthusiasm as well as his unfailingly kind and helpful assistance throughout the process. Alison Mero, Managing Editor of the Press, was similarly kind and helpful. I also wish to thank all the contributors to the present collection for their hard work and kindness in making the book possible. Christine Jackson-Holzberg was an indispensable support in many ways.

The image used for the cover, the downward view of a staircase in Johnson's house at 17 Gough Square—his residence during his most productive literary period, the 1750s—is used by the kind permission of Dr Johnson's House, London. The image of the Dreadnought Hoax is used by kind permission of the National Portrait Gallery, London.

Finally, I dedicate my labors in bringing this book out to Richard Schumaker, a colleague and friend for many years. His friendship has been both life-affirming and a ceaseless source of intellectual stimulation.

It was his gift of a copy of Joyce's *Portrait* that re-sparked an interest in Modernism that had fallen into dormancy since its original kindling from my undergraduate days. I'd like to thank him for that, and much else.

# Short Titles

*Dictionary*—Samuel Johnson. *A Dictionary of the English Language*. 2 vols. London, 1755.

*JM*—G. B. Hill. *Johnsonian Miscellanies*. 2 vols. Oxford, 1897; reprinted New York: Barnes and Noble, 1966.

*Journey*— J. D. Fleeman, ed. *A Journey to the Western Isles of Scotland*. Oxford: Clarendon Press, 1985.

*Boswell's Life*—James Boswell. *The Life of Samuel Johnson, LL.D.* Edited by G. B. Hill, revised by L. F. Powell. 6 vols. Oxford: Clarendon Press, 1934–1964.

*Lives*—Samuel Johnson. *The Lives of the Most Eminent English Poets: With Critical Observations on Their Works*. Edited by Roger Lonsdale. 4 vols. Oxford: Oxford University Press, 2006.

*Letters*—*The Letters of Samuel Johnson*. Edited by Bruce Redford. 5 vols. Princeton: Princeton University Press, 1992–1994.

*Poems*—*The Poems of Samuel Johnson*. Edited by David Nichol Smith, Edward L. McAdam [and J. D. Fleeman]. 2nd ed. Oxford: Clarendon Press, 1974.

Yale *Works*—*The Yale Edition of the Works of Samuel Johnson*. General Editor Robert DeMaria, Jr. 23 vols. New Haven: Yale University Press, 1958–2018.

Short Titles

# Abbreviations

| | |
|---|---|
| *AJ* | *The Age of Johnson: A Scholarly Annual* |
| *BCP* | *Book of Common Prayer* |
| *ECS* | *Eighteenth-Century Studies* |
| *ELH* | *English Literary History* |
| *JNL* | *Johnsonian News Letter* |
| *MLN* | *Modern Language Notes* |
| *MP* | *Modern Philology* |
| *OED* | *Oxford English Dictionary* |
| *PMLA* | *Publications of the Modern Language Association* |
| *RES* | *Review of English Studies* |
| *SEL* | *Studies in English Literature* |
| *TLS* | *Times Literary Supplement* |

# Introduction: Modernity Johnson?

*Anthony W. Lee*

## I. Entrée

The traditional view of Samuel Johnson has been that of a quaintly nostalgic figure redolent of days long past, or that of a narrowly bigoted High Anglican Tory, insular and xenophobic, resistant to innovation and experimentation. Many mid-twentieth-century scholars and critics worked indefatigably to undermine the simplicity of the stereotype; in the process, they have enriched our understanding of this complex human being and inexhaustibly fecund writer.[1] However, perhaps just enough of the old stereotypes linger to make the claim of Johnson as a representative of modernity, one who has significant and enduring connections with such Modernists as Virginia Woolf and Samuel Beckett, seem idiosyncratic, if not downright wrong-headed. But the time has come to adjust our notion of Johnson through the prisms of Modernism and modernity.

The first maneuver substantiating this contention must consist in trying to establish what we mean by Modernism. Forty or fifty years ago, this would have been a fairly simple procedure. In the 1960s and 1970s, most teachers and critics in the academy identified Modernism with an elite cadre of white (and largely male) creative writers flourishing from around the turn of the century roughly up to World War II. And there is a kernel of validity to this. Such figures as Joyce, Eliot,

Pound, and Yeats redefined the terms of European literature by instituting an alternative to nineteenth-century traditions of realism and compositional convention. They initiated radical experimentation and established an avant-garde movement that worked to creatively deform and reinvigorate inherited genres, modes, and expectations. However, this conveniently tidy picture has been disrupted by challenges in recent decades that question the Eurocentric and masculine biases embedded in it, extending the concept to include signal feminine and global contributions.[2] In 2017, the *Routledge Encyclopedia of Modernism*, an online project presenting materials from nearly twenty different global cultures and regions, was published.[3] Its chronological scope encompasses the nineteenth century to the present day and includes entries ranging from the can-can to Petrushka, the Shinkankakuha of Japan to William S. Burroughs, Charles Mingus to Thomas Adès. Such dazzling diversity, however, flirts with the danger of stretching the concept to an almost all-inclusive inanity. While honoring the noble generosity underlying such expansions, the present volume strategically restricts its focus primarily to the Anglo-American Modernist tradition that coheres most naturally around the target figure here, Samuel Johnson.[4]

## II. Johnson's Modernity

Before examining Johnson's possible alignments with Modernism, we first need to explore the larger topic of Johnson and modernity.[5] His 1755 *Dictionary of the English Language* offers an initial point of departure. Under "modern" (adj.) the first definition is, "late; recent; not ancient; not antique," followed by this illustrative quotation:

> Some of the ancient, and likewise divers of the *modern* writers, that have laboured in natural magick, have noted a sympathy between the sun and certain herbs.
>
> Bacon.[6]

Under the noun definition, "those who have lived lately, opposed to the ancients," he appends:

Some by old words to fame have made pretence;
Ancients in phrase, mere *moderns* in their sense!

Pope.[7]

The cultural referent indirectly underlying Johnson's inclusion of these entries is the so-called *Querelle des Anciens et des Modernes*. This first developed in France in the seventeenth century and erupted in England during the fray over Phalaris between Sir William Temple and Richard Bentley in the 1690s.[8] In a very real sense, the "Battel of the Books" (Jonathan Swift's coinage) marks the emergence of literary modernity in European culture, the attempt to shrug off the yoke of antiquity that had helped creatively shape Renaissance culture, but which was now found by many to be constrictive and oppressive. Johnson's attitude toward this development cannot be directly determined by the textual evidence that we have. He refers to it twice, once in the "Life of William King" and later in the "Life of Swift." While he dismisses Swift's "digressions relating Wotton and Bentley" as exhibiting either "want of knowledge, or want of integrity," his attitude may indicate as much his characteristic dislike of Swift rather than his advocacy of the two champions of the moderns.[9] His indirect references to the notion tend to be even-handed as well.[10]

More telling is his critical mistrust of literary imitation. For example, in *Adventurer* 84 he rejects the "servility of imitation," while in *Rasselas* he proclaims that "no man was ever great by imitation"; in the "Life of Milton" he states that "the highest praise of genius is original invention" and values the writer who, like Milton, "was naturally a thinker for himself, confident of his own abilities and disdainful of help or hindrance."[11] Originality, or the emphasis placed upon individually expressive creative genius, is a trait not typically associated with the neoclassical Augustan literary mode that Johnson often reflects, yet his embrace of it suggests a literary temperament more sympathetic with both Romanticism and Modernism.

Viewed retrospectively, Johnson emerges as a compellingly modern figure. We can trace this aspect most cogently by looking at a handful of issues that suggests that he is in many respects refreshingly *au courant*— at least for a man born more than two and a half centuries ago. Take, for example, his literary criticism—the early champion of Modernism F. R. Leavis described it as "alive and life-giving"[12]—which at times exhibits a very modern sensibility. One of the most frequently quoted slogans of Modernism is Ezra Pound's imperative "make it new." Johnson was not a neoclassic critic in the sense of a Boileau or a Malherbe—or even a Dryden or an Addison—but nonetheless he imbibed from the neoclassic fount and redirected what rivulets he found serviceable into the crafting of his own critical and literary voice and identity. Put another way, Johnson took the materials of his cultural heritage and made them new—fresh, novel, and relevant—to his contemporary audience, but also in ways that, like Joyce's *Ulysses*, continue to resonate with modern readers.

The nimble empiricist base and supple rationality of Johnson's criticism are compatible with the expectations of the modern reader, especially when compared with the doctrinaire heaviness of such immediate predecessors as John Dennis and Thomas Rymer. But more importantly for our purposes, Johnson practices the kind of hard-nosed, textually oriented approach to texts associated with I. A. Richards and William Empson. A discrete example of this may be found in *Idler* 60, where Johnson, in the voice of the character Dick Minim, analyzes a passage from Samuel Butler's *Hudibras*:

> The wonderful lines upon honour and a bubble have hitherto passed without notice.
>> Honour is like the glassy bubble,
>> Which costs philosophers such trouble,
>> Where one part crack'd, the whole does fly,
>> And wits are crack'd to find out why.
> In these verses, says Minim, we have two striking accommodations of the sound to the sense. It is impossible to utter the two lines emphatically without an act like that which they describe; "bubble" and "trouble" causing a momentary inflation of the cheeks by the retention of the breath, which is afterwards forcibly emitted, as in the practice of "blowing bubbles." But the greatest excellence is in the third line, which is "crack'd in the middle to express a crack, and then shivers into monosyllables." (Yale *Works*, 2:189)

Johnson's intent here is to ridicule Minim for being a small critic (cf. the Latin root, "minimus," "creature of the smallest size; a small or insignificant creature," OED); hence, the ludicrous image of a mouth contorting to blow bubbles. However, the observation of the final cracked line shivering into monosyllables is fine—genuinely of the "greatest excellence"—and anticipates the methodologies of the New Criticism and other twentieth-century formalisms that form an important element in literary Modernism.[13] As we see in this instance, Johnson's stature as a close reader of poetry is formidable.[14]

Johnson's attitudes toward female education, slavery, and colonialism have long been recognized for their progressiveness. He championed the notion of women as being intellectually equivalent to men; he declaimed against the patriarchal mistreatment of women forced into unhappy marriages and prostitution; he promoted the concept of women as public intellectuals; he supported their writings and spent time with them in serious intellectual conversation.[15] While it would be a mistake to claim him as a feminist,[16] he possessed, when compared with the vast majority of his male (and many female) contemporaries, a clear-eyed grasp of the harsh limitations imposed by a society based upon patriarchal premises.

Johnson's fierce hatred of slavery—to say nothing about his far-sighted advocacy of native American rights—marked him off from many of his contemporaries (including his most famous biographer, James Boswell).[17] His vehement rejection of imperial rapaciousness—expressed heatedly and courageously in his Literary Magazine, just as Britain began waging the Seven Years' War (or the Great War for Empire, as it is sometimes called)—is an indisputable mark of a mind able to look past local prejudices and take the long view that would be verified by history. As Clement Hawes has previously observed, when comparing Johnson with one of his more vociferous Victorian detractors, with respect to his attitude toward non-European people and cultures "it is he [Johnson], rather than the relentlessly progress-oriented Macaulay, whose work now seems prescient and anticipatory."[18]

Perhaps the decisive impetus to the development of cultural modernity—the one that mostly distinctly differentiates the modern period from the classical and medieval eras—was the impact of science and technology. Beginning in the seventeenth century, the age of Descartes and Newton, the instrumental rationality—i.e., the rigorous application of human reason to the self-interested subjugation and exploitation of nature—championed by Bacon became *the* operative force in fundamentally transforming European society (and by extension, over time, that of the entire globe), entailing consequences that we are still grappling with today. Johnson's embrace of this historical development is remarkably forward-looking. He was fascinated by electricity, and he delighted in conducting chemical experiments. His writings have been shown to be thoroughly impregnated with "philosophick words" or the language of science.[19] He took an active interest in the practical application of technology to daily life, as seen, for example, in his support of Lewis Paul's cotton-spinning machine, and he astounded his hosts during a tour of the island of Skye by providing "an account of the whole process of tanning."[20] In fact, the overall thought process shaping his travel book, *A Journey to the Western Islands of Scotland* (1775), is frequently scientific in orientation and inductive in approach, ensuring a careful and comprehensive inquiry into human life and society in the Hebrides.

In all of the ways detailed here and more, Johnson must be seen as no hide-bound reactionary figure clinging desperately to a vanishing past: he is rather a writer and thinker who offers a sympathetic and often enthusiastic acceptance of modernity. Nonetheless, in fairness it must also be acknowledged that in some important respects he resists modernity—at least as seen from our present perch—most especially, perhaps, in politics and religion. He is not a card-carrying member of the eighteenth-century Enlightenment that is often associated with modernity, and his feelings about its two greatest contemporary exponents in Britain, David Hume and Edward Gibbon, were far from complimentary.[21] His staunch support of the High Anglican Church would seem to place him firmly in opposition to the secularizing tendencies often seen as characteristic of modernity.

Yet even this last statement requires qualification. Johnson was theoretically an untiring advocate for the Church, yet, in practice he was at times rather lax. As Virginia Woolf's father noted:

> Johnson, as we know him, was a man of the world ... . He represents the secular rather than the ecclesiastical type. So far as his teaching goes, he is rather a disciple of Socrates than of St. Paul

or Wesley. According to him, a "tavern chair" was "the throne of human felicity," and supplied a better arena than the pulpit for the utterance of his message to mankind.[22]

An anecdote that Boswell recorded in his journal reinforces this view:

> Beauclerk said Johnson did not practise religion. He seldom went to church. He was with him three Sundays at [Windsor], and never once went. One Sunday he went and lay on a tombstone in the churchyard, and was in that posture when the people came out of church. Beauclerk said to him he was like Hogarth's Idle Apprentice.[23]

From this perspective, Johnson seems rather more at home in the Enlightenment's public sphere of coffee-house culture rather than an example of "the ecclesiastical type." Even without these qualifications, many of the things often said regarding Johnson's politics and religion may be said also of T. S. Eliot, one of the classic instantiations of Anglo-American High Modernism. This sort of mingling speaks to the complexity of modernity and the Modernist responses to it themselves—responses that could be wildly enthusiastic or warily suspicious of the great political and economic transformations preceding the early twentieth century. Johnson's own temperamental and intellectual complexity thus may be said to cohere importantly with many of the figures we associate with the Modernist phenomena.

As Leslie Stephen noted, Johnson typically prioritizes the urban setting in ways not dissimilar to Modernism's attraction to the city. If not an outright *flâneur*, he is persistently associated with London to the point that it has become part of his identity: "When a man is tired of London, he is tired of life; for there is in London all that life can afford" (*Boswell's Life*, 3:178). He was a curious traveler to other capitals as well—Edinburgh and Paris, for example—and he would have visited the great cities of Italy had not his aspirations been foiled by adverse circumstances.[24] Yet, his enthusiasm for urban life should not occlude the more unsavory elements he discerned within it. See, for example, his description of one entering London for the first time:

[A]n inhabitant of the remoter parts of the kingdom is immediately distinguished by a kind of dissipated curiosity, a busy
endeavour to divide his attention amongst a thousand objects,
and a wild confusion of astonishment and alarm.
The attention of a new-comer is generally first struck by the
multiplicity of cries that stun him in the streets, and the variety
of merchandise and manufactures which the shopkeepers expose
on every hand…. (*Adventurer* 67; Yale *Works*, 2:384)

His epic simile from *Rambler* 14 offers an implied description of the
British capital:

A transition from an author's books to his conversation, is too
often like an entrance into a large city, after a distant prospect.
Remotely, we see nothing but spires of temples, and turrets of
palaces, and imagine it the residence of splendor, grandeur,
and magnificence; but when we have passed the gates, we find
it perplexed with narrow passages, disgraced with despicable
cottages, embarrassed with obstructions, and clouded with
smoke.[25]

The smells of pollution, the shrill cries invading the ear, the disorienta-
tion induced by visual congestion—all conspire to produce a repulsion
that later writers will dilate upon in their depictions of an alienated
urban modernity. But the seeds for such alienation are already implicit
in Johnson, whether in his frenetic cityscapes or in his depiction of the
degradations imposed by a society increasingly governed by principles of
transactional exploitation.[26]

We see the latter in the plight of his character Misella, who, reduced
by adversity to hunger, despair, and prostitution, is

[D]riven again into the streets, I lived upon the least that could
support me, and at night accommodated myself under pent-
houses as well as I could. At length I became absolutely pennyless
… having strolled all day without sustenance.

> In this abject state I have now passed four years, the drudge of
> extortion and the sport of drunkenness; sometimes the property
> of one man, and sometimes the common prey of accidental lewd-
> ness; at one time tricked up for sale by the mistress of a brothel,
> at another begging in the streets to be relieved from hunger by
> wickedness; without any hope in the day … .[27]

Johnson's deeply empathic depiction of Misella's psychic dissociation
from her environment, his protest against the inhuman degradation of
the vulnerable female, eloquently collapses into an expository vignette
arousing concerns that will be taken up with greater degrees of specificity
and intensity by such later writers as Mina Loy, Djuna Barnes, and Zora
Neale Hurston.

To this example might be added his vivid description of urban squalor
found in the 1744 *Life of Savage*:

> He [Richard Savage] lodged as much by Accident as he dined,
> and passed the Night sometimes in mean Houses, which are set
> open at Night to any casual Wanderers, sometimes in Cellars,
> among the Riot and Filth of the meanest and most profligate of
> the Rabble; and sometimes, when he had no Money to support
> even the Expences of these Receptacles, walked about the Streets
> till he was weary, and lay down in the Summer upon a Bulk, or
> in the winter, with his Associates in Poverty, among the Ashes of
> a Glass-house.
>
> In this Manner were passed those Days and those Nights,
> which Nature had enabled him to have employed in elevated
> Speculations, useful Studies, or pleasing Conversation. On a
> Bulk, in a Cellar, or in a Glass-house among Thieves and Beggars,
> was to be found the Author of the *Wanderer*, the Man of exalted
> Sentiments, extensive Views, and curious Observations; the Man
> whose Remarks on Life might have assisted the Statesman, whose
> Ideas of Virtue might have enlightened the Moralist, whose
> Eloquence might have influenced Senates, and whose Delicacy
> might have polished Courts.[28]

The reduction of the man of artistic talent—even genius—to utter abjection by an unfeeling commercial society foreshadows the alienation and isolation depicted in such characters as Stephen Daedalus, J. Alfred Prufrock, and Belacqua Shuah. Put pat, in both his innovative prose artistry as well as some of his thematic preoccupations, Johnson exhibits a disposition that may be seen as exemplifying modernity, if not directly plunging into Modernism outright.

### III.  Johnson Amongst the Modernists

If we resist taking this plunge, it is nevertheless striking to observe how so many of the writers we associate with High Modernism responded positively and productively to Johnson. The following excursion parses but a few salient examples.

T. S. Eliot's defense of Johnson as a poet (which intertextually echoes Johnson's own defense of Pope against the strictures of Joseph Warton) is perhaps familiar:

> Those who demand of poetry a daydream, or a metamorphosis of their own feeble desires and lusts, or what they believe to be "intensity" of passion, will not find much in Johnson. He is like Pope and Dryden, Crabbe and Landor, a poet for those who want poetry and not something else. … if lines 189–220 of The Vanity of Human Wishes are not poetry, I do not know what is.[29]

Eliot's letters also reveal the high place Johnson held in his estimation.[30] But perhaps less well known is that Eliot took his inspiration for "Of the Awefull Battle of the Pekes and the Pollicles" (in *Old Possum's Book of Practical Cats*) from Johnson's schoolboy translation of a Latin poem of Addison's, "Battle of the Pygmies and Cranes."[31] Johnson's influence appears at numerous other points in the poetry. For one example, see line 3 of "Sweeney Erect," which has "paint me the bold anfractuous rocks"; elsewhere Eliot noted of the penultimate word that it was "a favourite … of Dr. Johnson's."[32] Eliot's employment of the unusual term possesses a bivalence that may indeed be traced directly back to Johnson. The *Dictionary* defines "anfractuous" as "Winding; mazy; full of turnings and winding passages." The definition may be applied to the physical properties found in the poem's "waste shore." This material sense is brought even more fully by the illustrative quotation Johnson uses under his definition, from John Ray's 1691 *The Wisdom of God Manifested in the Works of Creation*:

> Behind the drum are several vaults and *anfractuose* cavities in the ear-bone, so to intend the least sound imaginable, that the sense might be affected with it; as we see in subterraneous caves and vaults, how the sound is redoubled.

This heightens the verses' evocative power by calling attention to the element of sound in the stanza: Ray's "sound" rolling through the "subterraneous caves and vaults" itself "redoubles" the echo of "the snarled and yelping seas" echoing through Eliot's "cavernous waste shore."

But a conversational quotation snatched from Boswell's *Life of Johnson* suggests a deeper, psychological level: "Sir, among the anfractuosities of the human mind, I know not if it may not be one, that there is a superstitious reluctance to sit for a picture."[33] The anaphoric echo found at the beginning of Eliot's first and third lines, "paint me," "paint me," clearly draws directly upon the *Life* anecdote, but complexly. For the injunction "paint me" takes the dative rather than objective grammatical form: "paint *for* me," not "depict me." Hence the intertextual appropriation reinforces the sense of resistance against receiving interrogative scrutiny, reflecting the neurotic mental state that dreads "sprawling on a pin" by "eyes that fix" "on the wall."[34] This poem deploys a dense intertextual allusiveness that ironically contrasts Sweeney's sordid plight with the healthy wholeness that Eliot discovered in the literary tradition of Homer and Shakespeare—and Johnson.

Ezra Pound shared Eliot's enthusiasm for Johnson in general and for *The Vanity of Human Wishes* in particular. The compliment he bestows in the *ABC of Reading* is of the highest order: "Very possibly the best mind in England of his day, save for the months that Voltaire spent in London."[35] And Pound devotes a chapter to *Vanity* in the *Guide to Kulchur*, "Human Wishes," where he offers such observations as,

> Where it is most typical of its mode, and where it most brilliantly illustrates and attains the apogee and top notch of that mode ...

[is a] triumph … of the perfectly weighed and placed word. Its general statements, slickingly epigrammatic, give the reader what he himself brings to the text.[36]

And,

Johnson has enough thought to carry the uniform *to a reader searching* for the thought and the technique of its expression. Almost nothing suffers by being excerpted, line, distich or four lines at a time. (*Guide to Kulchur*, 180)

Pound's more general assessment that "the WHOLE of 18th century literature was a cliché" (*Guide to Kulchur*, 180) considerably sharpens the generosity of his praise for Johnson. And in Pound's landmark poetic critique of modernity, *Hugh Selwyn Mauberley* (1919), the cheapened cultural standards of contemporary London are brought home by reference to a countervailing nostalgia for the age of Johnson:

> Conduct, on the other hand, the soul
> "Which the highest cultures have nourished"
> To Fleet St. where
> Dr. Johnson flourished;
>
> Beside this thoroughfare
> The sale of half-hose has
> Long since superseded the cultivation
> Of Pierian roses.[37]

As Hugh Kenner has observed, "patronage is trivial, and the Fleet Street for which Dr. Johnson forsook patrons is [now] venal."[38] Given his hostility toward Western culture as "an old bitch gone in the teeth, / … a botched civilization,"[39] Pound's apparent affection for a Johnsonian literary and cultural plenitude is striking. Modernists have often been noted for their hostility to the past, to history. Clearly, some exceptions were made.

The impact of Johnson upon another Samuel—Beckett—was immense and enduringly important. He read the elder author's works and

Boswell's *Life of Johnson* avidly (visiting the birthplace house in Lichfield in July 1935) and incorporated Johnson's words and sensibility into his own work at various points.[40] Like Pound, Beckett wrote a piece called "Human Wishes"—not an essay but rather a dramatic fragment. For many years he contemplated a play centered upon Johnson and Mrs. Thrale, one that would have focused especially upon the sexual tensions he discerned between the two after the death of her husband Henry. Beckett filled three notebooks with these ideas, but only a part of one act was eventually written, set in "A room in Bolt Court. Wednesday, April 14, 1781" (the date of Henry Thrale's death). A recent commentary concludes:

> What took its place (but was unsuited to dramatic expression) was the image of the melancholy hypochondriac in physical decline, the horror of annihilation and fear of going mad, yet self-consciously intrigued by the shabby spectacle of his own deterioration, the "necessity of suffering" (Smith, 115). SB's reading and personal sense of Johnson were thus sublimated into *Watt* and *Three Novels*.[41]

Even more to the point is Becket's own admission of the importance of the connection: "They can put me wherever they want, but it's Johnson, always Johnson, who is with me. And if I follow any tradition, it is his."[42]

Beckett's mentor James Joyce was also impacted by Johnson, if to a somewhat lesser degree. Joyce's use of intertextuality to create meaning may be found in *A Portrait of the Artist as a Young Man*. Near the beginning of chapter three, Daedalus recalls "the words, the words of Shelley's fragment on the moon wandering companionless, pale for weariness."[43] Here we find Joyce's allusion used to illuminate the conditions of Stephen's consciousness. The moon's airless aridity operates as an objective correlative that reflects the character's spiritual barrenness. He too wanders "companionless"—that is, without authentic companionship as he shifts amongst the prostitutes who offer fleeting physical contact devoid of interpersonal authenticity. At the end of the chapter, after his confession and consequent joyfulness, Stephen walks the streets of Dublin, "and life lay all before him." The allusion is of course to the end of *Paradise Lost* (12:646), as Adam and Eve hopefully depart from the Eden they have forfeited. And if Joyce read *Rasselas*, which he surely did, given his University College, Dublin education, he would have seen the title character's Miltonic declamation, after the escape from the Happy Valley, "I have here the world before me" (Yale *Works*, 16:68). So, Joyce employs allusions to Shelley, Milton, and Johnson to depict a miniature moral lapse and spiritual reclamation.

Not quite halfway through the same third chapter we read, "Was it not Addison, the great English writer, who, when on his deathbed, sent for the wicked young earl of Warwick to let him see how a Christian can meet his end?" (*Portrait of the Artist*, 105). This stems from a passage in Johnson's 1781 "Life of Addison":

> Lord Warwick was a young man of very irregular life, and perhaps of loose opinions. Addison, for whom he did not want respect, had very diligently endeavoured to reclaim him; but his arguments and expostulations had no effect. One experiment, however, remained to be tried: when he found his life near its end, he directed the young lord to be called; and when he desired, with great tenderness, to hear his last injunctions, told him: *I have sent for you, that you may see how a Christian can die.* (*Lives*, 3:19)

The verbal resemblances are compellingly: "the wicked young earl of Warwick" and "Lord Warwick was a young man of very irregular life"; "see how a Christian can meet his end" and "see how a christian can die." Joyce's appropriations are apt, for they express Stephen's spiritual and psychological torment when facing his own departures from Catholic orthodoxy. His sinful behavior forces him to confront "last things": death, judgment, heaven, and hell. This battery of doom relentlessly assailed Johnson's consciousness in his life as well, from his earliest writings up to his own deathbed.[44] And so, in the depiction of Stephen's existential confrontation with death and damnation, the allusion to Addison's demise and Johnson's "horror of the last" is doubly appropriate: the former taunts Daedalus while the latter commiserates with his plight.

In an autobiographical piece, Virginia Woolf mentions "gnawing my way through the eighteenth century."[45] Her encounters with Johnson and his representation in the *Life* form a significant portion of this gustatory assimilation. In "Dr. Burney's Evening Party," Woolf wrote of Mrs. Thrale: "She understood—her anecdotes prove it—that Dr. Johnson was somehow a rare, an important, an impressive human being whose friendship might be a burden but was certainly an honour."[46] The title of an early review of three editions of Boswell's *Life* is tellingly expressive: "Saint Samuel of Fleet Street."[47] Like Beckett, she visited—at least from the outside—one of Johnson's surviving houses.[48] If Johnson was an influence on Joyce and was admired by Eliot and Pound, we find in the work of Beckett and Woolf more potent and penetrating points of creative influence. Here is Woolf:

> There was the little shadow with the pouting lips, fidgeting this way and that on his chair, uneasy, petulant, officious; there was the bent female shadow, crooking a finger in the cup to feel how deep the tea was, for she was blind; and there was the Roman-looking rolling shadow in the big armchair—he who twisted his fingers so oddly and jerked his head from side to side and swallowed down the tea in such vast gulps. Dr. Johnson, Mr. Boswell, and Mrs. Williams, those were the shadows' names. … At length Mr. Boswell rose. He saluted the old woman with tart asperity. But with what humility did he not abase himself before the great Roman shadow, who now rose to its full height and rocking somewhat as he stood there rolled out the most magnificent phrases that ever left human lips; so Orlando thought them, though she never heard a word that any of the three shadows said as they sat there drinking tea.[49]

We witness in this remarkable passage not only her abiding affection and admiration for Johnson—alongside her bemusement at his idiosyncrasies—but as well a capacity for entering into the Johnsonian universe with imaginative creativity.

For a further example of this, in *To the Lighthouse* we read, "The very stone one kicks with one's boot will outlast Shakespeare."[50] This likely recalls a famous passage from Boswell:

> After we came out of the church, we stood talking for some time together of Bishop Berkeley's ingenious sophistry to prove the

nonexistence of matter, and that every thing in the universe is merely ideal. I observed, that though we are satisfied his doctrine is not true, it is impossible to refute it. I never shall forget the alacrity with which Johnson answered, striking his foot with mighty force against a large stone, till he rebounded from it,— "I refute it *thus*." (*Boswell's Life*, 1:471)

The possibility of the connection of these passages is strengthened by the direct solicitation of George Berkeley a little later, when Mr. Ramsay imagines talking "nonsense" about Berkeley, among other things, to students at Cardiff (62). It is Ramsay who imagines kicking the stone, so he may be associated with Johnson in Woolf's mind. Without going too far down the autobiographical trail (Boswell's Johnson was the favorite book of the model for Ramsay, Leslie Stephen—who also wrote his own biographies of the great lexicographer), it is enough to point out the correlation between Woolf's character, later described as so "absorbed in himself, he is tyrannical, he is unjust" (64), with the Johnson she described as a burdensome "monster" to Mrs. Thrale.[51] In this reading, Mrs. Thrale serves as a template in part for the character of Mrs. Ramsay, in that both possess deep imaginative inner worlds not entirely understood by their sometimes blundering male counterparts.[52] Thus, Woolf's reading of Johnson (and his great biographer) importantly informs the thematic and character development in her fiction, as the phrase "the influence of somebody upon something" that flashes throughout the first section of the novel suggests.[53]

## IV. Chapters

The preceding surveys only the surface of Johnson's impact upon the Modernist imagination; the essays collected in this volume work to explore that impact more deeply and in variously fertile ways.

In "Johnson, T. S. Eliot, and the City," Melvyn New re-examines Johnson's relationship with Modernism by discussing the shared experience of two young writers adjusting to life in the city, an adjustment worked out respectively in Johnson's *London* and Eliot's *Love Song of J. Alfred Prufrock*. The essay argues that Christianity plays a more important role in their poems than the label Modernism might otherwise suggest. For both poets, the city represents science, progress, and Enlightenment, but equally the delusions of pride and perfection that tie both poems to *Paradise Lost* and the Fall in the Garden. New concludes that Johnson and Eliot shared a Modernism that looked backward in despair over an ever-receding sea of religious faith and ahead in equal despair over the Enlightenment secular faith that was replacing it.

Both Samuel Johnson and Virginia Woolf excelled in several genres—fiction, essay-writing, journals and diaries, biography, and criticism—and both held common attitudes toward a number of important topics. Furthermore, Woolf's writings betray an admiration for and attraction to Johnson, as is suggested in the title of my own chapter "'Saint Samuel of Fleet Street': Johnson and Woolf," which contrasts and compares a number of topics linking the two. The chapter then looks more closely at two particular genres, literary criticism and biography, and concludes with a meditation upon Johnson and Woolf's intertextual engagements.

In "'Intellectually "Fuori del Mondo"': Pound's Johnson," Joe Moffett observes that, despite Ezra Pound's repugnant anti-Semitism and questionable support for the Mussolini regime, he continues to be viewed as one of Modernism's most influential artists. In works such as *The Spirit of Romance*, *The Guide to Kulchur*, and *ABC of Reading*, Pound argued for the literature and ideas he felt were most vital for preservation and study. Among these great works and writers stands Samuel Johnson. Pound praises Johnson as "admirable because he will not lick boots, but intellectually 'fuori del mondo,' living in the seventeenth century, so far as Europe is concerned." The chapter explores important connections between these two writers, with special attention paid to direct citations of Johnson in Pound's poetry and prose.

Clement Hawes's "The Antinomies of Progress: Johnson, Conrad, Joyce" examines its three authors from a post-colonialist perspective. Hawes discovers affinities among Johnson, Conrad, and Joyce that valuably involve the long arc of British expansion, North American dominance in the New World, and the freighted notion, on at least three levels—personal, literary, and political—of "progress." Deploying analyses of periodization, rhetorical strategies, and colonial exploitation, Hawes's chapter subtly repositions Johnson as a presence in the broad expanse of literary history.

Jack Lynch's "Johnson Goes to War" observes that literary histories conventionally link the rise of literary modernism to the collective physical and psychological trauma inflicted by the war of 1914–1918. Lynch observes that, when we think of Great War literature, we include writers who wrote during the war, such as Siegfried Sassoon and Wilfred Owen; those who reflected on it shortly afterward, such as Ford Madox Ford and Erich Maria Remarque; and those who said little about the war itself but whose sensibilities were shaped by what happened there, a category that contains nearly all the writers usually grouped under the rubric of High Modernism. But Johnson was there too and played a series of important roles. These include how he sometimes served as a reassuring reminder of the civilized world to which the country hoped to return; while others viewed him as a harsh critic of war and empire. If Johnson influenced thinking about the war, thinking about the war also influenced Johnson. It was the year after the end of the Second World War that the Great Cham became *Johnson Agonistes*—the conception of him that emphasizes the writer and thinker instead of a Boswellian stereotype—but that was the culmination of a process of rethinking literary icons in general and Johnson in particular that began in Flanders Fields.

In "Samuel Beckett and Samuel Johnson: Like-minded Masters of Life's Limitations," Thomas M. Curley suggests that Johnson's overall philosophy of life was traditionally and emphatically Christian. But he was a fearful believer, part of whose anxiety, Curley argues, stemmed from a sense of existential emptiness flowing from his abiding vision that we do not really live in the present but exist primarily by means of past or future apprehensions of living. Perhaps no famous modern author, Curley contends, was more fascinated by Johnson and his anxieties than Samuel Beckett. Beckett turned a blind eye to the traditional magisterial figure of the Great Cham and instead focused upon a doubt-ridden and phobia-filled persona, a subversive Johnson wrought in the Irishman's own image and serving as a formative influence on his canon. Johnson's influence upon Beckett— however unlikely—proves upon deeper scrutiny to be profound.

Carrie D. Shanafelt's "The 'Plexed Artistry' of Nabokov and Johnson" notes how, in the 1962 experimental novel *Pale Fire*, Vladimir Nabokov invokes Samuel Johnson as the prototype for the poet John Shade. Shade is described as a rather old-fashioned but brilliant poet whose last poem interrogates his own subjective experience of meaning-making in a world that stubbornly refuses either to make sense or to be meaningless altogether. Nabokov's affinity for Samuel Johnson, Shanafelt argues, operates in important ways as a recognition of the latter's similar aesthetic resistance to the dominant secular empiricist models of linguistic meaning of his time. Exploring their epistemological contexts as well as their literary productions, her chapter delineates parallels between Johnson and Nabokov with respect to similar investments in the aesthetics of desire and trauma in relation to linguistic meaning.

Greg Clingham's "Johnson and Borges: Some Reflections" considers whether (and how) Johnson's cultural value changes when he is placed in relation to Jorge Luis Borges, the great modern fantasist, conversationalist, essayist, poet, and director of the National Library of Argentina. It explores Borges's life-long love of and imaginative engagement with Johnson found not only in his literary and cultural criticism, but also in fifty-five years of recorded conversations with his Argentine colleague and friend Adolfo Bioy Cesares (and others, such as Willis Barnstone), and in the fact that Borges and Bioy translated the *Lives of the Poets* into Spanish (a work that was, lamentably, never published). Clingham argues that Borges saw in Johnson not the embodiment of Enlightenment hegemony—and thus a figure to be spurned or patronized—but (along with Shakespeare) the quintessential writer of the English language, and a radiant image of the blind modern writer's own magical poetic and expansive self.

In "Ernest Borneman's *Tomorrow is Now*: Thoughts about a Lost Novel, with Glances toward Samuel Johnson and other Modernists," Robert G. Walker situates Samuel Johnson with the German writer, filmmaker, and jazz critic Borneman, who, owing to the rise of Nazism, fled to Britain, where he assimilated Anglo-American Modernist currents. Asking how we can apply the slippery term "Modernist" to someone who falls so far outside the chronological limits as Samuel Johnson, Walker suggests that the empirical approach Johnson often used can lead to valuable and interesting insights about a twentieth-century writer largely unknown to mainstream criticism, yet one who is undoubtedly a Modernist. The chapter contends that Johnson would be among the very best readers of Borneman, since both showed themselves to be comfortable with mixing compositional conventions and defying narrative expectations.

In conclusion, the perhaps unexpected perspective this book's collation offers will bring Johnson more sharply into focus by casting him amongst an unfamiliar milieu and company; likewise, it is hoped that by bringing Johnson to bear on the various authors and topics gathered, *Samuel Johnson Among the Modernists* manages to foreground some aspects of Modernism and its practitioners that would otherwise remain elusively hidden. If it is unlikely that the phrase "Modernity Johnson" will eclipse such better-known appellations as "Dictionary Johnson" and "the Rambler," this volume urges a rethinking of both Johnson and Modernism in ways that seek to be at once compelling, illuminating, and critically productive.

# CHAPTER ONE

# Johnson, T. S. Eliot, and the City

## Melvyn New

Now Johnson was, in his day, very much a modern; he was concerned with how poetry should be written in his own time.

T. S. Eliot, *Milton* (1947), 2.

Aliterary scholar spending years in the company of Laurence Sterne will, if only as a defense mechanism against the many assertions of Sterne's anticipation of postmodernism, find himself arguing for his far more interesting, if less obvious, relationship to modernism. Hence, in a series of essays over the years, I have brought Sterne's writings into proximity with the novels of Marcel Proust, Italo Svevo, Bruno Schulz, and Virginia Woolf; with the philosophy of Friedrich Nietzsche; and with the autobiographical *Sentimental Journey* of Viktor Shklovsky—an erratic but sufficiently representative sampling of the modernist movement.[1] What I learned from these excursions, however, was not only that Sterne anticipated modernism, or that the predilection among modernists for Sterne's writings (several were enthusiastic admirers) was of particular importance to their own endeavors but that great authors of any era and any "ism," when placed in proximity by attentive readers, will be overheard engaging in conversations well worth chronicling.

For example, when reading *Tristram Shandy* alongside *Mrs. Dalloway* I believe I heard a conversation between the two works about the modern worship of proportion, order, and unstoppable progress through science and technology. Herself a reader of Sterne, moreover, Woolf had a different conversation with him, one sufficient to induce her to write an introduction to an edition of *A Sentimental Journey* that is still a very valuable commentary on that work.[2] On the other hand, the Polish writer Bruno Schulz might never have encountered Sterne, but a reader putting his work in proximity with Sterne's may well hear the two authors speaking to one another across languages, countries, and generations. This conversation among the best authors is, I believe, what too many teachers of literature have tended to ignore in a postmodernist era dominated by socially and politically determined reading lists alongside a desire to eschew all that is past in order to emphasize their own agenda of freedom and nonjudgmental evaluation.[3] Modernism, I would argue, instinctively and pervasively sensed and addressed the hazards of leaning too far forward without also looking back.

If Sterne then proves to be an eighteenth-century author in conversation with modernists, is Samuel Johnson another? And, if so, would it be wise to listen first to any conversation that might be heard between Sterne and Johnson, before moving on to Johnson and modernism? We know that he offered several of his patented jibes at Sterne's expense, including one that has proved a wonderful failure of prescience: "Nothing odd will do long. 'Tristram Shandy' did not last."[4] It is a fact, however, that within the single annus mirabilis of 1759, Voltaire's *Candide* was followed closely by Johnson's *Rasselas*, and by the first two volumes of Sterne's *Tristram Shandy*. It is certainly possible to align all three authors on numerous topics; I have recently suggested, for example, that their works share a core interest in exposing the flaws of Enlightenment thought.[5] Indeed, the most important conversations modernism has had with the eighteenth century seem always to be reducible to this concern with Enlightenment's implications for both the inherited past and the promised future.

Twenty-five years ago, in a short essay on teaching *Rasselas*, I aligned Johnson's apologue with two modernist texts, Joseph Conrad's *Lord Jim* and Andre Gide's *The Counterfeiters*, three chronicles of a young man's attempt to find meaning in a world in which, as Gide's Bernard is told, "you can only learn how you ought to live by living" and where Stein's advice for Jim is "to the destructive element submit yourself, and with the exertions of your hands and feet in the water make the deep, deep sea keep you up. So, if you ask me—how to be?"[6] The advice is vague enough to include the characters of Candide and Tristram as well within a modernism that seems to accept the existential autonomy of the individual, but in each instance the author has raised sufficient obstacles to any interpretation that accepts human autonomy as absolute. Rather, these authors across two centuries seem committed to holding fast to an essentialist vision of "how to be" within the jointly perceived "destructive element." Their shared solution entails not only one's own efforts but assistance from higher powers as well, defined as an inherited religion or inherited culture, or perhaps as both. That is to say, we are inheritors as well as innovators, imitators as well as originators. Perhaps the most pertinent distinction to be observed between modernism and academic postmodernism is precisely this, that, despite its many quarrels with, deviations from, and innovations to its nineteenth-century inheritance, modernism recognized its inescapable position as heir to Enlightenment and Romanticism. One suspects that the present professorial commitment to starting anew (*ab ovo*) is already a fading blip, but perhaps that is only a hope. Certainly, for many in the eighteenth and twentieth centuries, whether as writers or as citizens of the world, their grave suspicions concerning Enlightenment have already been realized; it seems quite likely that our century will come to the same conclusion.

Christianity was one inheritance received by both Johnson and Sterne, an inheritance rich enough to encompass two figures who have come down to us as very different Christians indeed. For the present discussion, the nature and depth of their faith is not as important as its service to both authors, an impediment to the century's emerging and alternative belief system, a newly constructed faith in constant and ameliorating progress, the result of an awakening in the eighteenth century to scientific method, to social improvement, and to political utopianism. Moreover, both authors, while undeniably innovative in thought, form, and style (had anyone before—or after—Johnson written a similar prose sentence?), looked to the past, classical and Christian, early and late Renaissance, for much of their inspiration. It is this mindset, I would argue, that most surely binds Johnson and Sterne together, as two centuries later it would bind Eliot and Woolf.

In a fine essay on "Johnson and Modern Poetry" (1985), David Perkins noted, as have others, the appearance of Johnson in *Little Gidding*, and the strong influence that *Vanity of Human Wishes* played throughout T. S. Eliot's career. However, it is another observation, concerning Pope's suppressed presence in *The Waste Land*, that suggested to me a path worth pursuing in quest of Johnson's "modernist" links to Eliot, namely Perkins's explanation as to why Eliot thought of including in the archetype of modernist poetry a seventy-line passage imitative of *Rape of the Lock*:

> [The poem] was about contemporary life in Pope's London (thus extending Eliot's panorama of the city back in time), and, like virtually every other allusion in *The Waste Land*, showed the same life persisting through time: the life of men and women in a bored, materialistic society, aimless and frivolous, in which the cross Pope's Belinda wears about her neck is merely an ornament.[7]

Perkins adds the further astute comment that, as the Romantics rebelled against the Augustans, it was only natural for the modernists, in rebellion against the Romantics, to turn back to writers such as Dryden, Pope, Goldsmith, and Johnson, and he quotes Eliot's 1930 introduction to Johnson's *London and The Vanity of Human Wishes*: "Those who demand of poetry a day dream, or a metamorphosis of their own feeble desires and lusts, or what they believe to be 'intensity' of passion, will not find much in Johnson."[8]

While *Vanity* has been combed for its interactions with Eliot's poetry, *London* has remained relatively unexamined, although clearly it pursues, through the genre of "imitation," the city "back in time," importantly so since Juvenal's Rome is certainly among the first to be characterized as "aimless and frivolous." Indeed, in his introduction to the two poems, Eliot returns again to urbanization:

> The verse after Pope, Swift, Prior, and Gay seems an age of retired country clergymen and schoolmasters. It is cursed with a Pastoral convention … and a ruminative mind … . In this rural,

pastoral, meditative age Johnson is the most alien figure ... .
Johnson remains a townsman ... with no tolerance of swains and
milkmaids. He has more in common in spirit with Crabbe than
with any of his contemporaries; at the same time he is the last
Augustan. (15)

Eliot does judge *Vanity* to be the "finer poem," but then adds that "both of
them seem to me to be among the greatest verse Satires of the English or
any other language ... . They are *purer* satire than anything of Dryden or
Pope, nearer in spirit to the Latin" (15).

In the Christopher Ricks and Jim McCue edition of Eliot's poems there
are several allusions noted to Johnson's writings, but none to *London*, and,
indeed, this essay will not attempt to establish verbal influence.[9] Rather, I
will be discussing "modernism" as a reaction to urban life, but a reaction
significantly different from that of a pastoral-leaning Horatian comparison between city and country life, or a Wordsworthian return to Tintern
Abbey, where the country restores the innocence and energy sapped by the
city. I will also limit my discussion to Eliot's *Love Song of J. Alfred Prufrock*,
although one might suggest the themes to be discussed are more overtly
evidenced in *The Waste Land*. But *London* and *Prufrock* have an important
biographical connection, being the first successful poems by two young
men encountering the city as the place of their chosen residence for the
remainder of their lives.[10] Johnson and Eliot (and perhaps Juvenal before
them) seem to share the view that the promise of progress, ameliorative
change, and, in brief, enlightened modernity that seems always to accompany urban dwelling is indeed a hollow promise. Yet Eliot remained in
London throughout his life and never returned (except for occasional
visits) to his native country; it would not be far afield to suggest for him a
seemingly paradoxical agreement with Johnson's famous paean that "No,
Sir, when a man is tired of London, he is tired of life; for there is in London
all that life can afford" (*Life*, 3:178), delivered some forty years after writing
*London*. Nor would Eliot disagree with Johnson's many pronouncements
marking London as the center of science and learning: "no man, at all
intellectual ... is willing to leave."[11] By placing *London* alongside *Prufrock*,
Johnson in proximity to Eliot, I believe we may uncover a foreshadowing
of the one aspect of modernism that seems out of place for both authors:

their Christian faith. Needless to say, as the careers of both writers developed, this faith became quite overt, but few have wanted to suggest that at this early stage in their careers it was already shaping their vision. I shall argue that this is indeed the case. They portray urbanism as the only environment left to writers and thinkers, but the city confines, corrupts, and finally exhausts everyone; it leaves the writer with no exit, trapped in a violent and corrupt landscape. The choices presented to modern man seem to be limited to adapting to the "destructive element" or withering away; if this is so, modernism, I would suggest, can be defined as a persistent state of psychic depression inherent to this urban experience.

A minor poet, Amy Levy, on the cusp of English modernism in 1889, captured the essence of this urban depression in what is perhaps her best poem, "A London Plane-Tree":

> Green is the plane-tree in the square,
>     The other trees are brown;
> They droop and pine for country air;
>     The plane-tree loves the town.
>
> Here from my garret-pane, I mark
>     The plane-tree bud and blow,
> Shed her recuperative bark,
>     And spread her shade below.
>
> Among her branches, in and out,
>     The city breezes play;
> The dun fog wraps her round about;
>     Above, the smoke curls grey.
>
> Others the country take for choice,
>     And hold the town in scorn;
> But she has listened to the voice
>     On city breezes borne.[12]

Needless to say, any London poet is bound to comment on its fog, although Eliot insisted he had never experienced a London fog before he wrote lines

15–16 of *Prufrock* (*Poems*, 380, n.15), but what interests me here is the poet's strained attempt to thrive in London, to ignore the city's destructive environment for all but the one species able to survive amid the fog and smoke and whatever else is borne on "city breezes." It is perhaps unfair to note that Levy committed suicide the year this poem was published, at the age of twenty seven, but, despite the poem's struggle to be positive, it seems pregnant with a despair generated by entrapment. It is therefore important to point out that in Juvenal's poem (and in Johnson's imitation) the poet is seeing his friend out of the corrupt city but is himself remaining behind. The first thing we might discover by putting *London* into proximity with *Prufrock*, then, is the value of treating the latter as partaking of elements of classical "verse satire"—most particularly here a separation of the speaker from the observing poet. In *Prufrock*, I would suggest, the young poet accompanies an older man on his city tour, listens to his lament, and ends, as in Juvenal's original poem, on the beach, looking for an exit.

To be sure, that would suggest that the four poets I have invoked, Juvenal, Johnson, Levy, and Eliot, are all *modernists*, an absurdity on the surface but a possibility I nevertheless want to pursue. What the modernist label most suggests to me is a point of view trapped between a worldly dream of a return to an imagined halcyon past (whether a Golden Age or an Eden) and the counterdream of an equally worldly golden or edenic future. Christian theology and literature are built on an alternative vision, a lost Eden, by which time, sin, and death entered the world, and a possible timeless future in the company of an eternal God, but only through faith in the sacrifice of Jesus Christ. That both Johnson and Eliot famously held tight to this alternative is manifest in their biographies and their writings, although both were also quite cognizant of its failure any longer to organize the society around them. Rather, hope for the future had now passed to the promise of a rational political and social amelioration through science and human intellect, the pillars of the urban structure, ancient or modern. Johnson and Eliot envision for us the despair generated by our permanent estrangement from this mythic (as it is to rationalist eyes) story and our equally permanent compensatory commitment to utopian fantasies of progress. Many possibilities have been offered as to the nature of Prufrock's "overwhelming question" (l.10), but the best answer, I think, is one provided in the Ricks–McCue edition, from Pascal's *Pensées*: "every man who thinks and lives by thought must have his own scepticism, that which stops at the question, that which ends in denial, or that which leads to faith" (*Poems*, 1:379). What most establishes Johnson and Eliot as "modernists" is, I believe, their simultaneous and contradictory embrace, here at the beginning of their careers, of the fraught role of being displaced (or unplaced) *urban Christians*, fully aware of the oxymoronic character of the term. Their response was to undergird their portrait of the city with faint but still audible echoes of scripture, echoes of doctrine, and echoes of *Paradise Lost*.[13]

Twenty years after *Prufrock* was published, Eliot presented a lecture, "The Christian in the Modern World," to the Church Union Literature Association, that remained unpublished until appearing in the *Times Literary Supplement* in 2017 (July 7, 16–18).[14] To my mind, it offers the best commentary on *Prufrock* and urbanism that I have found, beginning with the observation that

> so long as people were able to believe—most of them—that the world was making continuous progress in civilization, it was possible for most people to make easy terms with contemporary society … . The social and economic order was far from perfect, but it was on the way towards perfection.

For Eliot this progress had one exception, namely that everything was improving "except belief in Christ," and possibly this accounts for his making space for exceptions in his phrasing: "most of them," "most people."

The period 1920–1935 (the aftermath of World War I, the ensuing economic collapse, and the preparations for World War II) broke these illusions of progress according to Eliot, but surely the poets of *London* and *Prufrock* were never fully vested in them. As Eliot explores the inevitable failure of the League of Nations, fascism, and communism, he notes that all of them absorbed elements of Christianity: "Various publicists will tell you, that either Marxism, with a few important modifications, is the real Christian attitude; or that Fascism, again with a few important modifications, is the Christian attitude." His own view is crucial: before accepting any political or social system, "consider those Christian elements which are omitted, as well as those that are included." Those elements can be narrowed to two essentials, less familiar in modern times than they were to Johnson, for whom they were the profound bedrocks of the Anglican faith he professed: first, in Eliot's words, "one of the dangerous delusions that the Christian must avoid is that of the perfect human society situated somewhere in the future"; and second, that the "eventual perfection of human nature [can be] brought about exclusively from outside."[15] Johnson would perhaps have been more scriptural: the breach between God (perfection) and humankind, caused by the first Adam's fall into sin and death in the Garden of Eden, can only be healed by absolute faith in, and the assistance of, the second Adam, his sacrifice for—and restoration of—grace to humanity.[16]

In a very useful chapter on *London*, David Venturo notes the poem's contrast between the "georgic existence in lines 210–23 and the 'Dangers' (line 236) of an urban night in lines 224–41," and suggests that because Eliot failed to recognize these "specifically ideological foundations," he questioned the "'sincerity' of Johnson's praise of the country": "[T]hat Johnson should ever have contemplated leaving London for the remote promontory of St. David's is so inconsistent with his character, and his confessed sentiments in later life, that we cannot believe he ever meant it."[17] Venturo goes on to express surprise that Eliot would so confound the poet and the poem's "rhetorical spokesman"—that is, his persona (Thales)—and makes the point that "Eliot, of all authors, who could write *The Waste Land* and yet delight in living and working in London, should have been more careful ... " (76). The point is important because, as Howard D. Weinbrot long ago demonstrated, there is almost certainly no irony in Juvenal's "georgic existence"—nor would Johnson have believed there was.[18]

It is of course possible that Eliot was simply careless here, but I would suggest another explanation, namely that when Thales speaks of "Some pleasing Bank where verdant Osiers play, / Some peaceful Vale with Nature's Paintings gay" (ll.45–46), or later, when the poet instructs Thales to "There prune thy Walks, support thy drooping Flow'rs, / Direct thy Rivulets, and twine thy Bow'rs" (ll.216–17), Eliot correctly recognized the diction of satiric parodies of the pastoral tradition, while failing to acknowledge that the same language was edenic as well. Thus, when

Samuel Richardson wants to ridicule the pastoral, he has Sir Charles Grandison talk of a "mossy bank of a purling stream, gliding thro' an enamelled mead … the feathered songsters from an adjacent grove, contributing to harmonize and fan the lambent flame"; and when Milton wants to describe life in Eden, his language is similar: "what we by day/ Lop overgrown, or prune, or prop, or bind, / One night or two with wanton growth derides / Tending to wild."[19] Johnson may well have built this ambiguity into his poem because while the georgic seems to offer a valid alternative to the city it ultimately fails—as does the city—to answer the question "how to live?" The eternal oneness with God, represented by Eden or by the pastoral, is now possible only through the mediation of Christ and only after death; it is no accident that Johnson places signs of Christianity not in the country but in the past, the "consecrated Earth" of Elizabeth's time (1.24) or "her Cross triumphant on the Main" (1.27). The tendency to believe the world after the expulsion from Eden to be in a steady and continuing retreat from perfection is precisely the opposite of Enlightenment thought, and hence the story of the Fall becomes the fundamental notion that puts Christian city dwellers in conflict with themselves.[20]

The attempt to find an edenic existence in the countryside, a mythic return to innocence and harmony, is, within a Christian view, as hopeless a dream as a social and political creation of perfection within the secular state. Given our fallen natures, however, it is highly likely that, even while writing his imitation, Johnson recognized his own "delight" in urban life, the same delight that Venturo notes in Eliot. For both, the city gathers all the conflicts and contradictions of leading a secular life in a God-created world—of being an urban Christian—but there is no other place in which they are willing to live. The past is unrecoverable, at least on earth, but not irredeemable; the future is utterly tainted, both by the impossible dreams postulated but even more so by the tactics those in power will resort to in the belief that they can do what divine power will not do. In Eliot's lecture, he opportunely turns to Jacques Maritain:

> In this way (the separation of the secular from the spiritual) the action of States as well as the conduct of wars and conspiracies, revolutions, acts of violence and the rest came to be the work of a tiny group of men who sacrificed their virtue on the altar of

public welfare in much the same way that prostitutes sacrifice
their honour to maintain the peace of families. (17)

As Johnson's poem suggests, he and those he allied himself to had already
identified Robert Walpole and his cohorts as one such "tiny group."[21]

Even as we accept Weinbrot's argument that Juvenal was indeed
sincere about a return to country life, and Venturo's assertion that the
"pastoral/georgic tradition gives [Johnson] the ideal vehicle for linking
rural husbandry and private virtue with the public realm of political
virtue" (76), I suspect that Johnson would have had some reservations,
not because he scorned the countryside but because he realized it was no
longer a viable alternative, from either a religious or a secular viewpoint;
his empiricism and his faith would both inform against the pastoral. In
this regard, Eliot's reading of the georgic in *London* is valid. He found in
Johnson's poem the same inescapable environment into which he impris-
oned his own urban dweller. Unlike Thales, however, Prufrock, although
equally without "Youth, and Health, and Fortune" (l.256), cannot (or
will not?) escape the city; and, unlike the satirist, he no longer has the
"angry Numbers" (l.259) of Johnson's heroic couplets, backed by Juvenal's severity, but only the fragments of experiences he fears to confront.
While both Johnson and Eliot are equally adept, in their different voices,
at pointing to the truly destructive and confining environment of urban
life, both recognize it as the only life now available for them. The pastoral
alternative, not so much a place as a concept, is no longer possible, and we
can perhaps capture their shared dilemma by pointing to the word itself,
*pastoral*, denoting as it does both a rural and a religious setting.[22]

Put another way, if one can believe in Lazarus, one can find an alternative to urban life, but Prufrock is not "Lazarus, come from the dead. /
Come back to tell you all" (ll.94–95). The promise of eternal life, figured
as the pastoral in literary tradition, as prophecy ("I am no prophet" [l.83;
cf. Amos 7:14]) in the Old Testament, and as John the Baptist in the New
Testament ("my head (grown slightly bald) brought in upon a platter")
[l.82; cf. Matthew 14:6–11]) is now lost to urban dwellers, and its evocation is a hollow promise from the past, no longer functional in the brave
new world emerging from that "mythic" spiritual hope into the new
secular expectations of modernity.

These overt scriptural allusions are reinforced by less obvious ones. For example, the section begins with the simple "Shall I say ... " (l.70), which Ricks and McCue tie to Isaiah 38:15 ("What shall I say ... ") and John 12:27 ("Now is my soul troubled; and what shall I say"). The speaker in Isaiah is Hezekiah, who is punished by God for displaying all his wealth—an Orgilio of biblical times, a Great Gatsby of the modern era.[23] In John, the speaker is Jesus, contemplating his own coming death, which will re-establish the connection between God and humanity; significantly, the chapter opens with an allusion to Lazarus, "which had been dead, whom he raised from the dead" (12:1). It is appropriate, therefore, that after invoking the prophets, John the Baptist, and Lazarus, Prufrock should confront his fear of death, "from whose bourn / No traveller returns," thus leading us to the Hamlet allusion (l.111) that has seemed abrupt to some readers.[24]

Unhappily, the lost promise of salvation, a return to wholeness with God that existed before the Fall, is combined for both poets with a cityscape that makes the new promise of progress equally empty. The result is well described by Andrew Varney, in one of the better essays written on *London*: "Johnson fuses with his public satire a deeply impassioned presentation of the mind in distress that is almost wholly absent from Juvenal and from his other translators and imitators ... . [T]he strains of querulousness, alarm, unease, fear, and testiness that complicate and enrich the poetic texture of *London* may be missed" if readers concentrate only on the physical and political aspects of the poem.[25] Varney centers attention, instead, on the impact of the city on its inhabitants, bringing Johnson's poem much closer to *Prufrock*, although Eliot is not invoked: "Human minds in this society are fractured, hypocritical, deluded, deceived, or otherwise divorced from their own better interests" (204). For Varney, the poet chronicles the fact that the "social and mental fabric of the city is falling apart," leaving us "nowhere to turn for an assurance of stability" (212), surely a useful reading, although it does cause him to downplay two additional insights that reading *London* as a modernist poem has perhaps helped bring into focus.

Varney uses a quasi-theological diatribe by Dr. Sacheverell on the moral degeneracy of the times to serve as a contrast to Johnson's more subdued and anguished utterance.[26] The comparison is unfair, reducing the spiritual dimensions of the poem to the caricature of Sacheverell's excessive (and political) certainties; surely, however, when one speaks of the "social and mental fabric" of London, at least in the eighteenth century, one must consider the "spiritual fabric" as well, since most in the century thought of self and state as still fully informed by their religion. Johnson, for example, with poetic subtlety rather than sermonic bombast, several times addresses the presence of religious belief within the land-scape of a city without faith. From the "female Atheist" who talks "you dead" (l.18) to the "Crimes" that "inflame the Wrath of Heav'n" (l.66), from the often discussed line on the artful French sycophant who will go to hell on your behalf (l.116) to the invocation of "Heaven's just Bolts" to confound "*Orgilio's* Wealth" (l.194) with "angry Heav'n's ... fire" (l.209), one finds glimpses of Johnson's Christianity, heavily marked, even at this early date, by three of the four last things that would become the preoc-cupations of his mind: Death, Judgment, and Hell. Heaven, the end that imparts meaning to a virtuous life, is absent, and in the most famous para-graph in the poem Johnson makes its absence the center of his indictment of London:

> Has Heaven reserv'd, in Pity to the Poor,
> No pathless Waste, or undiscover'd Shore?
> No secret Island in the boundless Main?
> No peaceful Desart yet unclaim'd by SPAIN? ...
> This mournful Truth is ev'ry where confest,
> SLOW RISES WORTH, BY POVERTY DEPREST. (ll.170–73, 176–77)

Obviously, there are economic, social, and political dimensions to this passage, but framing it, I believe, is the now forsaken promise, "Blessed are the poor in spirit: for theirs is the kingdom of heaven" (Matthew 5:3; cf. Luke 6:20). Matthew Henry's traditional commentary on the passage provides a context for *London* that seems particularly pertinent, as, for example, when he argues that the entire Sermon on the Mount

> is designed to rectifie the ruining Mistakes of a blind and carnal World ... [in which] most *mistake* the End and form a wrong notion of Happiness ... [they] spend their Days in Mirth, and

their Years in Pleasure, … eat the Fat and drink the Sweet, and carry all before them with a high Hand.[27]

This may strike one as more pertinent to *Vanity of Human Wishes*, where a more confident Johnson will break away from Juvenal for his own overtly Christian conclusion, but I believe that already in *London* Johnson manifests his world as within and not distinct from his Christian inheritance. It is a perspective that we have difficulty recapturing and crediting after two hundred years of enlightened urbanization, so that if we hear it repeated by a modernist like Eliot, our hackles are raised, and "reactionary" may be the kindest of epithets sent in his direction. Nonetheless, I will here suggest that both *London* and *Prufrock* are guided by a similar scriptural response to the modernist question: how are we to live in the destructive element when it is the *only* element in which we can keep afloat? Henry's *Exposition*, in explaining Matthew's difficult phrase "poor in spirit,"[28] may provide their answer: "a gracious Disposition of Soul, by which we are *emptied of self*, in order to our being filled with *Jesus Christ*" (5:24).

The second aspect of *London* downplayed in Varney's reading is what many critics have noted as Johnson's fondness for city life, and that the poem projects that view in various ways, both overt and covert. John Wain perhaps expressed this view most strongly: "the poem welcomes London. In tone, in strategy, in the nature of its art, it is metropolitan. It signals an acceptance of the values of eighteenth-century civilization at their most urbane and sophisticated."[29] If observing this predilection serves only to further a political reading of the poem, the critic's incipient leaning toward Whiggism, it seems misapplied. If, instead, it accounts for the fact that neither Johnson nor Juvenal nor Eliot leave the city they deplore, it reminds us that the city has become the poets' place, the "intellectual and artistic centre" where they now must live, caught between the fading promise of heaven and the dubious dream of utopia that have become the defining boundaries of civilization.[30] Within those boundaries, moving from the city's streets to one's own home, the private "city" within the public one, one closes the door in the "*hope* … [of] the balmy Blessings of Repose," the "*sacred* Hour of silent Rest" (ll.236–40; my italics)—that is, escape from despair into hopefulness, or at least unconsciousness. At this point we are told that the "faithless Bar" is burst and a violent death ensues (ll.239–41). Johnson, always careful in his choice of words, makes the door complicit in the murder, a *faithless* abandonment of duty in a world emptied of hope, whether in the promise of scripture or enlightened amelioration.

For comparison, we can turn to a scriptural verse that may well have been on Johnson's mind when he reconstructed the passage in Juvenal: "But the day of the Lord will come as a thief in the night; in the which the heavens shall pass away with a great noise, and the elements shall melt with fervent heat, the earth also and the works that are therein shall be burned up" (2 Peter 3:10). Here the ancient promise is fulfilled, the true end time that is not the building of a perfected city in the future but the final undoing of human self-assertiveness and self-aggrandizement. This particular chapter of Peter's second epistle was, we note, burned into the historical consciousness of every Londoner because the great London fire of 1666 was at first taken as the fulfillment of its prophecy, and afterwards as one final warning to that fallen city:

> For this they willingly are ignorant of, that by the word of God the heavens were of old, and the earth standing out of the water and in the water: Whereby the world that then was, being over-flowed with water, perished: But the heavens and earth, which are now, by the same word are kept in store, reserved unto fire against the day of judgment and perdition of ungodly men.[31]

As Juvenal demonstrates, one does not need Christianity in order to condemn city life or the corruptions of human beings. My point here is that in eighteenth-century England it would have been impossible, especially given the recent historical past of both plague and fire, to think about London without scriptural reference—and most especially, perhaps, when identifying oneself with a political opposition ready to suggest, even if hyperbolically, that the corruptions and crimes of the Walpole administration were returning the country to all the vices that had justified disaster by plague and fire two generations earlier. Being steeped in scripture is natural enough for eighteenth-century writers, and almost as natural is an appeal to the authority of the ancients that is always implied by the genre of imitation. Paradoxically, it is this looking back that links Johnson most tellingly to modernism, for, like the modernist, his life and thought clearly committed him to urbanism and its Enlightenment ideals, including scientific progress, better education, and social amelioration. However, this commitment was impregnated with a skepticism concerning futuristic schemes inherent in Christian belief. In our own day, modernists, whether in reaction to nineteenth-century naiveté or twentieth-century reality, have exhibited a similarly directed skepticism in their writings. Many of these modern writers have also cast an equally skeptical backward look on Christianity,[32] but what binds Johnson and Eliot together is their effort, despite their skeptical empiricism, to retain the single most fundamental truth of their Christian heritage—namely, that we are fallen, mortal and immoral, and all our efforts to replace a virtuous and eternal life by means of the promise of God through Christ with the promise of self-made progress toward secular ideals are almost certainly futile—the city being built is only another Tower of Babel.[33]

The crux of the matter is in such qualifiers in my previous sentence as "efforts" and "almost certainly futile," because it indeed takes strenuous efforts within the cityscape to keep religious faith alive; and because the city dweller can never be certain that human reason will not ultimately reveal the sufficient knowledge and wisdom heretofore thought to be God's alone. We return thus to Varney's "mind in distress," the condition he finds in *London*, but which, I would suggest, is indicative of the more general aesthetic vision we know as modernism. Significantly enough, one sees this distress in a conflict that surrounded the rebuilding of London after the fire, well outlined by Nicholas Hudson. Caught between architects who saw the opportunity for a new rationalized cityscape and what today politicians would call "facts on the ground," "grand projects of urban redesign seemed out of step with the largely undirected and eclectic growth of England's booming metropolis" by the second half of the century.[34] Johnson's first encounter with London reveals, Hudson argues, "the distress and alienation of a small town teacher in the face of the bewildering modernism" of 1738; the fire of 1666 "seems still to be burning," a "particularly bleak and bewildered portrait of a city that other poets were celebrating for its commercial vigor and political liberty"— that is, its resistance to rational organization (584–85). Hudson then traces a change in attitude, whereby the city's "twisting alleys and obscure neighborhoods" came to symbolize "the irregular and detailed shapes of human truth, the fabric of 'nature' that he [Johnson] constantly celebrates as the substance of both true art and virtue" (589).

While this argument is quite valid, it may not sufficiently account for Johnson's moral and religious separation from the "commercial ideals" that generated an unplanned city of cosmopolitan complexity and confusion (think of Smollett's portrayals of London), not to mention the problems of crime, poverty, and filth that did not disappear after 1738. For Johnson, the city certainly meant intellectual fulfillment, but precisely for that reason, I would argue, it was a residence of lifelong conflict and tension, the modernist dilemma of dwelling in despair because there is no other place to dwell.[35] Johnson could never fully become a man of the city, if by that we mean, as we probably must, those occupying their lives only with getting and spending. Thus, although, as Hudson argues, he "rejected schemes informed by neoclassicism, rationalism, and an autocratic vision of government," preferring instead to embrace a city "essentially realist in its artistic outlook, empiricist in its epistemology, and democratic in its political orientation" (590), the fact remains, and Hudson acknowledges this, that he was far from "wholehearted" in embracing the "commercial ideals" that generated this vision of the ad hoc city, showing "little conscious sympathy with those who spent their lives making money … " (592).

Putting *London* in proximity with *Prufrock* helps divert attention from the physical, political, and economic aspects of urban life and steers us back to Matthew's "poor in spirit," and the expositor's "*emptied of self.*" Certainly, one dominant theme that Johnson imitates from Juvenal is the triumph of guise and pretense within the city, whether practiced by native inhabitants or invaders from foreign parts. These are the people who empty themselves of self in order to become what others want them to be, all the while ignoring the other half of Matthew Henry's exposition, "in order to our being filled with *Jesus Christ.*" Rather, they are literally "poor in spirit," willing to vote "a Patriot black, a Courtier white" (1.52), where words also are emptied of substance and a lie is given "the confidence of Truth." It is particularly telling in this regard that the French invaders are pictured by Johnson (as were the Greeks by Juvenal) as especially skilled in emptying themselves in order to play whatever part is necessary, an actor's talent no longer confined to the stage but now played out in the drawing rooms of the wealthy and powerful: these are the true villains of Johnson's London, those who "lye without a Blush, without a Smile; / Exalt each Trifle, ev'ry Vice adore, / Your Taste in Snuff, your Judgment in a Whore" (ll.147–49). The last line is one of Johnson's more Juvenalian moments, although without actual precedent in his satire, and it leads to what I would suggest is the culmination of Johnson's underlying Christian structure: "For Arts like these preferr'd, admir'd, carest, / They first invade your Table, then your Breast; / Explore your Secrets with insidious Art, / Watch the weak Hour, and ransack all the Heart" (ll.152–55). Venturo also centers attention on this passage, arguing the seriousness of the portrayal of the French: they are "more dangerous than contemptible. Their silly, protean exterior masks deadly and determined intent ... . This passage turns on a conceit based on the etymology of the word *insidious*, which is derived from the Latin verb, *insidere*, 'to ambush'" (72). For Venturo this is primarily of political importance, the Frenchman's design to "invade," "explore," and ransack" the "inner sancta of his patron's life and thought, but so subtly that the patron fails to notice"; it is, he concludes, "an 'insidious' invasion which results in tacit French rule" (72).

This very apt description of the import of the passage might also lead the reader to the Garden of Eden, indeed, to the already cited (for its pastoral description) Book Nine, where the temptation and fall of Adam and Eve take place. One might recall first the mask Satan assumes: "The Serpent, subtlest Beast of all the Field ... . / Fit Vessel, fittest Imp of fraud, in whom / To enter, and his dark suggestions hide / From sharpest sight" (9:85–91). In this guise, Satan will approach the "much deceiv'd, much failing, hapless *Eve*" (9:404), who will "never from that hour in Paradise" find "either sweet repast, or sound repose," and with *insidious intent* bring sin and death into the world: "Such *ambush* hid among sweet Flow'rs and Shades / Waited with hellish rancor imminent / To intercept thy way, or send thee back / Despoil'd of Innocence, of Faith, of Bliss" (my italics). If one accepts that Johnson indeed has this passage in mind when he recounts the several "ambushes" awaiting the walker in the streets of London, then surely those subsequent lines, in which the murderer, "Cruel with Guilt, and daring with Despair," disturbs one's hope for the "balmy Blessings of Repose" and "Invades the sacred Hour of silent Rest" (ll.237, 240), can also be seen as a replay of the first loss of innocence that underlies all Christian thought. Without doubt, Johnson's *London* addresses the social, economic, and political corruptions of London in 1738, but the poem is framed, I would argue, by a vision of a world in which the emptying of self is filled not with Christ but with Satan.[36] That being so, the Enlightenment ideals that shape the city must be measured against Eliot's warning: "our duty to change our environment, the environment of our fellow human beings, for the better, must be balanced by our duty to change ourselves" (*TLS*, 17).

Neither Milton nor Johnson used the phrase "insidious intent" as I did in the paragraph above, but it was easily recognized, I hope, as a borrowing from *Prufrock*; "Streets that follow like a tedious argument / Of insidious intent / To lead you to an overwhelming question ... " (ll.8–10). That question, I have suggested, may be Pascal's choice between denial or faith, but it is a question that Prufrock does not have the courage to ask, having become himself one of those who prepares every day "a face to meet the faces that you meet" (l.27). Ultimately, those who empty themselves of self only to be filled with the dreams of infinite knowledge and boundless self-sufficiency (the "sins" of Enlightenment) are not strengthened but weakened. Satan himself is merely a ludicrous pawn in God's divine plan, his existence made possible only through "the will / And high permission of all-ruling Heaven," in order that he can "Heap on himself damnation" (1:211–15). Prufrock's enervated state is what has become the archetype of the urban dweller, caught by temptation and indecision, by depression and despair, all "Youth, and Health, and Fortune spent" (*London*, l.256), but too exhausted to do more than listen to the mermaids of his imagination. Indeed, Prufrock becomes the archetype of modernism, living now in a world east of Eden because Adam and Eve partook of the fruit offered by an insidious flatterer, but himself now not daring to "eat a peach."[37]

It is widely acknowledged that neither Johnson nor Eliot was particularly fond of Milton, either as a "politician" or a "theologian," and only begrudgingly so as a poet. It is therefore counterintuitive, perhaps, to suggest that their first poetic successes revolve in some way or another around *Paradise Lost*. In justification, I would argue that we need not posit a concrete influence of Milton on either poet, but rather embrace a more abstract notion: namely, that literary genius is always in dialogue with literary genius, and that no English-language poet whose world has been shaped by Christian thought can avoid entering into a conversation with that one English poet who retold so brilliantly the most essential story of Christianity, from the Fall in the Garden to the redemption through Christ. Johnson quarreled with Milton's politics and Eliot with his poetics, but when Johnson set himself the task of summarizing *Paradise Lost* he did so in a manner that suggests a shared heritage of faith with Milton. Eliot, too, shared that faith, and, as well, shared with Johnson a modernism that looked backward in despair over an ever-receding sea of religious faith and ahead in equal despair over the Enlightenment secular faith that was replacing it. Clinging to both faiths would not be an easy task:

> We all, indeed, feel the effects of Adam's disobedience; we all sin like Adam, and like him must all bewail our offences; we have restless and insidious enemies in the fallen angels, and in the blessed spirits we have guardians and friends; in the redemption of mankind we hope to be included; and in the description of heaven and hell we are surely interested, as we are all to reside hereafter either in the regions of horror or of bliss.[38]

Not coincidentally, I hope, that word *insidious* occurs again. Ironically enough, the shared modernism of Samuel Johnson and T. S. Eliot takes rise in the fact that, despite Enlightenment, they both persisted in having faith in the inherited story that *Paradise Lost* told so well; perhaps that was Milton's own *insidious intent*.

# CHAPTER TWO

# "Saint Samuel of Fleet Street"
## Johnson and Woolf[1]

*Anthony W. Lee*

## I. Introduction

On February 10, 1910, the Royal Navy seemingly entertained a visit from the Emperor of Abyssinia. Admiral Sir William Henry May and other officers of HMS *Dreadnought*—the flagship of the Home Fleet—escorted the party on a tour of the battleship's armaments, wireless room, and other points of interest. Newspaper accounts a few days later revealed, however, that a hoax had been perpetuated upon the unsuspecting naval hosts. The party in fact consisted of a group of English, including Virginia Stephen, disguised as the emperor and members of his court (see image below. Virginia is the seated figure furthest to the left). The deception was masterminded by her brother Adrian and his college friend Horace de Vere Cole. Exposure of what came to be known as the "Dreadnought Hoax" led to public outcry and official embarrassment, precipitating a parliamentary inquiry.[2] For her part, Woolf, after learning that the escapade resulted in tightened naval regulations, drily remarked, "I am glad to think that I too have been of help to my country."[3] Taking a longer view, however, we may discern more pregnant dimensions looming from the episode. A *Times* article reporting the event identifies Stephen as "an Abyssinian prince."[4] Perhaps some will recall the original title page name of Samuel Johnson's 1759 masterpiece fiction *Rasselas, The Prince of Abissinia. A Tale*. Did Woolf think, if

perhaps only fleetingly, of the book and character that has come to rank among the touchstones of Johnson's art and moral outlook? Was she in 1910 at some level consciously aware of disguising herself as Johnson's most famous fictional character, of penetrating the Johnsonian literary universe, as well as the British naval defenses?

The anecdote symbolically suggests an important affinity that persists throughout Woolf's written record, one indicating that she indisputably held Johnson in the highest estimation. In her 1925 review "Saint Samuel of Fleet Street," she includes him, on the basis of being "one of the very few human beings who love their kind,"[5] in the company of Socrates and Christ, and, among authors, with Montaigne, Shakespeare, and—"perhaps," Sir Thomas Browne. (Woolf pointedly excludes Milton, Wycherley, Swift, Pope, and Congreve from this privileged list.)[6] And, apart from her appreciation of his humanity, she offers high praise for Johnson the writer:

His prose … appears brief, pointed, almost elegant; which alights with all its feet neatly together for the most part and exactly upon its meaning; which indulges frequently in a thrust or lunge of phrase of the utmost vigour and vivacity.[7]

In addition to his large humanity and impressive literary style, Woolf prized the cogent brilliance of Johnson's mind: "He said things casually that one never forgot."[8] She thought highly enough of him to name a collection of some of her best essays after a famous Johnsonian phrase, "the common reader."

There is a sentence in Dr. Johnson's Life of Gray which might well be written up in all those rooms, too humble to be called libraries, yet full of books, where the pursuit of reading is carried on by private people. "… I rejoice to concur with the common reader; for by the common sense of readers, uncorrupted by literary prejudices, after all the refinements of subtilty and the dogmatism of learning, must be finally decided all claim to poetical honours." It defines their qualities; it dignifies their aims; it bestows upon a pursuit which devours a great deal of time, and is yet apt to leave behind it nothing very substantial, the sanction of the great man's approval.[9]

Johnson appears frequently elsewhere in both her public and private writings.[10]

Upon closer inspection, numerous points of similitude connecting their literary careers and writings emerge. Both wrote a single play. Both produced voluminous life writings: biographies, diaries and journals, and correspondence. Both are masters of the essay. Both wrote enduringly relevant fiction. Both are superb literary critics. Both rank among the greatest prose stylists in English: each may be said to have crafted a style at once original and influential.[11] Both were library cormorants, omnivorous devourers of books.[12] Both wrote journalism for the popular press, including many outstanding literary reviews. And both, as practicing journalists and reviewers, were important contributors to their cultural moments.

Johnson and Woolf were, in their different ways, brilliant and charismatic conversationalists.[13] As such, they each helped found and centrally
inhabited the epicenters of two intellectual/artistic circles that attracted
some of the best minds of their respective generations and that potently
influenced their immediate and succeeding cultures: the Literary Club and
Bloomsbury.[14] The former has been lauded as a rare example of figures
from many different areas of expertise who could mingle and mutually
understand each other, especially before the advent of professional special-
ization in the nineteenth century.[15] Yet Bloomsbury may be seen in a
similar light, perhaps as a deliberate departure from this latter nineteenth-
century tendency, as Victoria Rosner has recently noted: "Bloomsbury's
willingness to integrate ideas from outside their individual specializations
is a signal reminder of the benefits that can accrue to the omnivorous
intellect."[16]

There are important differences, of course. But the affinities are striking
and compelling. Woolf and Johnson represent for their respective periods
the classic model of the (wo)man of letters—each of them, as Johnson said
of his friend Oliver Goldsmith, "touch[ing] almost every kind of writing,
and touch[ing] none that [s/]he did not adorn."[17] In the following pages, I
will first examine some topical facets that establish a network of shared—
as well as contrasting—values and practices. I will then move on to analyze
the intersection of Woolf and Johnson with respect to two particular
genres, literary criticism and biography—realizing that the boundaries
separating these are blurry and that they often intersect and overlap. I end
the chapter with a brief meditation upon the two as intertextual writers.

## II. Topics

There are a number of common topical points uniting the two. To begin
at perhaps the most mundane level, that of physical appetite, Woolf wrote
"One cannot think well, love well, sleep well, if one has not dined well."[18]
This is counterpointed by a Johnsonian conversational retort, recorded by
Boswell,

"Some people (said he,) have a foolish way of not minding, or
pretending not to mind, what they eat. For my part, I mind my

belly very studiously, and very carefully; for I look upon it, that he who does not mind his belly will hardly mind any thing else."[19]

Affinities of content aside, the remarks offer the basis for stylistic comparison. Woolf's is rather Johnsonian: she deploys such typically eighteenth-century rhetorical devices as isocolon, epistrophe, and the grand periodic conclusion—albeit with a quick, slender terseness that renders it her own. Johnson's declamation is, upon closer inspection, informed by a similar verbal craft. The first sentence and subsequent independent clauses are unified by verbal repetitions at their centers— "way of not *minding,*" "I *mind* my belly," "*mind* his belly"—simultaneously exhibiting the rhetorical tropes of conduplication and polyptoton. These repetitions are artfully contrasted: the generality of the first dilates into the specificity of the second, whose positive affirmation contrasts with the negativity of the last—"*does not.*" The ensemble concludes with a fourth repetition of the verb "mind," climactically tightening and drawing to a close the series by extending beyond dining toward larger dimensions of human life, just as Woolf's does in reverse.[20] Woolf and Johnson rank among the greatest stylists in the English language; an entire chapter, if not a book, could be devoted to this aspect of their art.

Moving from body to mind, of weightier import are their attitudes toward human psychology. Both suffered severely from depression. While in Scotland, Johnson related to Boswell: "I inherited (said he,) a vile melancholy from my father, which has made me mad all my life, at least not sober" (*Boswell's Life,* 5:215). He had two major breakdowns (that we know of). The first occurred in his twenties, shortly after poverty forced him to leave Oxford, and during which he contemplated suicide;[21] the second was when he was in his mid-fifties.[22] The latter introduced him to the mothering offices of Hester Thrale, who selflessly nursed Johnson back to mental stability and helped keep him healthily maintained until their break in 1784—likely precipitating his death a few months later. Woolf too died from complications arising from her depression. And, like Johnson, she suffered recurrent paralyzing (at times suicidal) collapses, sadly with much greater frequency.[23] Johnson's psychological debilities stem to a great extent from religious and familial—especially maternal—guilt, while Woolf's may be due in large part to a patriarchal oppression also involving familial issues, particularly with her father and step-brother. Awareness of Johnson's psychological struggles may have rendered him a more sympathetic figure to Woolf.

These personal perplexities enabled both writers to transmute their traumas, through deep introspection and careful intellectual analysis, into truths of larger, more general application. Both operate as masters of psychological insight: Johnson's meditative reflections led him to arrive at a wisdom that anticipates Freud.[24] Woolf was an early inhabitant of the Freudian age, who herself read (and, in 1939, met) Freud and took insights from him for fruitful introspective application.[25] And perhaps it is also safe to say that, for both Johnson and Woolf, immersion in social networks, engaging in conversations and sparkling intellectual conviviality, operated in part as a balm to the depression that assailed both.

Expanding outward from these privately subjective concerns, a larger topical element importantly uniting the two writers is their critique of colonialism. Johnson wrote essays and reviews—until he was (most likely) dismissed on account of his unpopular views—for the *Literary Magazine* that defiantly challenged the Great War for Empire that England embarked upon (quite successfully) between 1756 and 1763. Unlike most of his countrymen, he was offended by the manipulation of Native Americans in that conflict. For example, in "Observations on the Present State of Affairs. 1756," he wrote:

> The general subject of the present war is sufficiently known. It is allowed on both sides, that hostilities began in America, and that the French and English quarrelled about the boundaries of their settlements, about grounds and rivers to which, I am afraid, neither can shew any other right than that of power, and which neither can occupy but by usurpation, and the dispossession of the natural lords and original inhabitants. Such is the contest that no honest man can heartily wish success to either party. ... The American dispute, between the French and us is therefore only the quarrel of two robbers for the spoils of a passenger. (Yale *Works*, 10:186, 188)

Two decades later, in *Taxation no Tyranny*, he exposed the hypocrisy of the liberty-seeking Americans, who rhetorically bolstered their case against England by declaiming against their "Slavery and Oppression,"[26] with the retort, "If slavery be thus fatally contagious, how is it that we hear the loudest yelps for liberty among the drivers of negroes?" (Yale *Works*, 10:454). And Johnson once shocked a group of Oxford dons at table by proposing a toast to the next insurrection of the slaves in the West Indies.[27]

Woolf's opposition to colonialism appears throughout her writings, from her first published book, *The Voyage Out*, to the last, *Between the Acts*.[28] Indeed, the episode this chapter began with, the Dreadnought Hoax, may be parsed as an implicit rejection of imperialism, given its public humiliation of the primary instrument of British global supremacy since the mid-eighteenth century.[29] In *Three Guineas*, this opposition is unmistakable:

> There it is then, before our eyes, the procession of the sons of educated men, ascending those pulpits, mounting those steps, passing in and out of those doors, preaching, teaching, administering justice, practising medicine, making money. ... If you succeed in your profession the words "For God and Empire" will very likely be written, like the address on a dog-collar, round your neck. And if words have meaning, as words perhaps should have meaning, you will have to accept that meaning and do what you can to enforce it.[30]

Woolf's ironic scorn for the banality of the masculine professions denied to women here coalesces into her larger implicit rejection for the wider colonial apparatus that many actively served and to which most at least paid lip-service. Equivalizing the honorific Order of the British Empire into a dog-collar crystallizes the fury burning behind the words, words that *do* have meaning. Elsewhere in the book, Woolf writes:

> In short, all her conscious effort must be in favour of what Lady Lovelace called "our splendid Empire" ... "the price of which," she added, "is mainly paid by women." And who can doubt her, or that the price was heavy? (49)

Like Johnson, Woolf publicly—and in defiance of popular opinion—expresses anger and indignation at how the colonial apparatus harms and oppresses politically unrepresented or underrepresented populations.

Closely linked to this critique is the hostility both writers exhibited toward war. It is a point not often enough remembered that England was at war for much of Johnson's life: he died at age seventy-five, and Britain was engaged in major military conflicts for almost half of those years.[31] In the pamphlet *Thoughts on Falkland's Islands*, he remarks,

> As war is the last of remedies, *cuncta prius tentanda*, all lawful expedients must be used to avoid it. As war is the extremity of evil, it is surely the duty of those whose station intrusts them with the care of nations, to avert it from their charge. (Yale *Works*, 10:370)

In *Idler* 22 (September 9, 1758), he presents the reader with a modern beast fable in which an older vulture instructs the young:

> "When you hear noise and see fire which flashes along the ground, hasten to the place with your swiftest wing, for men are surely destroying one another; you will then find the ground smoking with blood and covered with carcasses, of which many are dismembered and mangled for the convenience of the vulture." "But when men have killed their prey," said the pupil, "why do they not eat it? When the wolf has killed a sheep he suffers not the vulture to touch it till he has satisfied himself. Is not man another kind of wolf?" "Man," said the mother, "is the only beast who kills that which he does not devour, and this quality makes him so much a benefactor to our species." (Yale *Works*, 2:319)

Johnson's satire, written in the second year of the Great War for Empire—one also sometimes called the first world war[32]—was so savage that when the *Idler* essays were reprinted in a collected edition (1761), No. 22 was removed, and the entire series was renumbered. His choice of a vulture—a bird possessing repellant connotations[33]—as the mouthpiece for a stinging indictment of warfare renders ironic comparison all the more ferocious. The slyly inserted allusion to the wolf as naturally superior to humans renders the jab even more acute.

Woolf's shorter lifetime witnessed the Boer War, the Spanish Civil War (in which hundreds of British volunteers fought, and where Woolf's nephew Julian Bell died fighting in 1937), and two world wars. Like many of her fellow Bloomsburians, Virginia Woolf is notable for her pacifist views.[34] This is a stance she maintained even in WWII, with its menacing threat of Nazism upon European civilization and the bombing of her own two London homes, at 52 Tavistock Square and 37 Mecklenburgh Square. Unlike Johnson, however—who vaguely gestured toward "lawful expedients" and "the duty of those whose station intrusts them with the care of nations"—she proposed specific solutions for the elimination of war. These are found most notably in *Three Guineas*, where she argued for the establishment of "an experimental college" that would eschew training for the professions, traditional ceremonies and rituals, and "the arts of dominating other people … the arts of ruling, of killing, of acquiring land and capital." Rather, "It should teach the arts of human intercourse; the arts of understanding other people's lives and minds." And, "It would be a place where society was free; not parceled out into the miserable distinctions of rich and poor, of clever and stupid; but where all the different degrees and kinds of mind, body and soul merit co-operated" (43). This forward-looking, visionary prescription is one clearly beyond Johnson's ken. And even had he been presented with it, in his own time and place, he likely would have found much to object to.

Nevertheless, Johnson himself was forward-looking enough to anticipate a predicament of war that Woolf personally experienced. In the midst of the Battle of Britain, during the summer of 1940, she wrote:

The Germans were over this house last night and the night before that. Here they are again. It is a queer experience, lying in the dark and listening to the zoom of a hornet which may at any moment sting you to death. It is a sound that interrupts cool and consecutive thinking about peace. Yet it is a sound—far more than prayers and anthems—that should compel one to think about peace. Unless we can think peace into existence we—not this one body in this one bed but millions of bodies yet to be born—will lie in the same darkness and hear the same death rattle overhead. Let us think what we can do to create the only efficient air-raid shelter while the guns on the hill go pop pop pop and the searchlights finger the clouds and now and then, sometimes close at hand, sometimes far away a bomb drops.[35]

In the winter of 1759, Johnson wrote "a dissertation on the art of flying." In it, the naïve Abyssinian prince asks the would-be inventor of a flying contraption—the "artist"—why such a boon should not be shared with all of humankind, "for universal good":

"If men were all virtuous," returned the artist, "I should with great alacrity teach them all to fly. But what would be the security of the good, if the bad could at pleasure invade them from the sky? Against an army sailing through the clouds neither walls, nor mountains, nor seas, could afford any security. A flight of northern savages might hover in the wind, and light at once with irresistible violence upon the capital of a fruitful region that was rolling under them."[36]

If Johnson can hardly be credited with the prescience to forecast the Nazi aerial assault upon the London capital and its outlying "fruitful regions," his insight into the terrible uses to which humans are capable of putting technology is clear enough. It is in part this insight, and the horrific consequences of its realization, that made him a vocal opponent of war.

In sum, Johnson and Woolf shared any number of views on topics important to their lives and writings. This brief precis is not intended to dilute or disguise the important differences separating the two; however, the affinities noted here—and many beyond them—are distinct, lucid, and incontrovertible.

## III.  Literary Criticism

Woolf and Johnson were among the leading literary critics of their respective generations. A good place to begin comparing their modes of literary criticism may be found in remarks each made upon *Paradise Lost*. Both were deeply impressed by it. Woolf was "struck by the extreme difference between this poem and any other," finding it "the essence, of which almost all other poetry is the dilution." And, "even Shakespeare after this would seem a little troubled, personal, hot and imperfect."[37] For Johnson, *Paradise Lost* "is not the greatest of heroick poems, only because it is not the first" (Yale *Works*, 21:205). That is to say, Homer is superior only because he possesses greater originality—always a plus on Johnson's critical score card. He says of Milton's language, "those who have a style of eminent excellence, such as Dryden and Milton, can always be distinguished" (*Boswell's Life*, 3:280).

Despite this shared praise, both critics home in on a negative characteristic they find in Milton: his lack of human sympathy. Woolf:

He deals in horror and immensity and squalor and sublimity but never in the passions of the human heart. Has any great poem ever let in so little light upon one's own joys and sorrows? I get no help in judging life; I scarcely feel that Milton lived or knew men and women; except for the peevish personalities about marriage and the woman's duties. He was the first of the masculinists, but his disparagement rises from his own ill luck and seems even a spiteful last word in his domestic quarrels. (*A Writer's Diary*, 5)

And Johnson:

But original deficience cannot be supplied. The want of human interest is always felt. *Paradise Lost* is one of the books which the reader admires and lays down, and forgets to take up again. None ever wished it longer than it is. Its perusal is a duty rather than a pleasure. We read Milton for instruction, retire harassed and overburdened, and look elsewhere for recreation; we desert our master, and seek for companions.

> Milton ... knew human nature only in the gross, and had never
> studied the shades of character, nor the combinations of concur-
> ring, or the perplexity of contending passions. He had read much,
> and knew what books could teach; but had mingled little in the
> world, and was deficient in the knowledge which experience
> must confer. (Yale *Works*, 21:196, 201)

(Significantly, Woolf read Johnson's "Life of Milton," as her approving comments upon it in "Saint Samuel of Fleet Street" reveal [*Essays of Virginia Woolf: Vol. 4*, 311]. Her objections to Milton's lack of passion may be a direct line influence from Johnson.) Both Woolf and Johnson respond in similar fashion to their perception of Milton's forbiddingness: in dealing with lofty epic affairs, "immensity and squalor and sublimity," he exhibits a "want of human interest." Woolf directly links this lacking "human heart" with misogyny, something indirectly evident in Johnson.

For example, Woolf's indictment of Milton as "the first of the mascu-linists" finds a correlation in some remarks Johnson made earlier in his Life of Milton, where he sympathizes with Milton's wife and daughters. His rehearsal of the details of the first marriage are bitingly acerbic:

> At Whitsuntide, in his thirty-fifth year, he married Mary, the
> daughter of Mr. Powel ... . He brought her to town with him, and
> expected all the advantages of a conjugal life. The lady, however,
> seems not much to have delighted in the pleasures of spare diet
> and hard study; for, as Phillips relates, "having for a month led
> a philosophical life, after having been used at home to a great
> house, and much company and joviality, her friends, possibly
> by her own desire, made earnest suit to have her company the
> remaining part of the summer; which was granted, upon a
> promise of her return at Michaelmas." ... Milton was too busy
> to much miss his wife: he pursued his studies; and now and then
> visited the lady Margaret Leigh, whom he has mentioned in one
> of his sonnets. (Yale *Works*, 21:123)

Here Johnson pointedly highlights Milton's egotistical self-absorption, one that blinds him to the needs and desires of his wife. Johnson soon details Milton's sending for his wife, only to be spurned; he then set about composing his first divorce tract.

Johnson's account of the treatment of Milton's daughters invites similar criticism of Milton's "masculinist" hardness. He includes, from Jonathan Richardson's early life, "he would sometimes lie awake whole nights, but not a verse could he make; and on a sudden his poetical faculty would rush upon him with an *impetus*, or *oestrum*, and his daughter was immediately called to secure what came" (Yale *Works*, 21:155). And he later quotes extensively from Edward Phillips' Life of Milton,

> yet excusing only the eldest daughter, by reason of her bodily infirmity, and difficult utterance of speech (which, to say truth, I doubt was the principal cause of excusing her), the other two were condemned to the performance of reading, and exactly pronouncing of all the languages of whatever book he should, at one time or other, think fit to peruse, viz. the Hebrew (and I think the Syriac), the Greek, the Latin, the Italian, Spanish, and French. All which sorts of books to be confined to read, without understanding one word, must needs be a trial of patience almost beyond endurance. (Yale *Works*, 21:161)

Detailing these trials of patience, Johnson unmistakably favors the daughters over a blind, peevish, domineering father—a set of traits with which Woolf herself would have been all too familiar with respect to the parent (nearly deaf, not blind) she wrote about near the close of her own life: "it was the tyrant father—the exacting, the violent, the histrionic, the demonstrative, the self-centred, the self pitying, the deaf, the appealing, the alternately loved and hated father—that dominated me then" (*Moments of Being*, 116). Hard masculinity indeed! In both cases we see the shading of critical assessment into biographical and autobiographical presentation, something apparent in the two writers. And, in this instance, we find evidence of "one of the very few human beings who love their kind" exemplified, in Johnson's generous sympathy for the wife and daughters of Milton, his reservations about the "peevish personalities about marriage and the woman's duties."

The sympathy both evince for the female emerging from their respective handling of Milton leads us to consider, as a kind of side-bar to this section, an additional correlation: their shared views upon the dignity of women and the importance of female authorship. Virginia Woolf is the doyen of twentieth-century Anglo-American feminism, and her importance in this role requires no further comment here. However, Johnson's intellectual respect for women is perhaps less obvious to some readers, and it is one demanding due consideration because of this famous observation:

> The woman composer stands where the actress stood in the time of Shakespeare. Nick Greene, I thought, remembering the story I had made about Shakespeare's sister, said that a woman acting put him in mind of a dog dancing. Johnson repeated the phrase two hundred years later of women preaching. And here, I said, opening a book about music, we have the very words used again in this year of grace, 1928, of women who try to write music. 'Of Mlle. Germaine Tailleferre one can only repeat Dr Johnson's dictum concerning, a woman preacher, transposed into terms of music. "Sir, a woman's composing is like a dog's walking on his hind legs. It is not done well, but you are surprised to find it done at all." So accurately does history repeat itself. (*A Room of One's Own*, 54)

Here is the actual anecdote:

> Next day, Sunday, July 31, I told him I had been that morning at a meeting of the people called Quakers, where I had heard a woman preach. JOHNSON. "Sir, a woman's preaching is like a dog's walking on his hinder legs. It is not done well; but you are surprized to find it done at all." (*Boswell's Life*, 1:463)

If this were the only evidence we had of Johnson's views, it would be damning indeed. However, compare it, for example, to a (undeservedly) less-reported remark, that Mary FitzHerbert (née Meynell) "had the best understanding he ever met with in any human being" (*Boswell's Life*, 1:83). In fact, given closer scrutiny, the evidence afforded by the surviving written record (in addition to the statements made above about Milton) suggests that the latter anecdote is far more indicative than the former, as an index for Johnson's genuine attitude toward women.

Johnson cultivated the friendship of numerous female authors—for example, Elizabeth Carter, Charlotte Lennox, and Frances Burney—many whose careers he actively supported.[38] In many respects, Johnson's attitudes toward women are surprisingly modern. This ground has already been well covered, and so there is no need to rehearse the details here.[39] As a thinker, as well as a critic, his views might be understood in certain respects to anticipate many feminist themes and concerns.

Despite the two authors' closeness, a distance separates them, and we can see Johnson's limitations from a feminist perspective quite clearly in their respective critical accounts of Swift's *Journal to Stella*. Johnson devotes a paragraph to it in his Life of Swift:

> In the midst of his power and his politicks, he kept a journal of his visits, his walks, his interviews with ministers, and quarrels with his servant, and transmitted it to Mrs. Johnson and Mrs. Dingley, to whom he knew that whatever befel him was interesting, and no accounts could be too minute. ... [T]he reader, finding frequent mention of names which he has been used to consider as important, goes on in hope of information; and, as there is nothing to fatigue attention, if he is disappointed he can hardly complain. It is easy to perceive, from every page, that though ambition pressed Swift into a life of bustle, the wish for a life of ease was always returning. (Yale *Works*, 22:990)

Here, Johnson's focus is upon the journalist. In the last sentence he extracts from his reading of the *Journal* aspects of Swift's psychology, his ambition mingled with his desire for retirement—two themes that preoccupied Johnson himself. He also notes the *Journal's* usefulness in discovering information about Swift's social and political context.

Woolf, on the other hand, devotes an entire essay to the *Journal to Stella*. Here are two representative passages:

> But the woman [Stella, Swift's name for Esther Johnson] he had chosen was no insipid slave. She had a character of her own. She was capable of thinking for herself. She was aloof, a severe critic for all her grace and sympathy, a little formidable perhaps with

her love of plain speaking and her fiery temper and her fearlessness in saying what she thought. But with all her gifts she was little known. Her slender means and feeble health and dubious social standing made her way of life very modest.

Stella was left to enjoy her intimacy alone. She lived on to practise those sad arts by which she kept her friend at her side until, worn out with the strain and the concealment, with Mrs. Dingley and her lap-dogs, with the perpetual fears and frustrations, she too died. As they buried her, Swift sat in a back room away from the lights in the churchyard and wrote an account of the character of "the truest, most virtuous, and valuable friend, that I, or perhaps any other person, was ever blessed with."[40]

Woolf, unlike Johnson, devotes the bulk of her account not to analyzing the text of the *Journal* but rather to imaginatively reconstructing the inner life and world of its addressee. She employs her novelistic art to present a deeply human portrait of a woman who, "no slave," and possessing extraordinary "gifts," was nonetheless "little known" and reduced to virtual servitude under the egotistic sway of a man "omnipotent" (68)—something that resonates with Milton's treatment of his wife and daughters noted earlier. Was the sacrifice of assenting to being a nonentity worth, Woolf implicitly asks, the drafting of a laudatory remembrance after her funeral—one she would never read?

The detail of Swift shunning the lingering light in the churchyard so he can pen his remembrance in the dark cloister of his study nicely sums up the dilemma. In the end, Swift preferred his own quill to Stella's candle. Did Esther choose wisely in subordinating herself to Swift? Or did she even have a choice—perhaps her culture allowed her nothing better? Both accounts are critical, in a larger sense: Johnson's in the service of recovering Swift's character and age, Woolf's in the service of recovering the woman who certainly catalyzed the *Journal* and who indisputably inspired other productions from Swift's pen. But it would have been impossible, given the gendered restrictions of his time and place, for Johnson to write the account Woolf did.

The two critics' assessments of Addison are significant. Johnson wrote a Life (published in 1781); Woolf wrote an essay for the *TLS*, published on June 19, 1919. Johnson was writing some seventy years after Addison's death; Woolf two hundred (almost to the day). But Johnson had grown up when Addison's works were still a major cultural presence; on the other hand, by Woolf's time Addison had become merely a name, a figure barely alive: "he still draws his faint, regular breath" (*The Common Reader, First Series*, 96–97). (Note Woolf's covert allusion to Johnson's observation in the Life of Addison, "He thinks justly; but he thinks faintly" [Yale *Works*, 22:649]. She read Johnson well.) In 1781, Johnson was coming to terms, late in his life, with a writer who had had a decisive influence upon his own thought and his career as a writer (the *Rambler* was in many ways a direct response to the *Spectator*[41]), while Woolf was working to bridge the "troublesome barriers between ourselves and Addison."[42]

From these two accounts important commonalties emerge. Neither Johnson nor Woolf are academic critics: rather, they write for the "common reader," for those "uncorrupted by literary prejudices ... and the dogmatism of learning" (Yale *Works*, 3:1470–71). Furthermore, they both write as much as poets as critics. Here is Johnson:

> His prose is the model of the middle stile; on grave subjects not formal, on light occasions not grovelling; pure without scrupulosity, and exact without apparent elaboration; always equable, and always easy, without glowing words or pointed sentences. Addison never deviates from his track to snatch a grace; he seeks no ambitious ornaments, and tries no hazardous innovations. His page is always luminous, but never blazes in unexpected splendour. (Yale *Works*, 2:678)

Implicit in the paragraph is the metaphor of fire. However, Johnson, with great subtlety, initially uses words that have an etymological root in fire or light, but that are overlaid with a more abstract meaning: "glowing words" (cf. *Dictionary*, s.v., "glow": "5. To feel passion of mind, or activity of fancy") and "always luminous" (*Dictionary*, s.v., "luminous": "2. Enlightened"). It is in the final phrase, "blazes in unexpected splendor," that the image leaps out from its subdued smolder into a climactic literal signification. Likewise, Johnson employs the art of allusion to convey and reinforce meaning: "snatch a grace" refers to Alexander Pope's "And *snatch* a *Grace* beyond the Reach of Art."[43] It is in himself "snatching" an allusion from another poet's exercise in critical theory where Johnson demonstrates himself a true poet in the guise of a critic.

Here is a representative passage from Woolf's "Addison":

> It seems so often scarcely worth while to go through the cherishing and humanising process which is necessary to get into touch with a writer of the second class who may, after all, have little to give us. The earth is crusted over them; their features are obliterated, and perhaps it is not a head of the best period that we rub clean in the end, but only the chip of an old pot. (*The Common Reader, First Series*, 97)

Like Johnson, she offers a statement initially couched in abstraction. This is quickly followed by a parallel statement that is purely concrete and figural. The metaphor is archaeological; its connotation of meticulous and labored digging past the "troublesome barriers" adroitly communicates the temporal distance Woolf must bridge. But her tactile, concrete diction—"crusted over," "rub clean," "chip of an old pot"—proleptically bring the "obliterated features" of her subject vividly to life, even as it poetically enlivens the nature of her critical procedure.

There are, of course, significant differences separating the two. Johnson is, as almost always, a moralist:

> As a teacher of wisdom he [Addison] may be confidently followed. His religion has nothing in it enthusiastick or superstitious: he appears neither weakly credulous nor wantonly sceptical; his morality is neither dangerously lax, nor impracticably rigid. All the enchantment of fancy and all the cogency of argument are employed to recommend to the reader his real interest, the care of pleasing the Author of his being. Truth is shewn sometimes as the phantom of a vision, sometimes appears half-veiled in an allegory; sometimes attracts regard in the robes of fancy, and

sometimes steps forth in the confidence of reason. She wears a thousand dresses, and in all is pleasing. (Yale *Works*, 22:677)

Woolf has little truck with this:

> In the first place, there remains the not despicable virtue, after two centuries of existence, of being readable. Addison can fairly lay claim to that; and then, slipped in on the tide of the smooth, well-turned prose, are little eddies, diminutive waterfalls, agreeably diversifying the polished surface. We begin to take note of whims, fancies, peculiarities on the part of the essayist which light up the prim, impeccable countenance of the moralist and convince us that, however tightly he may have pursed his lips, his eyes are very bright and not so shallow after all. (*The Common Reader, First Series*, 100–101)

Johnson's approval of Addison as a "teacher of wisdom" is unambiguously affirmative. Woolf, on the other hand, incisively probes the whims, fancies, and peculiarities that subvert "the prim, impeccable countenance of the moralist." Elsewhere in the essay she makes fun of his bourgeois pretensions, his *une petite morale*. However, she never allows this to distract her from the "head of the best period" that her critical faculties allow her to unearth. Hers was a largely aesthetic excavation, Johnson's a call to live life well beneath the eye of the Author of our being.

For both Johnson and Woolf, Addison was a contemporary—but for very different reasons. He represented to Johnson the Augustan culture that he himself sought to uphold, extend, and indeed explain throughout his *Lives of the Poets* to a literary culture that was rapidly moving into *terra incognita*, from Sensibility toward Romanticism:

> What he attempted, he performed; he is never feeble, and he did not wish to be energetick; he is never rapid, and he never stagnates. His sentences have neither studied amplitude, nor affected brevity: his periods, though not diligently rounded, are voluble and easy. Whoever wishes to attain an English stile, familiar but

not coarse, and elegant but not ostentatious, must give his days
and nights to the volumes of Addison. (Yale *Works*, 22:678)

Woolf, on the other hand, discovers—or imaginatively creates—a different
contemporary:

> In all these matters Addison was on the side of sense and taste
> and civilisation. Of that little fraternity, often so obscure and yet
> so indispensable, who in every age keep themselves alive to the
> importance of art and letters and music, watching, discriminating,
> denouncing and delighting, Addison was one—distinguished and
> strangely contemporary with ourselves. (*The Common Reader,
> First Series*, 101)

In this, Woolf was distinctly a Modernist—aesthetic, secular, skeptical—
while Johnson remains rooted in his tradition of Christian humanism:
moral, devout, and an unwavering disciple of absolute truth.

In "The Modern Essay" Woolf writes

> There is no room for the impurities of literature in an essay.
> Somehow or other, by dint of labour or bounty of nature, or
> both combined, the essay must be pure—pure like water or pure
> like wine, but pure from dullness, deadness, and deposits of
> extraneous matter. (*Selected Essays*, 14–15)

She is talking specifically about Walter Pater's "Notes on Leonardo da
Vinci," but she implicitly recalls Johnson's remark about his greatest
essay project: "My other works are wine and water; but my *Rambler* is
pure wine."[44] The same may be said of both Johnson and Woolf's literary
criticism: in its distillation of extraneous matter into the finest essence, it
repays repeated re-readings. Which is to say that, in their hands, when
they are at their best, when metaphorically pouring pure wine into
nonfiction prose, their literary criticism becomes literature itself. Despite
the gulf separating them, the Modernist Woolf found much to value in
the "conservative" Johnson, and this speaks as much to Woolf's fineness of
intellect as it does to Johnson's modernity.

## IV. Biography

Johnson and Woolf were at once important theorists and practitioners of biography. Johnson's biographical writings fill four of the twenty-three volumes of his collected works; his disciple James Boswell, who assimilated and further extended Johnsonian principles, composed what is still considered by many to be the greatest biography ever written. The influence of Woolf's father, founding editor and major contributor to the massive *Dictionary of National Biography*, is evident in and important to her own biographical project. She herself wrote the book-length biographies *Flush: A Biography* and *Roger Fry*, a fictional biography of Vita Sackville-West, *Orlando*, and numerous brief biographical sketches are scattered throughout her other work. In addition, both devoted themselves to autobiographical writings.[45]

In his most important theoretical meditation upon biography, *Rambler* 60, Johnson wrote:

> But biography has often been allotted to writers who seem very little acquainted with the nature of their task, or very negligent about the performance. They rarely afford any other account than might be collected from publick papers, but imagine themselves writing a life when they exhibit a chronological series of actions or preferments; and so little regard the manners or behaviour of their heroes, that more knowledge may be gained of a man's real character, by a short conversation with one of his servants, than from a formal and studied narrative, begun with his pedigree, and ended with his funeral. (Yale *Works*, 3:322)

Johnson's principal innovation is to shift the biographer's focus away from the public and external to the private and interior, "to lead the thoughts into domestick privacies, and display the minute details of daily life, where exterior appendages are cast aside" (321). His goal is to penetrate to the essential truth of the person.

An important tactic in this strategy of recuperation is to identify what he calls the "particular fact":

> If now and then they [biographers] condescend to inform the
> world of particular facts, they are not always so happy as to select
> the most important. I know not well what advantage posterity
> can receive from the only circumstance by which Tickell has
> distinguished Addison from the rest of mankind, *the irregularity
> of his pulse* .... (Yale *Works*, 3:322)

The particular fact is a small detail that operates as a revelatory portal
into the larger character and personality, the "manners or behaviour," of
the biographical subject. Johnson here dismisses the detail from Thomas
Tickell's 1721 Preface to the *Works of Addison* because of its insufficient
attention to Addison's individuation: an irregular pulse is a merely physical condition extraneous to the truth of who Addison was. Elsewhere in
the essay, Johnson provides a few positive examples of what he means,
including this one, from *De conjuratione Catilinae*: "Thus Salust, the great
master of nature, has not forgot, in his account of Catiline, to remark
that *his walk was now quick, and again slow,* as an indication of a mind
revolving something with violent commotion" (321). Here the particular
fact *does* involve a physical action, but one intimately connected with
Catiline's state of mind. One of Johnson's key interests in writing biography, then, is psychological: he is about mental states and the specific
details that reveal them.

In her important essay "The Art of Biography," Woolf wrote:

> When and where did the real man live; how did he look; did he
> wear laced boots or elastic-sided; who were his aunts, and his
> friends; how did he blow his nose; whom did he love, and how;
> and when he came to die did he die in his bed like a Christian,
> or ... . But almost any biographer, if he respects facts, can give
> us much more than another fact to add to our collection. He can
> give us the creative fact; the fertile fact; the fact that suggests and
> engenders. Of this, too, there is certain proof.[46]

Woolf here describes the ideal biographer, one who moves past the
mechanical "facts of science," which, she says, once discovered, are "always
the same" (121). That is to say, the true biographer goes beyond static and

superficial description to find things that disclose the fertile fullness of the self. Like Johnson's preference for the "particular fact" that reveals an inner truth over a "chronological series of actions or preferments," Woolf urges the creative fact that enables "that high degree of tension that gives us reality" (122). Both Johnson and Woolf value those specifics that culminate in a revelation of self that transcends the trivial trappings of superficial exteriority. As she says elsewhere, in discussing the "particular fact" of her inability to look into a mirror, "In spite of all this, people write what they call 'lives' of other people; that is, they collect a number of events ["a chronological series of actions or preferments"], and leave the person to whom it happened unknown."[47]

We find another example of Johnson's deployment of the significant fact in his Life of Swift. Johnson typically divided his major works in the *Lives of the Poets* into a tripartite structure. The first offers a biographical narrative of the life, the last a critical account of the author's works. These are separated by what the eighteenth century called a "character," a genre practiced by such seventeenth-century writers such as Joseph Hall and Thomas Overbury, who in turn revived it from the classical Greek author Theophrastus. Johnson defined the genre in his *Dictionary* as "4. A representation of any man as to his personal qualities": that is, the "character" is a brief distillation of the principal distinguishing aspects that form a person's identity.

It is in this middle, "character" section in the Life of Swift that the following passage is found:

> The person of Swift had not many recommendations. He had a kind of muddy complexion, which, though he washed himself with oriental scrupulosity, did not look clear. He had a countenance sour and severe, which he seldom softened by any appearance of gaiety. He stubbornly resisted any tendency to laughter. (Yale *Works*, 22:1014–15)

Swift's "muddy [*Dictionary*: s.v., "Dark; not bright"] complexion," which washing would not make "clear" (*Dictionary*: s.v., "Bright; not dark"), betrays a psychological insight. Despite his inability to "brighten" his countenance, Swift continues to wash his face over and over again, the passage implies, because he, like Woolf, is unwilling to accept the mirror's reflection. Johnson here lightly touches upon an aspect of Swift he takes up a little later in the Life—that which later writers have called his "excremental vision":[48]

> The greatest difficulty that occurs in analysing his character, is to discover by what depravity of intellect he took delight in revolving ideas, from which almost every other mind shrinks with disgust. The ideas of pleasure, even when criminal, may solicite the imagination; but what has disease, deformity, and filth, upon which the thoughts can be allured to dwell? (Yale *Works*, 22:1020)

Swift's "oriental scrupulosity," then, suggest ablutions attempting to purge the deformity and filth that apparently obsessed his mind. Johnson's precise choice of diction, "muddy," indexes the "filth" to be found within. Swift's corrupt imagination and depraved intellect are signs of a suspect character that baffle explanation. The tone of Johnson's biography of Swift is a dark one, and this darkness can be indexed by the particular fact of Swift's "muddy complexion." This particular fact not only offers a clue to Swift's character but also operates as an interpretive avenue into understanding Johnson's Life of Swift considered more generally.

My reading provides an interpretive angle to the concluding "character" by Dr. Delany that Johnson quotes at length two pages later—a character that seems to fly in the face of the dark tonality that precedes, as Johnson acknowledges: "I have here given the character of Swift as he exhibits himself to my perception, but now let another be heard who knew him better." Consider this extract:

> All this considered, the character of his life will appear like that of his writings … . They will bear to be considered as the sun, in which the brightness will hide the blemishes; and whenever petulant ignorance, pride, malice, malignity, or envy, interposes to cloud or sully his fame, I will take upon me to pronounce that the eclipse will not last long. (Yale *Works*, 22:1022)

Johnson's "particular fact" of the "muddy countenance" ironizes Delany's hyperbolic puffery, and, indeed, Johnson's darkening "eclipse" has lasted much longer than Delany's putative "brightness."

To these remarks we might compare an example from Woolf, her description of H. G. Wells:

> Wells rather shrunk. Hair still brown, but has the dyed appearance of hair that is brown on an old face. Lines more marked: skin less plumped out. He was very affable: put both hands on top of L.'s to signalise his regret I suppose for their quarrel.

This is shortly followed by:

> Then we go on to Russian politics, so, somehow to Tom Eliot. Tee Ess he called him with a hiss of despite; & then proceeded to say how he, which I think meant we, had been the death of English literature. Afraid of being vulgar, thats what was at the root of it.[49]

While not a biography strictly speaking, this and the larger sketch from which it is drawn possess a strongly biographical flavor. Indeed, like other such sketches,[50] it may be viewed as an informal reconstitution of the seventeenth- and eighteenth-century character genre practiced by Johnson. The example given here of Wells certainly demonstrates Johnson's "particular fact," or Woolf's "creative, fertile fact." The shrunken posture reflects his diminished status in the current literary scene (later Woolf observes his remark that Wells, hopefully, "remembers that he has done a vast mass of work & thinks it wont all die"). This diminishment is further brought out by the detail about his hair and its contrast with his countenance: the youthful color of brown jars with his "old face," and this physical discrepancy chimes with his dislocation from modern authors such "Tee Ess" and Woolf herself ("he, which I think meant we"). English literature is dying, proclaims this seventy-year-old man, himself in danger of becoming a cultural non-entity. Woolf observes in his "dyed" physical appearance an older literary world has died.

We see a similar technique in the more properly biographical sketch Woolf wrote of her father. There, she reports, "For, as his tailor remarked when he saw my father walk past his shop up Bond Street, 'There goes a gentleman that wears good clothes without knowing it.'"[51] The preposition "for" connects the quotation with her prior observation that, despite his "great learning and wide experience," Leslie Stephen "would never impose his own views or parade his own knowledge." Yet it may be said to extend to illustrate a larger and less generous truth about the man—that despite his extraordinarily massive accomplishments as a man of letters he was ever plagued by a gnawing self-doubt that blinded him to his own sterling qualities: he is oblivious to the "good clothes" that he in fact possessed: "grown solitary and very deaf, he would sometimes call himself a failure as a writer; he had been 'jack of all trades, and master of none'" (115). As we see in Woolf's depiction of her father as Mr. Ramsay in *To the Lighthouse*, this self-doubt and sense of failure manifested in a craving vacuity that demanded emotional ministrations at times almost unbearable to his wife and children.[52]

Both Johnson's and Woolf's biographical writings are marked by the implementation of specific physical details—"particular facts"—that do more than describe appearance. They operate as little windows fretted upon the external physique that allow us to peer into inner qualities that work to constitute, piece-by-piece, the whole of the person—according to Woolf's and Johnson's respective interpretive lights. Whether it be Catiline's revolving walk, Swift's obsessive face-scrubbing, Wells' "dyed" appearance, or Stephen's good clothes, these authors masterfully deploy surface tesserae that contribute to the larger mosaic of their full-fledged portraits. In this respect, then, Woolf may be viewed as a successor to the Johnsonian school of biography.

Despite these summoning similarities, there are of course important differences—ones echoing those found in the earlier discussion of their literary criticism. Johnson preached and practiced biography as subsidiary to his overarching preoccupation with morality. For him, we read biographies because they help make us better people: "no species of writing seems more worthy of cultivation than biography, since none can … more widely diffuse instruction to every diversity of condition," and "Biography is, of the various kinds of narrative writing, that which is most eagerly read, and most easily applied to the purposes of life."[53] For Johnson, the purpose of life is to be an ethically responsible agent. For Woolf, biography is more of an aesthetic performance; at its highest level, it operates as a rival, but a lesser one, to literature: "Even Dr. Johnson as created by Boswell will not live as long as Falstaff as created by Shakespeare."[54]

Woolf's word "created" in the last sentence is highly suggestive. For her, the art of biography was just that—an art. It is not a precise science. She remarks in the same paragraph of a passage quoted above, "… it is so difficult to give an account of the person to whom things happen. The person is evidently immensely complicated. … I do not suppose that I have got to the truth" ("Sketch of the Past," 69). For Johnson, truth in biography as in all other things was fundamental: "A strict adherence to truth he considered as a sacred obligator insomuch that in relating the most minute anecdote he would not allow himself the smallest addition to embellish his story."[55] Johnson seeks the truth of the individual because (s)he is representative of a larger species: "All joy or sorrow for the happiness or calamities of others is produced by an act of the imagination, that … plac[es] us, for a time, in the condition of him whose fortune we contemplate."[56] That the individual person becomes subsumed within this larger moral purpose is a paradox—or perhaps a blind spot—in Johnson's biographical project. His commitment to the truth of individual subjectivity becomes an instrument for moral instruction. Woolf sees her subjects as more individual, unique, and hence more interesting precisely because of that particularity. Johnson's biographical subjects present us with a mirror in which we are able to view ourselves more clearly; Woolf's offer us a perspective upon other vistas that take us outside of ourselves to examine another. The particular fact, the creative fact, despite their technical similarities, are deployed for quite different biographical procedures.

## V. Conclusion

David Denby has written of *To the Lighthouse*, "the entire tradition of Western literature could be heard breathing through that book."[57] Johnson's own inspiration may be traced in the novel. For example, Woolf shifted the setting of the events based upon her own life from Cornwall to the Hebrides. I suspect that this was inspired by an imaginative evocation of that exotic place based upon her reading of Johnson and Boswell's actual journey there, a conjecture supported, for example, in the reference to emigration because of economic hardship—a key theme of the 1773 visit—in "that book" (*To the Lighthouse*, 127). Johnson's presence there may also be discerned in Ramsay's reflection, "The very stone one kicks with one's boot will outlast Shakespeare" (50). This, along with the presence elsewhere of Bishop Berkeley, suggests a famous passage from Boswell:

> After we came out of the church, we stood talking for some time together of Bishop Berkeley's ingenious sophistry to prove the nonexistence of matter, and that every thing in the universe is merely ideal. I observed, that though we are satisfied his doctrine is not true, it is impossible to refute it. I never shall forget the alacrity with which Johnson answered, striking his foot with mighty force against a large stone, till he rebounded from it,—"I refute it *thus*." (*Boswell's Life*, 1:471)

The kicks are complementary: Johnson's insists upon the reality of the empirically perceived world so that we may trust its actuality; Ramsay's thought hauntingly contrasts the ephemeral fleetingness of the actuality that Johnson insists upon with the stability of a larger geological reality. Johnson affirms the dignity of humanity, Ramsay diminishes it. The vague remark in the novel on Tansley's dissertation, about the "influence of somebody on somebody," repeated twice for emphasis (91, 140), operates as a sly synecdochal reference, perhaps, to Johnson's influence—among many others, as Denby observes—upon Woolf.[58]

Woolf, High Modernist *par excellence*, revitalized and made her own key elements from the "great books." Johnson, drawing upon the well-springs of biblical and classical antiquity, and the cultural heritage of the Renaissance, did the same thing for his day and age. Put another way, both Woolf and Johnson were densely intertextual artists.[59] Of course, all writers are intertextual. These two, however, were acutely aware of their debt to the tradition and of the peril and potential that this entailed. As should be clear, Woolf's intertextual assimilation and redeployment of Johnson exemplifies how the materials of the past may be appropriated to make new art of the highest order.

# CHAPTER THREE

# "Intellectually 'Fuori del Mondo'"

## Pound's Johnson

*Joe Moffett*

## I. Introduction

At a 1984 meeting of Johnsonians, David Perkins argued for the importance of Johnson and his peers to the Modernist poets, especially T. S. Eliot.
"Praise of the Augustans in Modernist criticism," he contended, "is ordi-
narily combined with an attack on Romanticism. The Augustan mode is
presented as a possible deliverance from error, yet a deliverance that only
the strong-minded can receive."[1] In Perkins's model, the Augustan poets
offer the Modernists an alternative approach to poetry not centered in
the emotional life of the speaker, as associated with Romantics poetics.
Instead it is a more cerebral and intellectually demanding method, as one
finds in Pope or Johnson. Perkins shows how Pound helped Eliot edit the
early lines in *The Waste Land* that aspired to Augustan verse but were not
successful. He says little about Pound's own work, however. In efforts such
as *The Spirit of Romance* (1910), *ABC of Reading* (1934), and *The Guide
to Kulchur* (1938), Pound identified the literature and ideas he felt most
worthy of preservation and study. His writing on poets was almost always
polemical, and his statements on Johnson are accordingly complicated.

Part of this conflict can be understood by thinking about the
immense pressure associated with poetic influence. One of the best
known and longest enduring models for assessing a later writer's grappling with his influences is Harold Bloom's "anxiety of influence." This

is not to say that Bloom's model escapes criticism or that it is without its problems. Aside from blind spots with regard to gender and sexual orientation, Bloom's theory presents a metanarrative of literary transmission, and metanarratives have long been an object of postmodernist thinkers' critique.[2] Nevertheless, Bloom's ideas offer a useful heuristic if not an infallible model, and they shed light on the writers under study here. Bloom famously contends that "the anxiety of influence *comes out of* a complex act of strong misreading, a creative interpretation that I call 'poetic misprision.'"[3] He believes that this is a universal issue: "influence-anxieties are embedded in the agonistic basis of all imaginative literature."[4] Indeed, he goes so far as to argue that "The largest truth of literary influence is that it is an irresistible anxiety."[5] This anxiety is detectable in the case of Pound and Johnson: the later poet praises his precursor for his general intellectual ability but grows more parsimonious when it comes to assessing Johnson's verse. There, Pound's views change, and one of Bloom's "six revisionary ratios" of influence—he calls it "tessera"—is particularly applicable. Bloom explains that "A poet antithetically 'completes' his precursor, by so reading the parent-poem as to retain its terms but to mean them in another sense, as though the precursor had failed to go far enough."[6] Later, in his study, Bloom adds to his definition of tessera by noting, "the later poet provides what his imagination tells him would complete otherwise 'truncated' precursor poem and poet."[7] Seen in this way, Pound attempts to "complete" Johnson's project of serving as an influential literary thinker *and* a groundbreaking poet. As seen below, his comments show that he does not perceive Johnson as both. Pound fails to fulfill this task and struggles in his own work with defects he finds in Johnson's.

Pound's view of Johnson should be understood in the context of the later poet's understanding of history. For Pound, the Enlightenment was generally a period of decline from what he saw as a cultural high point in the Renaissance. Given his historical setting, then, it makes sense that Johnson would stand out as a figure of consideration for Pound. One of Pound's enduring preoccupations, of course, was his concern with monetary systems, particularly the disastrous effects of usury, in the post-Renaissance period.[8] In this regard, *The Cantos*' famous "usury canto," XLV, is especially instructive.[9] A note at the end of the canto explains,

"Usury: A charge for the use of purchasing power, levied without regard to production; often without regard to the possibilities of production."[10] Pound posits that the corrupting influences of this financial institution filter down to the work of artisans, whom he suggests demonstrate failing skills: "With usura hath no man a house of good stone / each block cut smooth and well fitting." Pound memorably and emphatically argues that art loses its fine detail through the advent of usury: "with usura the line grows thick," he argues, "with usura is no clear demarcation."[11] This "thickening" of the line will be detectable by future scholars of the period and proves one indication by which modern economics have compromised society.[12]

The deleterious effects of usury extend to other areas as well. From depictions of the paradise and the Annunciation ("with usura / hath no man a painted paradise on his church [...] or where virgin receiveth message / and halo projects from incision"), to the commerce of art ("no picture is made to endure nor to live with / but it is made to sell and sell quickly"), to even the basis of bodily sustenance ("with usura, sin against nature, / is thy bread ever more of stale rags / is thy bread dry as paper"), Pound offers a vision of usury that leaves all it touches suffocating in mediocrity. As if the far-reaching effects of usury in various types of economic exchange were not enough, he suggests "Usura slayeth the child in the womb."[13] The unborn child's life is already decided by usury's influence on society; there will be no escape from its crushing effect until reform comes.

With this view of the trade-off society has made in financing modern life, Pound can only conclude that quality of life drops sharply in the post-Renaissance period. Perhaps not surprisingly, then, in *Guide to Kulchur*, Pound identifies the eighteenth century as "cliché."[14] This is not to say, however, that he dismisses all its writers. Pound examines many literary juggernauts in his prose, but it is in the course of discussing Voltaire in *ABC of Reading* that Pound engages with Johnson.[15] As a leading eighteenth-century figure, Johnson might seem unlikely to receive praise from Pound, and yet Pound calls him "Very possibly the best mind in England of his day, save for those months that Voltaire spent in London."[16] Pound notes Johnson is "admirable because he will not lick boots, but intellectually 'fuori del mondo,' living in the seventeenth century, so far as Europe is concerned." Placing Johnson in the seventeenth century, intellectually if not historically, Pound dissociates him from the purported decline of art and life brought on by practices such as usury. It is worth underscoring, too, that Pound's Johnson is a fiercely independent figure ("will not lick boots"), one whom Pound himself attempts to embody. Johnson cuts a path that later strong figures, such as Pound, can then widen and extend.

## II. Johnson's *The Vanity of Human Wishes*

Pound does not have more to say about Johnson in *ABC of Reading*, but elsewhere he discusses *The Vanity of Human Wishes* at some length. This engagement should not be surprising given Pound's indefatigable staking of territory in the field of verse. The poem was written in 1748 as an imitation of Satire X of Juvenal, and it is considered Johnson's finest. There are some timely replacements made, such as trading Juvenal's reference to Hannibal for Charles XII of Sweden (1697–1718). Johnson also relies on Christian spirituality to supply a hopeful end message to what is otherwise a rather dark and moody poem. Completed while Johnson was working on his *Dictionary*, the poem stretches over 368 lines and is written in a favorite eighteenth-century form: the heroic couplet. The poem opens with a reflection on the rise and fall of nations and "How rarely reason guides their stubborn choice" (l.11). The tension between reason and emotion runs throughout the poem, establishing a duality that accounts for human unhappiness but also suggests its remedy. The value of reason is typically seen as an Enlightenment touchstone, and so this feature of the poem throws an interesting light on Pound's desire to disassociate Johnson from this "cliché" of eras. The poem's speaker identifies an accumulative process: "Wealth heaped on wealth, nor truth nor safety buys. / The dangers gather as the treasures rise" (ll.28–29). If commerce and wealth undermine more fundamental values, including truth and well-being, they endanger the very heart of society. These perceived threats resonate with Pound's feelings that art and culture have grown coarser with the influence of what he calls "usury age-old and age-thick."[17]

There is a melancholy and nostalgia in Johnson's poem that foreshadows what appears later in Pound. Bringing to mind the theme of *ubi sunt*, Johnson writes, "For now no more we trace in every line / Heroic worth, benevolence divine" (ll.87–88). The speaker offers the present as a time of belatedness, but also, by extension, a time of transition from one great age into a future of uncertainty. It may be the case that there will arise again those of "heroic worth" and "benevolence divine," but, for that to happen, society itself would need to improve, and individuals would need to rise to the challenge. Before the poem strikes a more hopeful note, it grows even darker: "life protracted is protracted woe" (l.258); "New sorrow rises as the day returns" (l.301). This dim mood carries on until near the poem's end, where Johnson intones, "Where then shall Hope and Fear their objects find? / Must dull Suspense corrupt the stagnant mind? / Must helpless man, in ignorance sedate, / Roll darkling down the torrent of his fate?" (ll.343–47). There is a very modern feel to these lines; their sentiment anticipates some of the darker moods of Modernism. Indeed, there is almost an unbreakable pessimism, a fundamental mistrust in the possibility of improvement of the human condition. This mistrust would be confirmed later when poets such as Pound wrote in the aftermath of World War I, which proved to undermine any notion of society's "progress." Sedated by ignorance, the "helpless man" cascades down into his "fate" as humanity's downfall is all but certain under the present circumstances.

Johnson's lines strike an elegiac tone that has been shown to undergird much of Modernism.[18] The melancholy mood presages and is then amplified by further terseness in such work as *Hugh Selwyn Mauberley* by Pound. The speaker there imagines himself "out of key with his time," pursuing poetry despite having "been born / In a half savage country."[19] The early hopefulness that America might be able to sidestep the long-standing problems of Europe has proven baseless. By the turn of the century, the United States was still, regrettably, a "half savage" country largely inhabited by philistines who cared little for the higher powers of poetry. Nevertheless, Europe proves just as savage in its own way by wasting unfulfilled young lives in war: "Died some, pro patria / non 'Dulce' non 'et decor' / walked eye-deep in hell / believing in old men's lies."[20] Unfortunately, those who had been told it was "sweet" to die for one's country and who paid the costs in blood had sacrificed themselves in World War I: "There died a myriad / And of the best, among them, / For an old bitch gone in the teeth, / For a botched civilization [...] For two gross of broken statutes, / For a few thousand battered books."[21] Society's achievements—broken statues, battered books—offer little compensation for the spoken lies that lead to a "botched civilization." The human costs are immeasurable; "the best, among them" are now gone and cannot aid in the rebuilding of society. In Pound's view, society's wrongheaded faith in profit over the value of art and human wellbeing has created a civilization that is anything but civilized.

The elegiac tone of *The Vanity of Human Wishes* grows nationalistic: "will not Britain hear the last appeal" the speaker asks (l.91). This updating of the source text with a nationalistic bent is similarly reflected in one of Pound's own creative translations, that of the Old English lyric "The Seafarer," from early in his career (1911). There, he mistranslates the spiritually aspirational line of "lifge mid englum" ("live among the angels") as "And his laud beyond them remain 'mid the English."[22] Hugh Kenner notes this alteration "has long been pointed to as a prize howler, but he did it deliberately."[23] Aside from clearing the poem from what he viewed as later Christian insertions into a pagan text, Pound retroactively posits a literary origin point in Anglo-Saxon verse.[24] The history of England and the stately resolve of the English are burnished by their association with such a deeply felt originary literature. By this point, Pound had left America behind and had lived in England for a handful of years. Johnson too updated Juvenal's poem to place it in his contemporary England and thus, like Pound, brings the past into the present in a compression of time that is accommodated by the compressed nature of poetry. Unlike the insertion of Christian spirituality in Johnson's poem, however, Pound's translation cuts the end part of "The Seafarer" where the poem deepens its spiritual longing.

Despite the darkness that runs throughout *The Vanity of Human Wishes*, there is the recurring appeal to reason: "Reason guide thee with her brightest ray" (l.144). Reason is presented as the light that will lead humankind to an understanding of peace: "Reason frowns on war's unequal game" (l.186). Faith, too, offers a respite from humanity's lesser urges:

> For faith, that panting for a happier seat,
> These goods for man the laws of heaven ordain,
> These goods he grants, who grants the power to gain;

With these celestial wisdom calms the mind,
And makes the happiness she does not find. (ll.362–67)

The Christian overtones of heaven and its "celestial wisdom," she who "calms the mind" and "makes [...] happiness," help Johnson recontextualize the poem into his own time, although by the era of Pound even this kind of hopefulness in the salvific promise of religion will be largely absent from literature, as evident by his selective editing of "The Seafarer."[25] Nevertheless, for Johnson's speaker, recognizing "celestial wisdom" and its teaching that "these goods for man the laws of heaven ordain" indicate that, even if humanity may be challenged to do what is right, God has already "ordained" the proper path and it will remain available until humanity is ready to follow it.

## III.  Pound on *The Vanity of Human Wishes*

In "Human Wishes" from *Guide to Kulchur*, Pound responds directly to Johnson's poem. The immediate occasion is a new edition of *London: A Poem and The Vanity of Human Wishes*, replete with an introduction by T. S. Eliot. Edited by Frederick Etchells and Hugh Macdonald, published by Haslewood Books/Chiswick Press, the book appeared in 1930. Pound praises his friend Eliot (his "preface is full of urbanity"[26]), but less so Johnson, who in this case presents a monumental figure with whom he must struggle, Bloom's anxiety of influence coming into full view. Pound's praise of Johnson in the Voltaire passage is absent here; yet, it is little surprise that Pound would be less generous when it comes to his primary genre: poetry. Pound was ever the propogandist for his vision of a new poetics, quick to point out the problems with past literary movements and the weaknesses of their artists. Pound's main grounds for criticism are what he perceives to be the intellectual shortcomings of Johnson's poem:

> I intended to praise both the poems and their introducer, but the poems are facile, they are not really thought at all, or are thought only in reflection (using the term as of a reflection in a mirror), thought remembered in a moment of lassitude.[27]

Whereas earlier Pound had celebrated the acuity of Johnson's mind, here he dismisses the poem's "thought" as superficial or exhausted. This thought is not at all the product of a man who "will not lick boots," but rather of one who has little to say. Indeed, a significant portion of Pound's criticism of Johnson's poem hinges on his feeling that the poem is intellectually weak. He complains,

> You are never for an instant permitted to forget that the thought is in full dress uniform. Johnson has enough thought to carry the form *to a reader searching* for the thought and the technique of its expression. Almost nothing suffers by being excerpted, line, distich or four lines at a time.[28]

Pound's description of "thought remembered in a moment of lassitude" recalls Wordsworth's "emotion recollected in tranquility." Pound offers a revision of Wordsworth's dictum whereby Johnson's futile attempt at "thought" takes the place of emotion; similarly, exhaustion takes the place of reflection. For Pound, the very premise of the poem is dubious: "yet taking it by and large the poem is buncombe. Human wishes are not vain in the least," he contends but offers no qualification.[29] Pound follows these lines by repeating his message: "The age was decadent. It was going bust."[30] Part of what makes it decadent is the superfluous detail Pound finds in the work: "Gongorism was the excess attention to high-coloured detail. The 18th century English verse from this angle is a very superior kind of intellectual gongorism, if you compare it with *Madame Bovary*."[31] Pound believes the Romantics played an important role in repudiating this excessive detail that leads to decadent art, but the Romantics themselves did not have the sophistication necessary to remedy the situation: "The 'whole of the 18th century' was a cliché which the Romantics broke up, in disorderly and amateur manner. The distressing Rousseau etc. .... . ending with Whitman."[32] By alluding to Whitman, Pound brings in the American tradition from which he himself descends, like it or not, and which offers a less ornamental approach to verse. Whitman was an ambivalent figure for Pound, as shown in his early poem "A Pact" (1916). There, the speaker admits he has "detested" Whitman "long enough" and must make some amends with him as a precursor ("Let there be commerce between us"[33]).

As we find with his shifting perspectives on Johnson, Whitman too is an object of conflicted feelings for Pound.

Using a comparison with one of the few Americans he does admire, Pound notes that Johnson's poem is not as good as Thomas Jefferson's prose.[34] In considering the comparison of Johnson's verse with Jefferson's prose, one might recall Pound's famous injunction (following Ford Madox Ford) that "poetry should be written at least as well as prose."[35] In this case, Pound seems to suggest it is not. When it comes to Johnson's versification, Pound admits his poems are skilled but not flowing: "The Cadence comes to an almost dead end so frequently that one doesn't know the poem is going on."[36] A skeptic might counter that such a choppy rhythm is inevitable when using heroic couplets. Thus, Pound may be quibbling with the form Johnson adopts rather than Johnson's ability in particular. Nevertheless, Pound does offer some begrudging praise, finally:

> Looking at Johnson's *The Vanity*, where it is most typical of its mode, and where it most brilliantly illustrates and attains the apogee and top notch of that mode, being "as good as Pope with a touch of Saml. J. into the bargain," its triumph is of the perfectly weighed and placed word. Its general statements, slicklingly epigrammatic, give the reader what he himself brings to the text.[37]

If Johnson's poem reflects back on the reader his own associations and thus offers general enough "statements" that they can be read in differing ways, it would succeed in being able to sustain multiple readings, as one expects of great literature. Still, Pound's own criteria about the efficacy of "thought" suggests that a poem should not promote ambiguity but rather be driven by its ideological underpinnings and make its points succinctly and unflinchingly.

Reflecting his belief that one of the strengths of Johnson's work is its precision with language,[38] Pound offers Johnson some of his due as a celebrated figure just entering his mature phase at the time of the poem's composition:

> The "slowly wise, and meanly just" summarize long observation. They are verse for the man of fifty, who has a right to metrical

pleasures perhaps as much as his juniors. Yet the whole poem is, as the intervening century plus has judged it by relative neglect, couched in style of "senate's thanks and gazette's pompous tale."[39]

Pound's math is a little off here: Johnson would have been thirty-nine at the time of writing his poem. Pound, on the other hand, would have been forty-five in 1930 and fifty-three in the year of *Guide to Kulchur*'s first publication. He was, in other words, in the middle age that he projects onto Johnson. The anxieties that stem from losing a feeling of relevancy and the exuberance of youthful vigor haunt Pound's description. He presents himself as the irreverent young upstart compared to the stolid progenitor who holds on to outmoded ideas and approaches—even if such a comparison makes little sense age-wise.

Like the image of the brazen young man who defies canonized literary figures, Pound suggests that Johnson and the other standout poet of the time, Pope, "are mainly a negative statement." He notes that "Their positive implication is the value of intelligence, the right to be impatient with fools, the value of being undazzled."[40] Not content to give Johnson and Pope this one victory of intellectual superiority over their peers, Pound presents a comparison between himself and Eliot a few pages earlier that makes clear that Johnson and Pope have nothing on them: "Has Eliot or have I wasted the greater number of hours, he by attending to fools and / or humouring them, and I by alienating imbeciles suddenly?"[41] He and Eliot represent the new approach in English-language verse, both of whom have spent time in the British literary scene and thus work as twentieth-century equivalents to Pope and Johnson. Since Johnson and Pope never met, Johnson and Swift might have been the better pair. In any case, it is noteworthy how Pound creates a modern equivalent to Pope and Johnson where he and Eliot are similarly beset by fools, but they are an improvement over the earlier pair by generating fresh verse rather than the staid mediocrity of Johnson in *Vanity*, which excels only in strong word choice. When writing on a later poet's "misreading" of a precursor's work, Bloom notes, "That reading is likely to be idiosyncratic, and it is almost certain to be ambivalent."[42] "Idiosyncratic" and "ambivalent" characterize Pound's highly individual reading of Johnson in this essay. He demonstrates ambivalence at Johnson's successes as a poet, and his doubting of Johnson's intellectual abilities in the poem might be described as idiosyncratic. Bloom adds that "As the poets swerve downward in time, they deceive themselves into believing they are tougher-minded than their precursors."[43] This is surely the case with Pound, who dismisses the thought and poetics of Johnson as if the earlier poet were not disciplined enough to carry out the task he set for himself.

It should come as little surprise at this point that Pound works in a comment about economics in his short essay on Johnson. He writes, "I am looking even at: 'His bonds of debt and mortgages of lands' which ought to melt a credit-crank if anything cd., and soften his judgement."[44] Pound has in mind the following passage from Johnson:

> Unnumber'd Maladies each Joint invade,
> Lay Siege to Life and press the dire Blockade;
> But unextinguish'd Av'rice still remains,
> And dreaded Losses aggravate his Pains;
> He turns, with anxious Heart and crippled Hands,
> His Bonds of Debt, and Mortgages of Lands;
> Or views his Coffers with suspicious Eyes,
> Unlocks his Gold, and counts it till he dies. (ll.283–90)

This image of the man with "unextinguish'd Av'rice" who "counts" his money "till he dies" is hardly the non-judgmental view suggested by Pound's taking the lines out of their context. It is unclear whether or not Pound's appellation of the "credit-crank" is intended as a jibe at Johnson or as a reference to the type of figure Johnson here describes. One would guess the latter, although Pound's phrasing is ambiguous. Certainly, one could not accuse Johnson of preying on others' debts; he himself was arrested for debt in 1756 and 1758. In *Idler* 22, from Saturday, September 16, 1758 (Imprisonment of debtors), he writes,

> Those who made the laws have apparently supposed, that every deficiency of payment is the crime of the debtor. But the truth is, that the creditor always shares the act, and often more than shares the guilt, of improper trust. It seldom happens that any man imprisons another but for debts which he suffered to be

> contracted in hope of advantage to himself, and for bargains in
> which he proportioned his own profit to his own opinion of the
> hazard; and there is no reason, why one should punish the other
> for a contract in which both concurred.

There is certainly little sympathy for the creditor here, who, Johnson
suggests, is just as much at fault as the borrower and might be similarly
punished. In any case, Pound follows up his comments on the "credit-
crank" by moving into the passage quoted previously that "The age was
decadent," which he immediately emphasizes by writing, "It was going
bust." No doubt the term "going bust" carries special resonance as Pound's
book is published during the Great Depression, which suggested a failure
of capitalism generally and furnished evidence for Pound's assertions
about the problems of the western economic system.

One final point worth examining in Pound's essay on Johnson's
*Vanity* is his comments on elegiac poetry. Pound writes, "Even Elegiac
poetry at its best is not mere senile blubber or the pleasure of crab-
bing something, it is an 'And yet … .'"[45] We have seen how Pound's own
nostalgia for an imagined English origin, without Christian influence,
marked his idiosyncratic translation of "The Seafarer." His interest in
loose translation and Anglo-Saxon poetics also informs the opening of
his long poem *The Cantos*. Here Pound offers his own version of Andreas
Divus' Latin translation of the *Odyssey* but utilizing the alliterative style
he learned from his study of Old English verse. A fragment of a translation of a translation, framed by a later culture's literary aesthetics, canto
I thus demonstrates the continuum of literary traditions at the same
time as it launches Pound's own epic. Not insignificantly, the poem's first
line is "And then went down to the ship," which suggests a continua-
tion of a story already in progress, just as Pound is producing an elegy
for epic poetry in canto I while he produces his own, modern equivalent of the epic in the pages to follow. The "And yet" of his praise of the
elegy is the "And then" of *The Cantos*: the poem is both homage to that
which has been lost in the past while it also establishes a poetics for the
future. Although he might fail to see the point of Johnson's reinvention
of Juvenal, Pound thus proceeds with his own revivification of Divus,
and, through him, Homer, in his modern long poem.

## IV.  Johnson in *Hugh Selwyn Mauberley* and *The Cantos*

Johnson makes an appearance in two of Pound's most important poems: the aforementioned *Hugh Selwyn Mauberley* and *The Cantos*, which remained unfinished at the time of his death, making it impossible to know who or what may have appeared in the final version. He famously admitted in the poem itself, "I cannot make it cohere."[46] It is no coincidence that Pound would namedrop Johnson in *Hugh Selwyn Mauberley*, a poem premised on the notion that the speaker comes from a half-savage country and thus must go elsewhere to find the kind of cultivated intellect and appreciation of art he so desires. Johnson can serve as the model of the sophistication sorely lacking in the United States. Nevertheless, his appearance is brief:

> Conduct, on the other hand, the soul
> "Which the highest cultures have nourished"
> To Fleet St. where
> Dr. Johnson flourished.[47]

Here Pound reminds the reader of Johnson's home in London. Of course, Fleet Street was famously the center of printing and journalism, from Johnson's time up until the 1980s, when newspapers began an exodus from the area. The reference to Fleet Street helps to reinforce the urbane, worldly nature of Pound's poem while also drawing upon the breadth of British history. British landmarks such as Johnson's Fleet Street communicate the intellectual and literary traditions to be found in Pound's adopted Europe. Only in the nineteenth century did the United States begin to accrue similar literary landmarks, such as Emerson's Concord, Dickinson's Amherst, or Hawthorne's Salem. This shallow literary history—not quite a century old in Pound's time, could not "nourish" "the soul" like Great Britain's could.

The Cantos could be a case study in influence itself. The references to other writers, artists, politicians, and thinkers are staggering. Given this labyrinth of allusions, echoes, and citations, it may be surprising that Johnson appears only once in direct reference in the *Cantos* despite the hundreds of other figures who parade in and out of the poem, sometimes in direct quotation. Nevertheless, Johnson shows up in a crucial place: the Pisan Cantos. These cantos, written while Pound was detained before being taken back to the U.S. to stand trial for treason, represent some of the most moving lyrical moments in the poem.[48] Contrary to his typical archival approach in other parts of the *Cantos*, Pound was left without his usual access to source texts and therefore worked primarily from memory.[49] The cantos grow more intimate as a result. In this way, the people and events cited might be understood to hold an even greater personal relevance for the speaker insofar as they are references he has internalized and that now spring to mind at the moment of his most intense crisis. Surely one would waste little thought on matters of small significance in this kind of situation.

A case in point is canto LXXX. Here Pound references Johnson, in addition to a wide swath of personal topics. Pound notes his declining personal wealth, suggesting that his alleged treasonous acts in supporting Mussolini were not for financial gain: "so that leaving America I brought with me $80 / and England a letter of Thomas Hardy's / and Italy one eucalyptus pip / from the salita that goes up from Rapallo."[50] In moving from a small quantity of cash, to a letter, to a pip, Pound is demonstrating both his diminishing wealth, and therefore his repudiation of the prevalent economic system, but also how the exchange value, to borrow Marx's term, of the items may be of decreasing value but their personal significance is great, especially the pip, which Pound took with him as he was lead to his incarceration. The pip thus proves emblematic of his leaving of freedom and the Italy he loved. This symbol would be used years later by another American poet, Charles Wright, to reflect his debt to Pound as a progeniture.[51]

In LXXX, the reader finds references to topics as various as Pound's friend Eliot,[52] the familiar American nationalistic hymn, "The Battle Hymn of the Republic,"[53] and one of Pound's favorite philosophers: Confucius.[54] This is to say that personal relationships are juxtaposed with representative symbols, such as the hymn, as well as a global awareness, in the form of Asian philosophy. The speaker even reports the prison guard's sympathetic assessment of his predicament: "'Ain' committed no federal crime, / jes a slaight misdemeanor.'"[55] The connection between politics and poetics is underscored by Pound's reference to the figure for whom he once served as secretary, W. B. Yeats, and Yeats's struggles in serving as a senator for the Irish Free State: "the problem after any revolution is what to do with / your gunmen / as old Billyum found out in Oireland / in the Senate."[56] Pound makes broad statements about love ("Amo ergo sum, and in just that proportion"[57]) and the dangers of ignorance ("'There is no darkness but ignorance'").[58] Even by the *Cantos'* standards it is a heady brew of declarations and overlapping allusions.

As far as that goes, however, for all their complexity, the Pisan cantos offer insight into the friends, mentors, and texts that matter to the speaker. While some references may seem trivial on the surface, such as Pound's note, "It is said also that Homer was a medic,"[59] they show the mind in action and that which rises to it, from its preoccupations to its obsessions. Even one of the literary "fathers" with whom Pound had struggled early on, Whitman, emerges, and the speaker seems to make some kind of peace with him through similarly trivial detail.[60] In this way, the quotidian becomes the universal in Pound's Pisan cantos, and each minor allusion brings up a network of personal associations.

The reference to Johnson occurs when Pound cites a line (IV.ii.37–38) from *Twelfth Night* that does not appear in Johnson's Shakespeare: "'There is no darkness but ignorance,'" spoken by the clown to Malvolio.[61] Pound writes, "the trope is, as the accurate reader will have observed, not to be found in Sam Johnson's edition."[62] The Shakespeare quote reminds the reader of how Pound spent a career attempting to bring the willing out of the darkness of ignorance. Works such as *ABC of Reading* and *Guide to Kulchur* demonstrate this point. The breezy way Pound cites the various figures may seem on the surface to be superficial and unworthy of note. Rather, the opposite is true. The fact that Johnson appears among this host of figures offers some sense of his enduring importance in Pound's mind; his emphatic criticism of Johnson in *Guide to Kulchur* is underscored by Pound's memory in the Pisan Cantos. Indeed, the reference suggests that Johnson's job at editing Shakespeare was inadequate, as such an important quote had been lost. Pound implies that he would have been more meticulous. Here again we see him seeking to supplant Johnson as his precursor.

Near the end of *The Cantos* Pound contends that "One single falsehood does more in a murderous world / Than all my outbreaks."[63] While this may be demonstrably true, it nevertheless proves to be the case that

Pound failed to bring the poem to a satisfactory close. Most of the poem's final fragments contain a regretful, exhausted tone rather than the righteous indignation that comes through here and was evident in his earlier stridency. He movingly writes, "I have tried to write Paradise" but relates, "I lost my center / fighting the world."[64] His final hope, "To be men not destroyers,"[65] does not sound far off Johnson's hope in *The Vanity of Human Wishes* for reason to win the day and stem the tide of humanity's self-sabotage with war and inequality. If Pound had written his essay on Johnson in these later years, one wonders if it would have been much different, perhaps more sympathetic to the weariness he identifies in Johnson's poem? One thing is certain: "completing" what Johnson could not eludes Pound, and his debt of influence appears far from discharged as Pound is unsuccessful in finishing his own master poem.

# CHAPTER FOUR

# The Antinomies of Progress
## Johnson, Conrad, Joyce[1]

*Clement Hawes*

It ought to be the first endeavour of a writer to distinguish
nature from custom, or that which is established because it is
right, from that which is right only because it is established.

Samuel Johnson, *Rambler* 156

## I. Introduction

Anomalies of literary reception and periodization surround Samuel
Johnson. He embraced such key features of domestic progress as the ability
of the public sphere to problematize neglected social issues: domineering
fathers, cruel rural landlords, inadequate clothing for French prisoners
of war, resistance to the rise of women authors, and the list goes on.
Johnson (1709–1784) was caricatured as retrograde by Thomas Babington
Macaulay[2] (1800–1859) precisely because he opposed a certain very
particular "progress": that is, imperial domination. Even worse, Johnson
dared in *Rasselas* (1759) to endow "filthy savages" (Africans) with rationality.[3] Some critics and literary historians have similarly found it more
enticing to focus on Johnson's superlatively witty biographical presence
than to engage fully with his provocative written *oeuvre*.[4] A vast discrepancy separates Macaulay's version of Johnson, still far too influential, from
the author known to the sizeable enclave of Johnson Studies.

One exception to this ungenerous reception of Johnson, however, is the moment of High Modernism in the early twentieth century. It is well known that Samuel Beckett (1906–1989) admired his eloquent brother in stylized gloom. Virginia Woolf (1882–1941) was likewise alive to Johnson's extraordinarily bracing *oeuvre*. Exploratory connections and comparisons, even when not directly intertextual, remain to be teased out. Indeed, because Johnson's nimble critique of progress is still sometimes misunderstood, it can usefully be brought into focus through comparison with closely related reflections about leading exemplars of Modernist fiction as Joyce and Conrad. The obvious breaks that separate the eighteenth-century Enlightenment from twentieth-century High Modernity obscure illuminating links. This recognition, indeed, might serve subtly to reposition Johnson as a presence in the broad arc of literary history.

## II.  A New Constellation

As is also noted by the editor of this volume, Woolf in her *Orlando* (1928) presents Samuel Johnson through the eyes of her time-traveling narrator Orlando. Johnson figures as a "great rolling shadow, who now rose to its full height and rocking somewhat as he stood there rolled out the most magnificent phrases that have ever left human lips." Woolf's links to eighteenth-century art and literature are indeed strong and pointed. The name of the press she established with her husband Leonard, Hogarth Press, and the title of her collection, *The Common Reader*, confirm these patterns of affiliation. The latter, of course, alludes to Johnson's "rejoicing," when he came to discuss Thomas Gray's "Elegy Written in a Country Church-Yard," "to concur with the common reader."[5] Along with Joyce, Woolf is a founding Anglophone modernist. Why might Woolf have so pointedly looked back to Johnson in particular? What might this finally have to do with literary Modernism? A methodological question looms as well: does the break signaled by a period-marker such as *Modernism* necessarily entail an investment in a specifically literary "progress"?

Authors of literary Modernism mount aesthetic and political responses to the conditions of the early twentieth century. They all respond, that is to say, to the sheer productive power of capitalism; to the defeudalized social relations of capitalism at home; and, one way or another, to the expansion of western powers abroad. The Victorian exploration of the African interior had been racking up discoveries since about 1850, and the imperially "global" Crystal Palace exhibition appeared in 1851. About the same time, according to the doctrine of "manifest destiny," the United States began flexing its muscles in Mexico, then intervening in Nicaragua, Panama, and Honduras, on through the 1898 war with Spain. At the turn of the twentieth century, the European "scramble for Africa" had been a very recent geopolitical event. The Berlin Conference of 1884, which parceled out Africa to the "advanced powers," is among the conjuncture of historical factors that Fredric Jameson finds constitutive of Modernism.[6]

When in 1899 Rudyard Kipling had advised readers to "Take up the White Man's Burden," he had in mind the United States, the soldiers of which, soon to defeat their erstwhile allies among Filipino nationalists, had just wrested the Philippines away from Spain. Upon this development, an African-American newspaper opined that "the white man's burden is never so heavy that he cannot carry it out the door or window of the house he has just burglarized."[7] Kipling may have intuited that imperial power would one day devolve to the U.S. Over a century and a half before, George Berkeley (1685–1753), the Anglican bishop of Cloyne, had predicted the same westering trajectory for empire:

> WESTWARD the course of Empire takes its way.
> The four first acts already past,
> A fifth shall close the drama with the day:
> Time's noblest offspring is the last.

America must be the final act in the *translatio imperii*, as J. G. A. Pocock explains, because there would be no further land left in which traditional agrarian virtue might be cultivated.[8] The later-is-better theme, as Eviatar Zerubavel terms it, is constitutive of the notion of *progress*.[9] Meanwhile, claiming central and South America as its sphere of influence, the United States would indeed emerge as a muscular hegemon. The stoutest competition to Britain's early twentieth-century lead in multinational companies would come from American corporations.[10]

Imperial Japan, fresh off a victory over Russia, annexed Korea in 1910. The shortly ensuing First World War would of course disrupt a great deal. In the U.S. of the 1920s, during the aggressively racist presidency of Woodrow Wilson, a resurgence of the KKK occurred.[11] *Mein Kampf* appeared in 1925. As the Great Depression violently polarized public debates between the left and the right, geopolitics lurched toward a second war. With both the Japanese invasion of Manchuria and the appointment of Hitler as German Chancellor in 1933, another global conflagration loomed on the horizon. The Nazis, who agreed with Thomas Jefferson that racial coexistence was impossible, mined the history of American Jim Crow laws for models.[12] In the colonies, however, more than the impending war was stirring. Ireland had achieved the qualified home rule of the "Irish Free State" in 1921. After being in and out of jail during the 1920s, Gandhi launched in the 1930s a renewed *satyagraha* campaign, which would lead in 1947 to the negotiation of Indian independence. Within a year the twenty-six southern counties of Ireland likewise attained full independence from Britain. By the early 1960s, well after the deaths of Conrad and Joyce, the decolonization of Africa would be nearly complete. Given that an airing of the Nazis' genocidal atrocities had by this time been widely absorbed, the stage was set for a concerted revolt against the western politics of racism as such. At this writing—decolonization notwithstanding—the world continues to live "in the slipstream of colonialism."[13]

As a brutally compressed historical sketch, this frame provides a certain initial continuity—the longevity of western imperialism—for comparing authors as far apart in time as Samuel Johnson (who decisively enters literary history in the 1730s) and Joseph Conrad or James Joyce (whose moment arrives more than a century and a half later). A novel constellation of authors may reveal new patterns: a constellation that at once brings together, and is discovered by, the configuration of individual stars. Affinities between Johnson and Conrad and Joyce are valuable to explore: they involve the long arc of British expansion, North American dominance in the New World, and the freighted notion, on at least three levels—personal, literary, and political—of *progress*.

## III. Periodizing Modernity

Epochal breaks in literary history include the conjoined emergence in the early eighteenth century of the novel and the bourgeois public sphere.[14]

The demands of public rationality are tied to the emergence of the English novel as a genre. Indeed, rationality emerges conspicuously in connection with the first novel in European history: *Don Quixote* (Part I, 1605; II, 1615). The cure of the knight's delusion in *Don Quixote* seemingly announces the displacement of Romance by Realism. Modernism in turn defined itself in part by way of musing on the inadequacy of the mimetic project driving literary Realism. Though the best authors found in the awareness of succeeding literary periods many opportunities to claim "progress" *vis-à-vis* precursors, the most thoughtful express doubt and ambivalence.

The notion of *Modernity* remains among the most elusive terms ever fed to the hungry sheep. Let us stipulate that, for our purposes, it begins in earnest with William of Orange's landing at Torbay in 1688:[15] this is by way of highlighting unmistakably progressive developments: the Bill of Rights; the sovereignty of Parliament; the Lockean ideals of empiricism and popular sovereignty; the implementation of sophisticated Dutch techniques of banking and finance; and, on the darker but equally Lockean side, the trade in enslaved Africans, yet more war and land-confiscation in Ireland, and more British expansion.[16] A new toleration for dissenting Protestants was accompanied by intensified anti-Catholicism. In his *The Fable of the Bees* (1723) the Anglo-Dutch physician Bernard Mandeville subversively articulates the ways a commercially constituted society based on profit now renders ethical traditions obsolete and hypocritical. The seventeenth and eighteenth centuries had already been debating capitalism, a system as yet unnamed.[17] That Johnson admitted to learning a great deal from the scandalous Mandeville suggests his receptivity to select aspects of modern thinking. He remarked that Mandeville "had opened my views into real life very much."[18]

Meanwhile, in its more common usage, the term *Modernism*, usually spanning about 1899–1945, encompasses literary arts both radically experimental and often at odds with the political status quo. One finds authors of this High Modernism negotiating positions along both the spectrum of the traditional versus the *avant-garde* and that of a violently polarized left and right. The creative surge of twentieth-century Modernism may be among the most deliberately willed artistic ruptures in literary history. Determined to mark a break, Ezra Pound declared in a letter to H. L. Mencken in March, 1922 that the Christian era had ended on October 29, 1921—the day that Joyce finished *Ulysses*.[19] Despite the absurd extravagance of this assertion, however, Pound's famous battle-cry—*Make it new!*—perfectly sloganized the ambitions of literary modernism. An aesthetic war was underway between the tawdriness tolerated in mass-produced commodities and the craftsmanship cultivated in older social formations. Commercial values were among the chief stakes of the conflict. Such values, emergent in the eighteenth century, had initially challenged many a feudal remnant. The culture of commerce had critiqued murderous dueling over masculine "honor," aristocratic snobbery against merchants, and the blue-blooded genre of Romance itself. By the turn of the twentieth century, however, capitalism was legally and culturally dominant; aesthetic rebellion had now erupted against its shoddy and cheapjack products; and an emphasis on literary craftsmanship arose in response to commodification. These parallel aesthetic rebellions—for and then against "Realism"—mutually illuminate one another.

The obvious breaks that separate the Enlightenment from late nineteenth- and twentieth-century Modernity can obscure intriguing points of comparison. With Joyce, Johnson shared poor eyesight; he shared a susceptibility to depression with Conrad. Each of the three authors considered here wrote a brilliant *Bildungsroman*, a genre normally devoted to the progressive maturation and enlightenment of a youth: *Rasselas* (1759); *Lord Jim* (1899); and *A Portrait of the Artist as a Young Man* (1916). Each author was a formidable polyglot. Among the deepest connections that link an Enlightenment author such as Johnson to the high-flyers of Modernism is a sustained engagement with Britain's expansionist project. A pessimism shared by all three about the limits of progress leads them to a many-layered probing of its various antinomies.

An intermittent shifting of analytical scale down to the granular level of sentence and paragraph will help to throw in sharper relief the appearance, in Johnson, Conrad, and Joyce, of "progress" and its antinomies. For purposes of comparison, examples from each author of the rhetorical scheme of *chiasmus* will be found illuminating. As a quick reminder, here is an example of a chiasmus: *Love as if you would one day hate, and hate as if you would one day love.* Or again, the epigraph to this essay contains a chiasmus by Johnson, who distinguishes between "that which is established because it is right" and "that which is right only because it is established." This rhetorical scheme of reversibility, named after the resemblance of its elements to the shape of an "X," can also create a tiny epitome of broader temporal directionality. When the elements are arranged A—B—B—A, as in the example above—a classic chiasmus— the effect is often static. Blockage, regress, stasis, false progress: among such possibilities are a blocked mirroring or a circle.[20] Yet the potential for change built into the crisscross figure of the chiasmus also makes it the perfect scheme with which to convey a spiral of progress or regress (A—B—B—X). "Ask not what your country can do for you," JFK said: "Ask what you can do for your country." This famous chiasmus is progressive, crossing from selfish dependency to national service and from *ask not* to *ask*. A chiasmus distills conceptual movement (backward or forward), or its pointed absence.

Both rhetorical schemes such as the chiasmus and key tropes—say, leaving the dark cave for sunlight—can serve to epitomize attitudes towards progress. To be sure, for the three authors under consideration, the figuring of genuine progress can seem a *rara avis*. And indeed, though Johnson, Conrad, and Joyce all hold out hope for life-changing insights and telling interventions in tradition, each comes to frame "progress" as a dubious ideological theme.

## IV.  Hating Tradition Properly: Samuel Johnson

Library shelves justifiably teem with commentaries on the work of Samuel Johnson, and his memory footprint is, as it were, gigantic. Both by way of his delightful wit as a conversationalist and the brilliance of his written *oeuvre*, Johnson stands out against the setting of his era as the most vigorous and wide-ranging intellect; the most searching author; and, along with Jonathan Swift, the most prescient eighteenth-century critic of colonial exploitation. The editors of *The Dictionary of Global Culture* put it as follows: "he opposed war, censorship, colonialism, poverty, and the campaign launched against indigenous populations in Africa and North and South America."[21] Johnson was often fearlessly universal. Decades before there was a Society for the Abolition of the Slave Trade (1787), Johnson consistently condemned not just the slave trade but slavery as such. He inflects his many landmark contributions to a vernacular English literary culture in a pointedly cosmopolitan direction. In *Idler* 81, he imagines the Seven Years' War as observed in Quebec by a native American chief, who exhorts his companions as follows: "Let us look unconcerned upon the slaughter, and remember that the death of every European delivers the country from a tyrant and a robber." By way of contrast, the Anglo-American painter Benjamin West, in "The Death of General Wolfe" (1770), shows native American allies kneeling around the dying general. Johnson's word *robber* alludes both to settler appropriation and to the penal-colony nature of colonial America, a pre-Australian destination for transported British convicts. Through his writings, Johnson dramatically advanced both literary culture and political awareness in the later British Enlightenment.

Johnson's achievements illustrate his stratospheric expectations of himself—demands that could be debilitating. In his journals one meets a depressive Johnson who often berates himself for idleness and procrastination. Ford Madox Ford (1873–1939), who collaborated with Conrad and published Joyce, called Johnson "the most tragic of all our major literary figures."[22] For one man to have written the monumental *Dictionary of the English Language* (1755), with over 42,000 entries, is beyond extraordinary. As in the much later OED, these definitions are often accompanied by well-chosen illustrative quotations from important authors. As a lexicographer ("harmless drudge"), moreover, Johnson leavened his great work with occasional amusing asperities in the vein of cultural critique. (*Excise*: "a hateful tax levied upon commodities and adjudged not by the common judges of property but wretches hired by those to whom excise is paid.") Johnson's act of redefinition here launches a satirical subgenre with such followers as Gustave Flaubert and Ambrose Bierce (the American author in 1911 of *The Devil's Dictionary*). A gathering of Flaubert's satirical definitions was posthumously published in 1913 as *The Dictionary of Received Ideas*. Flaubert's point was of course a war on the latest clichés—a complaint, as Teju Cole puts it, against "automatic thinking."[23] We always need reminding that stupidity is a dangerous political weakness: a cliché both creates and solidifies intellectual sclerosis.

The scale of Johnson's literary ambitions begins to swim into view when we also take into account his edition of Shakespeare (1765) and, above all, the critical biographies gathered together as his *Lives of the English Poets* (1782). The latter, as Harold Bloom has put it, brim with "critical epiphanies."[24] To fill out his achievements, however, one must include the hundreds of superb essays written in the vein of wisdom literature for the *Rambler*, *Idler*, and *Adventurer*; and, of course, his philosophical novella *Rasselas* (1759). Johnson himself enacted a chapter in the historical progress of authorship. To his neglectful patron, the fourth earl of Chesterfield, Johnson wrote a scathing letter that is sometimes dubbed the author's declaration of independence. After promising him support while writing the *Dictionary*, Chesterfield had snubbed and neglected Johnson for some nine years, not even admitting him when he called, until word reached him that the mammoth project was almost finished. At that point Chesterfield suddenly wanted some reflected glory and attempted belatedly to patronize, in all senses of the word, the lexicographer. Johnson replied as follows:

> Is not a patron, my lord, one who looks with unconcern on a man struggling for life in the water, and when he has reached ground, encumbers him with help? The notice which you have been pleased to take of my labours, had it been early, had been kind: but it has been delayed till I am indifferent and cannot enjoy it; till I am solitary and cannot impart it; till I am known and do not want it.

Genius and immense labor trump, resoundingly, the usual deferential exigencies of rank and privilege. Difficult as the literary marketplace could be, Johnson embraced it by way of a very modern gesture: shaking off, in a telling gesture of defeudalization, his useless patron. To gain access to the public sphere without a patron's blessing registers genuine progress.

Against the grain of cultural nationalism, Johnson extended, critiqued, and renewed a many-tongued tradition that, for him, included Juvenal, Plutarch, Montaigne, Bayle, Boileau, Le Bossu, Boorhaave, and Cervantes no less than Milton or Shakespeare or Pope. Johnson everywhere pointedly acknowledges the international influences and borrowings that constitute English authors as thoroughly embedded in an intertextuality that exceeds national boundaries. Here is Johnson on Samuel Butler (1613–1680):

> We must not, however, suffer the pride, which we assume as the countrymen of Butler, to make any encroachments upon justice, nor appropriate those honours, which others have a right to share. The poem of Hudibras is not wholly English; the original is to be found in the history of Don Quixote; a book to which a mind of the greatest powers may be indebted without disgrace.[25]

As a crucial occasion of self-reflection inscribed within the tradition of English letters, this attitude exemplifies Johnson's habit of looking beyond national horizons. At such moments Johnson anticipates later disciplinary projects that register cross-national influences. Because Johnson was far too cosmopolitan to embrace, in Greg Clingham's phrase, "the sacralization of national boundaries,"[26] he resisted the trendy project of ballad-collection. Johnson's novella *Rasselas* (1759) not only centers on African characters, Coptic Christians, but takes those characters as universal.

*Rasselas* develops the theme of progress in all its double-edged glory. Rasselas and Nekayah are brother and sister; Nekayah and Pekuah are intimate friends; and Imlac and Rasselas are teacher and student. The novella's configurations avoid the marriage plot in favor of friendship. Rasselas and Nekayah had originally set out to learn enough to make the "choice of life": a commitment to the best and happiest way of being, whether through wealth or marital companionship or hermit-like withdrawal. A certain naïve "decisionism" underlies this quest—the sense that life is constituted above all by deliberate choices. The titular character and his companions encounter an inventor who hopes to fly by means of home-made wings. The topic of possible human flight leads almost immediately to Imlac's grim but accurate prediction of bombardment from above by flying machines: a prophecy fulfilled in World War I and every major war since. In the context of military technology, progress qualifies any larger sense that time's arrow is moving is the right direction. *Rasselas* includes such chiseled observations about human stasis as the following mirroring chiasmus, which comes from the mouth of Nekayah: "Age looks with anger upon the temerity of youth, and youth with contempt on the scrupulosity of age."[27] The endless cycles of generational antagonism persist as the arrogant young succumb in their turn to curmudgeonly old age—*sans* progress.

Johnson's novella famously concludes with "A Conclusion in which Nothing is Concluded." The characters return to Abyssinia. Rasselas occupies himself by tinkering mentally with various schemes of government. Nekayah busies herself with bringing higher education to women. This all seems to be wishful thinking. Meanwhile, Imlac and the astronomer— one imagines them in rocking chairs—just "drift along the stream of life." In the scheme of things, Rasselas's attempt to make the best *choice of life* proves to be of vanishing importance. The plot goes against the grain of the genre. In a classic instance of the *Bildungsroman* genre such as *Tom Jones* (1749), the protagonist develops beyond an initial imprudence and assumes an adult role in society. By comparison, the quasi-circular conclusion to *Rasselas* stubbornly resists any closure by way of maturation: no work ethic prevails, and drift conquers progress.

A formally daring Johnson, then—but surely Johnson's quaint strictures against puns, say, are to be read as aesthetically conservative? An example, that is, of Enlightenment self-policing at its fussy worst? For Shakespeare, Johnson famously writes, "a quibble was the fatal *Cleopatra* for which he lost the world, and was content to lose it."[28] The main point is that thought or speech is momentarily derailed by puns. A pun disrupts, in Derek Attridge's phrase, "communicational efficacy."[29] Perhaps Johnson's sense that human rationality is permanently embattled leads him here to paint with too broad a brush. This judgment represents a rare moment in Johnson of aesthetic obstructionism.

There is, however, another less officially rational, more embodied, and more aesthetically flexible Johnson. Anthony Lee notes, in the forthcoming annotated *Rambler*, examples not only of Johnson's anti-punning sentiments but also of his punning jokes. Both on the punning and bodily scores, Johnson has a more relaxed side.[30] It seems worth noting, first of all, that his *Dictionary*, citing Suckling and Swift, provides a definition— "wind from behind"—for the word *fart*. Moreover, Boswell recounts a conversation in mixed company in which Johnson said that a certain woman, a printer's devil, had "a bottom of good sense." When there were titters at the perceived *double entendre*, Johnson protested that he had meant that the person in question was "*fundamentally* sensible" (*Boswell's Life*, 4:99). Having doubled down with a new pun on "buttocks," Johnson in effect dared the gathered company to laugh. The whole scene would have been unbearably funny: Johnson was playing zanily both on his own position of dignified sobriety and on the difficulty of suppressing laughter. Johnson should not serve as the reified hyper-rational foil against which a supposedly more playful literary artist—a Shakespeare, a Joyce—can shine.

As a literary historian, Johnson focuses both on continuities and breaks without affirming overall "progress." The weightiest lives in *Lives of the Poets* are those of Milton, Dryden, Pope, Addison, Gray, and Cowley. Among his insights about Pope is the reflection that no later poet can go further in his refined mode. Insofar as Pope's poetry is infinitely polished, that is to say, "to attempt any farther improvement of versification will be dangerous."[31] Historical sequences of formal types, into which individual artists make "entrances,"[32] may set an aesthetic limit to the refining aspects of progress. Johnson prepares us to understand periodic gestures of rebarbarization. Too few serious critics elaborate on the formal possibilities confronting a literary artist of creating an original stance. Such is Johnson's understanding of the position, *vis-à-vis* the literary history of signal achievements in a genre, of the individual talent.

Johnson, however, did not need a major poet to write a major critical biography. His *Life of Savage* is among the most dazzling texts written in the eighteenth century, and perhaps the deepest interrogation of personal progress and maturation. Savage is among the great antiheroes in all of eighteenth-century English literature. Obsessed with the belief that he had been been unjustly dispossessed of an aristocratic rank and fortune, he felt entitled to live high on the hog; he was so embittered by the refusal of his mother, the countess of Macclesfield, to acknowledge his (supposedly true) paternity that he wrote a long poem about it called *The Bastard* (1743); he constantly borrowed money from friends and then immediately squandered it; he in effect stalked his mother; and he was eventually sent packing from London to Wales by those same exasperated friends.

Johnson observes that Savage was accused of borrowing expensive books; of then pawning them; of repeatedly drinking expensive wines in taverns and then—in company, when the bill came due—discovering himself to be without money. Such mooching was characteristic:

Whoever was acquainted with Mr. Savage easily credited both these accusations: for, having been obliged, from his first entrance into the world to subsist upon expedients, affluence was not able to exalt him above them; and so much was he delighted with wine and conversation, and so long had he been accustomed to live by chance, that he would at any time go to the tavern without scruple, and trust for the reckoning to the liberality of his company, and frequently of company to whom he was very little known. This conduct indeed very seldom drew upon him those inconveniences that might be feared by any other person; for his conversation was so entertaining, and his address so pleasing, that few thought the pleasure which they received from him dearly purchased by paying for his wine.[33]

A mirroring chiasmus then encapsulates the characteristic blockage haunting Savage's relationships:

It was his peculiar happiness that he scarcely ever found a stranger whom he did not leave a friend; but it must likewise be added that he had not often a friend long, without obliging him to become a stranger.[34]

Zero progress—and Johnson does not spare his friend the following absurdist description of a vicious cycle:

By imputing none of his miseries to himself he continued to act upon the same principles, and to follow the same path; was never made wiser by his sufferings, nor preserved by one misfortune from falling into another. He proceeded throughout his life to tread the same steps on the same circle; always applauding his past conduct, or at least forgetting it, to amuse himself with phantoms of happiness which were dancing before him, and willingly turned his eyes from the light of reason, when it would have discovered the illusion and shewn him, what he never wished to see, his real state.[35]

This is the compelling story of a non-epiphany, of an insight that, like Godot, never arrives. Written early in Johnson's career, the *Life of Savage* (1744) is wholly unlike any previous biography: a story of arrested development rather than maturation.

Progress, as Johnson conceives it, is rare, fragile, and reversible. In his estranging attacks on the march-of-progress theme, he did not spare scholars or authors. This bears heavily on the question of vocation, where the hopes of budding authors and scholars are invested. In *Rasselas*, Imlac provides such a demanding account of what is required to be a poet that Rasselas concludes it is impossible. One must know everything. So much for the vanity of vocational ambitions. Then there is this from *Rambler* 106:

> No place affords a more striking conviction of the vanity of human wishes than a public library. For who can see the wall crowded on every side by mighty volumes, the works of laborious meditation and accurate inquiry, now scarcely known but by the catalog, and preserved only to increase the pomp of learning, without considering how many hours have been wasted in vain endeavors ... .[36]

The shape of cultural time spirals entropically downward toward oblivion.

What to make of false or perverted claims to progress? Political hypocrisy disgusted Johnson, not least among American settlers and in the phony universalism expressed by their colony-cum-nation. Thomas Jefferson, that famous egalitarian—"All men are created equal," he wrote—knowingly assumed convenient exceptions. America's sometimes whiny Declaration of Independence indeed accuses George III of sponsoring "savages" to attack the (white) settlers for whom Jefferson spoke as if they constituted all humankind. Such is the false universality of Eurocentrism—but that, crucially and emphatically, is not Johnson's stance or framework. That Johnson is so firm, consistent, pointed, and acute on these same colonial issues testifies to his self-conscious refusal of Eurocentrism. He questioned "how it is" in *Taxation No Tyranny* (1775) "that we hear the loudest yelps for liberty among the drivers of negroes": perhaps the most succinct comment ever on such founders of the U.S. as Jefferson.[37]

Johnson wholly succeeded, to paraphrase Adorno, in "hating tradition properly."[38] "To hate tradition properly," according to Neil Lazarus, is "… to mobilize its own protocols, procedures, and interior logic against it—to demonstrate that it is only on the basis of a project that exceeds its own horizons or self-consciousness that tradition can possibly be imagined redeeming its own pledges."[39] This Johnson did often. Johnson deeply influenced not only individual writers from Austen to Beckett but whole genres, from essays to lexicography to biography. An author can be so culturally influential, however, as Johnson notes at the end of his *Life of Dryden*, that he is paradoxically invisible: as "natural" as dew on the grass and as vanishing. This passage, as Clingham observes, foresees erasure for even the great writer.[40] Literary immortality paradoxically ceases to be remarkable; it is naturalized and fades into the background of that which is already assumed. The cultural longevity of authors thus requires such a periodic gesture of estrangement as may be afforded by new constellations.

## V. Pessimistic and Avante-Garde: Joseph Conrad

"I've done enough for it [Kurtz's memory] to give me the indisputable right to lay it if I choose for an everlasting rest in the dustbin of progress, amongst all the sweepings and, figuratively speaking, all the dead cats of civilization."

Marlow, in *Heart of Darkness*

Library shelves groan with the weight of Joseph Conrad's achievements as a novelist, and one's bandwidth is quickly overwhelmed by his narrative sophistication. Conrad (1857–1924) has one foot in late Realism (in such French masters as Flaubert)—and one in an emerging Modernism that included Henry James. The critique of day-dreaming we noted above in Cervantes continues brilliantly in *Madame Bovary* (1856) and then in Conrad's *Lord Jim*. His sheer story-telling prowess appeals across the board. That Jameson uses *Lord Jim* for one of the great set-pieces of Marxist analysis in *The Political Unconscious* (1981) is scarcely accidental.[41] The title of Salman Rushdie's 2012 memoir of his life under a death threat, *Joseph Anton*, refers to his pseudonym while incognito, one designed to honor

Anton Chekov and Joseph Conrad. Conrad remains something of a writ-er's writer—and, perhaps above all, a subversive debunker of "progress."

Conrad depended on the marketplace, which took its time to reward his labors. His following famous sentence of 1897 constitutes a sort of statement about his calling: "My task which I am trying to achieve is, by the power of the written word … before all, to make you *see*."[42] The word *see* here, as Linda Dryden observes, "conveys a sense of visceral experi-ence, of instinctive understanding that cannot be contained in a word, a phrase, or even an entire paragraph."[43] In terms of literary advancement, this program amounts to aesthetic progress through a combination of limitation and intensification.

Conrad's prose is sometimes stylized not for visual power but for effects of elaborate pattern-making. Consider this sentence from his short story "An Outpost of Progress": "The courage, the composure, the confidence; the emotions and principles; every great and every insignifi-cant thought belongs not to the individual but to the crowd: to the crowd that believes blindly in the irresistible force of its institutions and of its morals, in the power of its police and of its opinion." Even as it throws final emphasis on "its police and its opinion," this sentence pivots around the chiasmus involving the repeated phrase *the crowd*—and the order that entity blindly provides. Amidst generational continuities of norm-giving, the individual—inevitably vulnerable to the crowd's false and triumpha-list definitions of progress—seems smaller and less independent than a microbe. Registering a sense of blockage, this is another "mirroring" chias-mus.[44] And so "a sense of hopelessness and nihilism," as Maya Jasanoff puts it, leaves room for little but pain.[45]

Conrad provides in *Heart of Darkness* (1899) one of the most resounding revelations in the novelistic tradition: the death-bed excla-mation of Kurtz, the arch-imperialist and exponent of late-Victorian "progress": *The horror! The horror!* This celebrated moment of self-judg-ment reflects not only on Kurtz but on the European imperial project as a whole. Granting that Conrad's representation of Africans is spectral at best, this nevertheless amounts to a major subversion of "progress" as a justi-fication for colonial exploitation. Although that insight itself represents a certain progress, Marlow's subsequent behavior—back in England he lies to Kurtz's fiancée about the latter's last words—suggests the possibility that this insight will be buried and his readers will continue to sleepwalk through colonial violence and exploitation.

*Nostromo* (1904), Conrad's fiercest attack on the rhetoric of progress and development, chimes with Johnson's unease about "American" settlers. The narrative chronology is scrambled, giving events a hallucinatory feel. In overturning the devices by which the novel had been devoted, in Jameson's phrase, "to the fictive, illusory assumption of reality,"[46] Conrad comments on the entire tradition of Realism. He brilliantly evokes the mentality of a more informal empire emerging, as Berkeley had foreseen, from the United States. Published in the same year that North America took over the building of the Panama Canal from the French, *Nostromo* figures the North Americans as plausibly in line for the next *translatio imperii*: a regional but rising hegemon. Teddy Roosevelt's regional policy called for the United States to act as "an international police force" in the Caribbean and Latin America.[47]

The plot of *Nostromo* illuminates the impact of capitalism—allegedly bearing the seeds of material progress—in a place rich in resources but poor in democratic institutions or political responsibility. The novel sketches out the misrule, following Spanish misrule, of a Creole oligarchy in the imaginary country of Costaguana on the western seaboard of South America. Costaguana is unstable—a "banana republic," as Jameson says[48]—and yet Conrad's creation is not without political insights well beyond the limits of such a stereotype. In *Nostromo* we see a new colonial commodity emerge by way of a second phase of silver mining in the New World. This occurs in the isolated port city of Sulaca. Sulaca seems lucky to have a few modern amenities, such as railway service and telegraphy. Just as Panama had been induced to secede from its previous union with Colombia, so the integrity of Costaguana is beset by internal and external pressures.

The mine in question, which is the focus of all anticipated progress, belongs to Charles Gould. Gould, a Costaguanero, has recently returned from England; he is of English descent. Also creole is Martin Decoud, of French descent, who advocates independence for the Occidental Province. The main cast of characters is fleshed out by old Giorgio Viola, an expatriate Italian republican steeped in nostalgia for the revolutionary views of Garibaldi; the English Emilia Gould, wife of Charles, who knows the earlier murderous history of the mine under Spanish rule; and Nostromo, the charismatic head of the longshoremen. After a coup, Nostromo, also an Italian expatriate, and Decoud work together under the orders of Charles Gould to hide silver ingots from political enemies offshore on the island of Great Isabel. Decould remarks as follows on the fatality of history in Costaguana: "There is a curse of futility upon our character: Don Quixote, Sancho Panza, chivalry and materialism, high-sounding sentiments and supine morality, violent efforts for an idea and a sullen acquiescence in every form of corruption." That which will again defeat progress is the contagious effect of the mine—and Nostromo will prove an anti-hero.

Progress at first seems possible: the mine proves to be a money-making "empire within an empire," a site where the economic future of the country seems to be at stake. Trying to redeem a contractual "concession" that ruined his father, Gould approaches the San Tomé Silver Mine as a rich man's hobby. He hopes in his dabbling way, by reviving the mine, to contribute to a general economic prosperity. Gould and Holroyd, the Gilded-Age financier from San Francisco, imagine enlisting Sulaca's local economy in the world credit market.[49] Gould had cooperated with the dictator Don Vincente Ribiera, however; and his political maneuvers in the end backfire.

Charles Gould has a quixotic faith that the "material interests" willy-nilly bring progress: "Only let the material interests once get a firm footing, and they are bound to impose the conditions on which alone they can continue to exist."[50] This never happens. Emilia gradually realizes that the entrancing mine has displaced her in her husband's affections. Meanwhile, the mysterious titular character, Nostromo, proves to be less than he seemed. A natural leader, Nostromo works on the docks and, as the foreman, acquires a reputation as personally incorruptible. He initially seems like a possible cure for what ails Costaguana. The latter part of the novel, however, recounts his descent into corruption by the silver mine. He begins stealing the hoarded silver for himself and—gradually, prudently—grows visibly rich. He loses his peace of mind, however, along with his integrity. While trying to smuggle his silver to safety, Nostromo is accidentally shot and killed by the old Garibaldino; and one looks in vain, at the end of the novel, for the faintest sliver of "progress." Emilia Gould, the novel's most sensitive and intelligent character, ponders the absence in

Costaguana of anything tying the past to the future. "It had come into her mind that for life to be large and full, it must contain the care of the past and of the future in every passing moment of the present."[51] For a life of integrity, as opposed to a shallow immediacy, history needs to be articulated in periods that both distinguish and connect. The novel concludes, however, with no plausible solution either to political instability or to the fetishistic allure of the silver mine. Emilia, the one truly incorruptible character, declines to hear from the dying Nostromo where his hoard of silver is buried. If eighteenth-century literary commerce had afforded Johnson a certain daylight within which to critique his stratified society, that commerce of the nineteenth century, as rendered here by Conrad, seems more profoundly veiled by the overwhelming fixation on extracting a valuable commodity.

Imperialism, that supposed bearer of progress, proves to be the very opposite. The real-life Latin American inertia described in *Nostromo* would eventually provoke "dependency theory," which cuts sharply against the template of progressive development by emphasizing the *creation* of prolonged underdevelopment in poor countries by wealthy and "developed" ones. Of most interest is the way this setting enables Conrad to imagine the early arrival of capitalism. The millionaire financier Holroyd, a key figure, refers below to North Americans collectively as follows:

> We shall be giving the word for everything—industry, trade, law, journalism, art, politics, and religion, from Cape Horn to Smith's Sound, and beyond too, if anything worth taking hold of turns up at the North Pole. And then we shall have the leisure to take in hand the outlying islands and continents of the earth. We shall run the world's business whether the world like it or not. The world can't help it—and neither can we, I guess.[52]

The bad faith of disclaimed agency—"we can't help it"—makes this an especially unappetizing brew of imperial posturing. Even the future-oriented, can-do Yankees, builders of the Panama Canal, bring not progress but ongoing exploitation. From "robbing" the indigenous inhabitants of North America, as Johnson had charged, so-called "Americans" would go on to exert a domineering influence over peoples and nations to the south. Here and elsewhere, Conrad's politics seem more pessimistically uncertain than (as used to be assumed) confidently reactionary.

Conrad continues to hold a foundational place in many things postcolonial: the popularity of revising his provocative works has made him difficult to avoid. The Colombian author Juan Gabriel Vásquez rewrites *Nostromo* directly in *The Secret History of Costaguana* (2012). V. S. Naipaul, scarcely less controversial than Conrad himself for unflattering depictions of "natives," belongs among his debtors. Also conspicuously in his literary debt debt are Graham Greene, F. Scott Fitzgerald, Virginia Woolf, Ernest Hemingway, and William Faulkner.

## VI.  Self-Exiled and Avant-Garde: James Joyce

[*Ulysses*] remains the twentieth century's most modern novel ... .
Saul Bellow

Library shelves veritably whimper with the literary burden of James Joyce; and the secondary fan comes on at the very presence of Joyce in one's storage device. Fiercely determined to be artistically autonomous at all costs, Joyce rejected as impediments to his artistic progress the three institutional and emotional "nets" (religion, language, nationalism) that might, in Catholic Ireland, ensnare his ambitions. He was broadly on the socialist left and thoroughly sympathized with Ireland's prolonged struggle for independence from Britain. And, though Joyce pointedly chose not to be, like Yeats, a literary voice for Irish nationalism, his major works are all set in Dublin. His first priority, however, was a towering literary ambition. Like Conrad, the early "naturalistic" Joyce especially admired the fanatically precise writing of Flaubert. A much deeper *agon*, however, in Harold Bloom's sense, can be traced in Joyce's competitive relationship with Shakespeare.[53] Joyce's subject matter, however, is sufficiently humble. In Richard Ellman's acute formulation, the work of Joyce is constituted by "the justification of the commonplace."[54]

Joyce was lucky with patrons. From the well-connected Pound he received a major boost for *A Portrait of the Artist as a Young Man*. Starting with *Ulysses*, he was fortunate to receive the timely patronage of Sylvia Beach (1887–1962), owner of the Parisian bookshop Shakespeare and

Company, which also published the book. This support was generously augmented by Harriet Weaver (1876–1961), the wealthy editor of *The Egoist*. Such backing enabled his creativity to flourish without much direct dependence on a market not necessarily geared to wild literary experimentation. That market, by now saturated with calculations about public opinion, had come to seem more barrier than opportunity, and Joyce made do by reviving patronage as a form of independence rather than dependence.

Joyce worked across several genres and made his mark in every variety of prose fiction. His *Dubliners* (1916) belongs in the company of the best short-story-collections ever. Joyce's happy use of the *epiphany* to structure these stories—an abrupt insight, often disillusioning—seems to demonstrate what the form was always meant to do. A Joycean epiphany, sometimes enigmatic and sometimes a clear hammer-blow, is a secular formal device. Consider the following epiphany from "The Dead," the final and climactic story in *Dubliners*. Gabriel Conroy, a sort of all-purpose everyman sleep-walking through daily existence, suddenly realizes the worst about his life:

> [Snow] was falling, too, upon every part of the lonely churchyard on the hill where Michael Furey lay buried. It lay thickly drifted on the crooked crosses and headstones, on the spears of the little gate, on the barren thorns. His soul swooned slowly as he heard the snow falling faintly through the universe and faintly falling, like the descent of their last end, upon all the living and the dead.

Gabriel suddenly realizes that his wife's memory of an old lover, Michael Furey, long dead and buried, is far more vivid to her than he is. The gorgeous concluding chiasmus ("falling faintly … faintly falling") formally clinches what is a devastating final sentence, not only for the story but the volume. The spiraling crisscross pattern does culminate here with an enlarged understanding.

The semi-autobiographical *Portrait*, though stylistically tame compared to the later Joyce, advances the claims and achievements of literary Modernism. Among the restrictive nets that Joyce's protagonist Stephen Dedalus sets out to escape, along with religion, is language: an issue with a long history of colonial antagonism. Although Joyce knew all the Irish politicking around languages—Stephen drops out of a class in (Gaelic) Irish—his literary ambition required him to compete with the best in Anglophone literary tradition. Meanwhile, the adolescent Stephen pursues aesthetic issues that emphasize both his implacable seriousness and his spooky distance from others. Stephen famously enumerates his artistic credo as "silence, cunning, exile":[55] the latter expressing the distance he needed from the third net: Irish nationalism. As the book closes he is preparing to depart for the continent. Samuel Johnson's loathing of cultural nationalism and its frequently kitschy solemnities constitutes a worthy precursor to Stephen/Joyce.

*Portrait* concludes with Stephen's commitment to a literary vocation. Switching abruptly from third-person narration to Stephen's diary from April 26 and 27, 1904, the novella makes interior the themes of pride, isolation, and productive solitude:

> 26 *April*. Mother is putting my new secondhand clothes in order. She prays now, she says, that I may learn in my own life and away from home and friends what the heart is and what it feels. Amen. So be it. Welcome O life! I go to encounter for the millionth time the reality of experience and to forge in the smithy of my soul the uncreated conscience of my race.
> 27 *April*. Old father, old artificer, stand me now and ever in good stead. (*Portrait*, 282)

Such a vocational moment, in which Stephen claims his last name, cannot be read as pervasively ironic. Stephen is at worst, as Ellman puts it, *young*.[56] It is worth noting that "race" here bears the older meaning of *lineage*. Stephen is creating, through Dædalus, his specifically literary ancestral line.[57]

In this conclusion to Joyce's *Künstlerroman*, the progress of an artistic sensibility is clinched. Stephen's "decisionism" contrasts sharply with the gentle irony, in *Rasselas*, against the all-or-nothing *choice of life*. Stephen's imagination sanctions his artistic project. Stephen experiences a *symbolic mandate*, a moment when he is "filled up" and "filled out," as Lawrence Kramer puts it, by surrendering to "the call, the gift, the name, the mandate" that marks the moment when he is invested with the license to remake tradition.[58] Stephen's imagination produces a fiery self-transformation; and Joyce, of the three authors under consideration, most wholeheartedly embraces that human faculty. Johnson's wariness on this score culminates in his famous and telling phrase from *Rasselas*, *the hunger of the imagination*: a watchword encompassing in ego-driven futility even such dazzling achievements as the Egyptian pyramids. Joyce's Stephen aspires, by way of contrast, to be "a high priest of the imagination."

*Ulysses* (1922), which achieves many literary breakthroughs, affords a bit of space also for the hope of individual and collective progress. A sharp change for Joyce artistically, it has often been judged the single greatest Anglophone novel of the twentieth century. The plot is compressed to a single day, June 16, 1904, the episodes of which are keyed to episodes in *The Odyssey*. Joyce's main characters are unquestionably objects of empathy no less than satire; and Leopold Bloom is certainly his richest and most sympathetic character. Bloom, a secular Jew, belongs to the tiny minority of Jews in Catholic and Protestant Dublin. Or so it seems: Bloom's mother is Catholic, not Jewish, so within the technicalities of a matrilineal tradition even his Jewishness is marginal. He works as an ad canvasser. The reader encounters nary an epiphany as such: instead, as Franco Moretti argues, we find a vast accumulation of deliberately banal details.[59] Poldy Bloom's clichés, Moretti goes on to argue, are precisely his "epiphanies."[60] Such is Joyce's departure here from Flaubert: an increasing investment, to look forward to *Finnegans Wake*, in the detritus of language, its *litteringture*.

From the first, the controversy around *Ulysses* has stemmed from Joyce's cutting-edge representation of the body. The bodily functions are all there, including urination, defecation, and menstruation. Bloom reads both *Don Quixote* and a daily newspaper while in the outhouse, and Joyce goes Chaucer one better by actually representing the sound of a fart (*Pprrpffrrppfff*).[61] Meanwhile, after the death of a son, Leopold and Molly find that sexual intimacy has departed from their marital bed. Molly has a lover, the boorish Blazes Boylan; and Bloom responds to his cuckoldry generously: he avoids confronting Molly and Blazes. Given that *The Odyssey* concludes with the disguised Odysseus's bloody massacre of the suitors wooing Penelope and living off his estate, Joyce provides us with a pacifist version of the story.[62] In terms of literary tradition and the notions of male honor that it has propagated, Joyce's plot here constitutes deeply considered literary and political progress.

Joyce's effort to dignify the commonplace—politically and artistically progressive—includes a candidly advanced description of sex. The events of Bloom's June 16 include both his own cuckolding and a masturbatory episode on Sandymount Strand, the latter helped along by the cooperative exhibitionism of Gerty MacDowell. The latter—lying on a beach—displays her drawers to him. This apparently mutual encounter culminates in Bloom's famous orgasm, set against a fireworks display:

> And then a rocket sprang and bang shot blind blank and O! then the Roman candle burst and it was like a sigh of O! and everyone cried O! O! in raptures and it gushed out of it a strand of rain gold hair threads and they shed and ah! They were all greeny dewy stars falling with golden, O so! O so soft, sweet, soft![63]

As Joyce understood, there is a vast gap between sexual norms (what society claims to believe about itself) and actual sexual behavior (what people do, however furtively). Joyce's texture of lived bodily funkiness expressed a reality very different from slick objects of commodified desire: the latter incite precisely the lazy fantasy that *Ulysses* works through. The deeper scandal of *Ulysses*, that pervy book, may be that it puts under a microscope the frailties, randomness, and routine backfires of actually existing erotic life. Unquestionably progress for candor in the public sphere, this novel angle of *Ulysses* provoked censorious legal battles that delayed the book's distribution.

Advances in literary technique are Joyce's imaginative specialty. The grand interior monologue of Molly with which *Ulysses* concludes ultimately affirms not just her life but specifically her imperfect marriage to Leopold. This monologue, concluding as she remembers with the word *yes* Leopold's proposal of marriage, is the single most famous stream of consciousness in literary history. The content of Molly's monologue makes clear her defiant awareness of living in a man's world, one defined by the sexual double standard. Molly remembers, for example, "pretending to like it till he comes and then finish it off myself anyway" (*Ulysses*, 610).

Here we learn that Leopold also has strayed from marital fidelity. Ultimately, however, Molly Bloom's final *yes* is not so much an epiphany as a state of mind.

An acute and highly advanced awareness of stylistic change is among Joyce's contributions to literary tradition. The English literary tradition, figured as a gestating embryo, achieves here a wryly amusing awareness of its own development. The later Joyce seldom charms by holding something in reserve. At the same time, one does not want to give ear to an unworthy complaint: that *Ulysses* is *hard*. Exuberant virtuosity is beauty. The complexity of styles and modes in *Ulysses* seems to illustrate the dictum of the art historian George Kubler: that in a sequence of artistic problems and their resolutions, later outcomes are "difficult, intricate, recondite, and animated."[64] Immediately from Joyce's generative text spring such progeny as Woolf's *Mrs. Dalloway* (1925), Beckett's *The Unnameable* (1953), and Anthony Burgess's *A Clockwork Orange* (1963).[65] Faulkner's *The Sound and the Fury* (1929), perhaps the single most brilliant Anglophone use of stream-of-consciousness narration, cannot be imagined without *Ulysses*.

Speaking of difficulty: was there ever a more *avant-garde* text than *Finnegans Wake*? Or a less readable one? If *Ulysses* is difficult, *Finnegans Wake* is exorbitantly opaque: the dark nocturnal counterpart to the daylight plot of *Ulysses*. What Kubler identifies as the busy intricacy of later artifacts in a formal sequence here reaches an astonishing intensity. To be sure, highly distinguished scholars, stepping up to fulfill Joyce's sardonic prediction that he had assured such professorial types their employment for several centuries, have greatly clarified the basic plot, its main "characters," and many other structural and verbal issues. The book, set in a dream that encompasses human history back to Adam and Eve, opens onto a dream-language, and gathers in many avatars for such collective "characters" as HCE and ALP. The *Wake* is more poem than novel and more puzzle than poem. It represents a violent break from *Ulysses*.

To read the *Wake* induces dizzying reflections on ordinary practices of reading; on the relations among a prodigious number of languages; and on the capacity of the humblest signifiers to condense infinite currents of meaning. One stumbles very soon on puns and Jabberwockian words and sentences that astonish with their sound and wit. Consider the following

Christmas greeting, sent to HCE by the children plotting to overthrow his rule: "With our best youlldied greedings to Pep and Memmy and the old folkers below and beyant, wishing them all very merry Incarnations in the land of the livvey and plenty of preprosperousness through their coming new yonks."[66] Here the annual repetition of Christmas-greetings clichés gets unraveled by a cheeky undertone of generational hostility. Elsewhere, the name *Corkcutta* links two city-spaces of anti-colonial struggle; *to westernize* re-emerges as *to westerneyes*; and *North Armorica*—a pun on the French region—nods to North American arms and imperialism. As night yields to the rising sun, the novel foretells—if not quite a fascist Japan—a rising Asia.[67]

Joyce's linguistic omnicompetence, however, sets a very high bar: *Finnegans Wake*, in which he invents a new language, could only work *as a story* for a very uncommon reader. Repeated references to *the murketplots* suggests that Joyce finds it idiotic to limit literary art to its market value: a gesture pointing to the superiority flexibility of discerning patrons. If the eighteenth-century literary marketplace affords Johnson some encouraging room for political critique, that of the early twentieth century, as rendered by Joyce, seems discouraging, without patronage, to radical literary innovation. While the market served as no check on Joyce, he was indulged by his patrons in what some critics have seen as a massive leg-pull.

Does artistic innovation count as "progress" if it results in little subsequent adoption, imitation, or development?[68] This is the question hanging over the method of *Finnegans Wake*, a text that seems, like Pope's consummate polish, "aesthetically terminal."[69] How could one take such a pun-happy linguistic mash-up any further? Punning in the *Wake* is not merely revealed by context: as Derek Attridge says, punning *is* context. Attridge also updates Johnson's verdict on Shakespeare's puns with this mock-paraphrase about Joyce's love of portmanteaux: "A portmanteau word, poor and barren as it is, gave Joyce such delight that he was content to purchase it by the sacrifice of reason, propriety, and truth."[70] Attridge's own more deconstructive view is that the effect of meaning is—in all texts—"unstable and uncontrollable."[71] It would be hard, however, to think of another single text in which such Derridean terms as *graft*, *citation*, *drift*, and *iteration* seem so thoroughly appropriate. As for that other favored concept of Derrida, *labyrinth*, we must recall that Dædalus devised wings precisely to escape a labyrinth of his own devising. Geoff Boucher, moreover, points out that "Joyce is exactly the opposite of what he should be for deconstruction—a signature."[72] Joyce ultimately does not disperse his authorial self. In reconciling aesthetic progress with infinite semiosis, he composes and recomposes that self, that signature. Though Joyce as an author did not, like Imlac and the astronomer, drift along the current of life, his last work is indeed all flow: a riverine experience of semiotic streams and counter-currents.

Joyce's larger structure emphatically refuses both closure and progress. Beginning in mid-sentence, *Finnegans Wake* famously concludes with the missing sentence-fragment that would complete its opening. The text is circular and infinitely repeating. The wake for Finn (again) puns on "awakening"; and that trope resonates with perhaps the most famous sentence, spoken by Stephen Dedalus, from *Ulysses*: "History is a nightmare from which I am trying to awake" (*Ulysses*, 28). Such a circular structure defies any notion of long-lasting "progress" or decisive awakening. Joyce now accepts, seemingly without gloom, this Viconian circularity. Starting with the trope of exile in *Portrait*, however, and concluding with *Finnegans Wake*, the fictions of James Joyce consistently recalibrate his unnerving distance from readers. This distance finally makes for his greatest difference from Johnson.

## VII. Conclusion: The Stale and the Fresh

What might this unusual constellation teach us? Reading the melancholy Conrad through Johnson, let us look unflinchingly at the history of western racism in the 1890s and after. Even as we acknowledge that Conrad often lacked the imagination to represent individuals from Asia or Africa,[73] let us tip our hat to his brilliant rendering of colonial futility and horror. Conrad did not shy away from showing the deepest experiences of political and psychological negativity. But let us also fully register the extent to which Samuel Johnson represents for English politics and letters *a path not taken*: the possibility, routinely dismissed in the nineteenth century as "Little Englandism," of refusing colonial expansion, exploitation, violence, and racist misrepresentation. Whereas Conrad too often recycles racial clichés, Johnson disputes the demeaning depiction of Africans in Portuguese voyage literature.[74]

Reading Joyce through Johnson, let us concede that Johnson, like almost every other renowned author, is more aesthetically conservative than the later Joyce. Johnson continually balances authorship with a reading public: he is willing to confront and push his readers in countless productive ways, including stylistically, but he attempts to stretch a readership that already exists. Joyce, by way of contrast, often had to *create* his own audience and to coach that audience in radically new ways of reading. The cerebral Joyce prized artistic autonomy above all, and in *Finnegans Wake* he shows us how it looks when the abstract process of signification itself, like Conrad's abstracted *seeing*, attains an autonomous life of its own. By creating a whole new language, one over-determined by the suggestive overtones of etymons in dozens of languages, including Irish, Joyce *made it new* with a great honking vengeance. The gnarliest of individualists, he risked eclipsing even the uncommon reader. And yet the sense that Joyce somehow touches the elemental is reflected in the adoption of the word *quark*, famously borrowed from the *Wake*, to represent a subatomic particle.

Conrad and Joyce cannot be said to represent, *vis-à-vis* Johnson, anything as straightforward as literary or political progress. Our trio of authors faced violent modernizing dynamics and all three responded with fictions that refreshed tradition and critiqued empire. We find in the threesome a persuasive key to understanding literary history: the practice of *defamiliarization*. As Johnson puts it in *Rambler* 125,

> There is ... scarcely any species of which we can tell what is its essence, and what are its constituents; every new genius produces some innovation, which, when invented and approved, subverts the rules which the practice of foregoing authors had established. (Yale *Works*, 4:300)

The dialectic of the stale and the fresh, as Johnson here anticipates Shklovsky, creates not so much progress or decline as an unpredictable pattern of zigs and zags.[75]

Samuel Johnson, both an anxious perfectionist and a laughing absurdist, has often been so far ahead of us that literary history has yet to catch up with him. He pointedly and consistently refuses the worst of "progress" as an ideological theme: its abuse as a racist and imperial mode of self-legitimation. Although he typically advocates for such possibilities of social and literary advancement as he could find, Johnson remains robustly skeptical of "progress" as an overall means of legitimating present arrangements of power. We certainly did not need to wait until the advent of postmodernism to see how often self-declared progress resolves itself into dead ends and dead cats—eventually to be exposed as "right only because they are established." Meanwhile, our broad literary histories, beyond the enclave of Johnson Studies, need to stop evoking Johnson as an obstinate conservative and to start recognizing him as a powerful enemy of received ideas and unexamined custom; as, indeed, the brightest star in an anti-colonial constellation that includes Conrad and Joyce; and, above all, as a far-sighted navigator across the rocky shoals of "progress." If Johnson was wary of claims to progress, those hoping for actual progress cannot afford to overlook his critical epiphanies.

CHAPTER FIVE

# Johnson Goes to War

*Jack Lynch*

## I. The Interests of Prince Charles Stuart

Samuel Johnson never went to war. That has not prevented a few eccentrics from considering the possibility that he somehow engaged in combat himself. Boswell records that his hero "was once drawn to serve in the militia, the Trained Bands of the City of London … . He upon that occasion provided himself with a musket, and with a sword and belt, which I have seen hanging in his closet."[1] Boswell found "the idea" of Johnson in uniform, "with all its circumstances, is certainly laughable," and any reasonable reader has to number this among Johnson's more ridiculous moments. But the evidence of a musket and sword prompted J. L. Ward to wonder conspiratorially in 1932,

> Where was Johnson in 1745? That year is an *annus candidus* in his recognised biographies, and no one has yet succeeded in finding out where Johnson was then, or what he was doing. Was he slaving at dull literary hackwork for Cave and the *Gentleman's Magazine*, or engaged as an active Jacobite in furthering the interests of Prince Charles Stuart, the Young Pretender?[2]

We know the answer to this question: "slaving at dull literary hackwork." It would be virtually impossible to for something like military service to escape biographical notice, and we would have to pity any commanding officer obliged to give orders to the authority-averse and half-blind Johnson. Whatever the exact nature of his "kind of *liking* for Jacobitism,"[3] it did not extend to defending the Pretender's interests on the battle-field. Even Ward calls it "admittedly difficult to picture the scholarly and myopic Samuel Johnson, armed with dirk and targe, tramping in the ranks of the Young Pretender's army." And yet he cannot forbear concluding that "some definite Jacobite activity may reasonably be suspected."[4] This stretches the definition of "reasonably" past the breaking point. Johnson never went to war.

Still, he thought a great deal about war. Johnson praised, and tried to account for, "The Bravery of the English Common Soldiers."[5] Colonel John Macleod of Talisker was among his friends, and Boswell himself longed for a career in the military. Johnson wrote about military action in Falkland's Islands. In the *Literary Magazine* for November 1756 he reviewed *The Cadet: A Military Treatise* by Samuel Bever and offered his opinions of standing armies and military academies.[6] *Idler* 20 reflects on the recent capture of Louisbourg and boldly tells the story twice, first from an English, second from a French, point of view (Yale *Works*, 2:62–65). He visited the École militaire in France; during the American war he went to Warley Camp in Essex, where he "took occasion to converse at times on military topicks," observed the drills, and quizzed the soldiers about the weight of musket balls (*Boswell's Life*, 3:361). In 1760 he reminded himself to "Send for books for Hist. of War," suggesting he was planning to write an extended work on the subject, though there is no agreement on whether this refers to the War of Austrian Succession, the Seven Years' War, or warfare in general.[7] Though no soldier himself, Johnson gave more thought than most to matters military.

## II.  Death and Destruction

It is only fitting, then, that those engaged in matters military gave thought to Johnson. Winston Churchill famously referred to the Seven Years' War as the "first world war,"[8] but my subject is the war that history has chosen to honor—if honor is the right word—with that title, the war that is often treated as the event that ushered in literary modernism. Though the First

World War broke out 130 years after Johnson's death, there are a surprising number of points of contact between the two.

For one thing, a generation of Johnsonian scholarship was put on hold. The second decade of the twentieth century has as fair a claim as any to marking the inauguration of serious scholarly attention to Johnson's works, a departure from the belletristic writing of the Victorians, but many of these new projects were halted aborning. David Nichol Smith, for instance, planned a new edition of Johnson's poems in 1913, but "its progress was checked by the events of the next five years."[9] The edition would not be realized until he teamed up with E. L. McAdam. Even then their collaboration was nearly scuttled by yet another world war, though the volume finally appeared in 1941.

More ceremonial activities were put on hold too: the Johnson Society of Lichfield published addresses in 1910, 1911, and 1912, and then not again until 1920. The Johnson Club of London, however, was heartier. After decades of meeting at the Cheshire Cheese, the group moved around the corner into the newly renovated house at Gough Square for their first dinner on December 13, 1913, and "even in the time of the War, and its food regulations," George Whale records, "we did not drop our quarterly meetings."[10] But the club nearly had reason to regret that move. The damage the Gough Square house suffered in the Second World War is part of the oral lore that docents share with visitors even today—on December 29, 1940, a German bomb sent a flaming oil-drum through the roof, destroying the garret—and the first few years' worth of James Clifford's *Johnsonian News Letter* from the early 1940s are filled with quarterly updates on the condition of the house.[11] Less well known is that the Gough Square was also targeted during the Great War, and that it happened during a meeting of the Johnson Club. On October 13, 1915, after the dinner had been eaten and the toasts drunk, the Conservative MP and publisher Arthur Baumann rose to deliver a paper on "The Cynicism of Dr. Johnson" before an audience of twenty-seven. In the discussion afterwards, someone asked Johnson's definition of *cynic*, and the secretary began turning the pages of the *Dictionary*. But "While he was doing so, a loud explosion was heard outside and near by." The face of publisher and bibliophile Clement Shorter fell as he realized what was going on: a German zeppelin was dropping bombs on the City of London. Together the club members watched as "The great airship was slowly sailing overhead, brilliantly illuminated by the flare of the searchlights and the explosion of shells." Publisher Thomas Fisher Unwin, eager to get a glimpse, leaned so far out the window that he nearly fell onto the street below. The gathering was interrupted by police, who "were shouting at us, and threatening to raid the house, if we did not … turn out the lights." Shells blew out most of the windows on Fleet Street and the Strand; they destroyed the porch of the Lyceum Theatre and most of a nearby pub; they set the *Morning Post* building on fire and killed several locals. One of the members reflected that "a chance bomb falling upon the house would, in all probability, have" wiped out a generation of Johnsonians.[12] Their survival was an occasion for a patriotic outpouring:

> We learnt, later, that death and destruction by bombs had been dealt around and very near, but Johnson's house, with our Club in it, had escaped, by what some would call chance. Could the patriotic Johnson have seen that Zeppelin, what tremendous lines had been added to his *London*![13]

This nearly fatal dinner featured not only a former Conservative MP as speaker but also Augustine Birrell, the Liberal chief secretary for Ireland. It serves as a reminder that some of the nation's most important political figures during the war—the very people who were conducting the war—were actively involved with Johnson. Prime Minister Herbert Asquith is described on the dustjacket of his *Studies and Sketches* as "a student and scholar as well as a statesman," and his résumé bears it out. Literature was for him a refuge from politics: "A man who spends most of his days and nights in the Law Courts and the House of Commons has a special need for the soothing and cleansing influences of literature and scholarship."[14] Shortly after the war, therefore, he addressed the Johnson Club on "Dr. Johnson and Fanny Burney," in which his attention is clearly on Johnson rather than Burney: he condescendingly calls *Evelina*, for instance, "still a readable book," but finds it "difficult now to understand its immediate and overwhelming success."[15] Asquith was well known as an admirer of Johnson; Max Beerbohm even did a sketch of Asquith in an armchair reading his wife's scandalous memoirs as a bust of Johnson looks down disapprovingly. That scandalous wife, meanwhile, had been so associated with Johnson's conversational style that in her social circle her name, "a Margot," became a common noun signifying someone marked by "social fearlessness or brutality, a sort of Dr. Johnson."[16]

An even greater Johnsonian enthusiast was Cecil Harmsworth, 1st Baron Harmsworth, the brother of the publisher Alfred, Lord Northcliffe, and undersecretary of state for the Home Department under Asquith in 1915 before becoming undersecretary of state for foreign affairs under Lloyd George. It was Harmsworth who bought the house on Gough Square in 1911 with his own money, renovated it in the nick of time before it fell down, and eventually donated the house to the nation. He published *Dr Johnson: A Great Englishman* in 1923 and wrote at length about the house.[17]

Not all the wartime interest, however, came from the politicians; most of the literary figures of the Great War were also Johnsonians to some degree. In 1903, Siegfried Sassoon bought the twelve-volume edition of Johnson's *Works* from 1801, with Arthur Murphy's Life, and in 1922 he praised Edmund Gosse with a Johnsonian quotation.[18] In late spring 1914, just months before the outbreak of war, Rupert Brooke was reading Boswell and declaring, "Dr. Johnson is the only man I love. An Englishman, by God!"[19] Ford Madox Ford in *Parade's End* focuses on Christopher Tietjens, "an eighteenth-century figure of the Dr Johnson type," who takes solace in his final illness by listening to his brother reading Boswell's *Life* to him.[20] Robert Graves, a passionate reader of Lucan, recalled Johnson's description of Nicholas Rowe's translation of the Latin poet. Graves memorably opens *Goodbye to All That* with a grudging acknowledgment of "autobiographical conventions," where Johnson is part of the idyllic antebellum world he was obliged to say goodbye to:

> Algernon Charles Swinburne … often used to stop my perambulator when he met it on Nurses' Walk, at the edge of Wimbledon Common, and pat me on the head and kiss me. … Swinburne, by the way, when a very young man, had gone to Walter Savage Landor, then a very old man, and been given the poet's blessing he asked for; and Landor when a child had been patted on the head by Dr Samuel Johnson.[21]

As George Saintsbury put it in *The Peace of the Augustans*, his influential history of eighteenth-century literature published in 1916, the culture of that century was "a Place of Rest and Refreshment." Asquith, too, calls the period "one of the eras in which it would have been most comfortable and restful to have lived."[22] For many of the writers whose world fell apart in 1914, Johnson represented a contrast to the modernity that had been thrust on them. Paul Fussell observes that "Eighteenth-century writing was popular" at the front because "It offered an oasis of reasonableness and normality, a place one could crawl into for a few moments' respite from the sights, sounds, and smells of the twentieth century."[23] And Johnson, who embodies all its essential qualities, stands synecdochically for the whole era. "Johnson," Saintsbury writes, "is not only by common consent one of the most striking figures of the eighteenth century, but he is, from a certain side and in a certain sense, *the* eighteenth century."[24]

## III. The Stricken Landscape

It is therefore only natural that soldiers brought copies of Johnson's works to the front. A series of pocket editions of Johnson and Boswell, as well as abridgments and vade mecums, seem to have been designed with soldiers' packs in mind. Three separate pocket abridgments of Boswell's *Life* were prepared during the war, by Gerard Jensen, Charles Grosvenor Osgood, and R. W. Chapman.[25] S. C. Roberts's *Story of Doctor Johnson* was completed in April 1918, while the war was still going on. There Roberts makes the case that Johnson's lifetime is uniquely relevant to his own:

> Kings and cottagers, statesmen and shopkeepers, bishops and play-actors, rich brewers and penniless poets, dukes and innkeepers, country parsons and gay young men of the town, street beggars and fashionable ladies—all play their part in the story and shew us a picture of the English world in the eighteenth century such as no history-book can give.[26]

We know at least a few of the readers of these books. Lieutenant Geoffrey Keynes of the Royal Army Medical Corps, brother of the famous economist, even passed his time at Ypres reading Courtney and Smith's newly published *Bibliography of Samuel Johnson*. As Fussell points out, "No book was too outré: in fact, the gross inappropriateness of certain books was part of their value."[27] The most remarkable front-line reader of Johnson's works, though, was a Scot who completed a first-class degree in classics at St Andrews, then took a double first in mods and LitHum at Oriel College, Oxford, and found employment as assistant secretary to the delegates at Clarendon Press. But the war called Captain Robert William Chapman from Oxford to the Royal Garrison Artillery, and he served in Salonika, on the Macedonian Front, as part of the effort to support Serbia against the Central Powers. There he did most of the work on his edition of Johnson's *Journey to the Western Islands* and Boswell's *Journal of a Tour*, as well as preliminary work on his hugely influential edition of Jane Austen's novels.

At this point neither Johnson's nor Boswell's works had been submitted to the kind of collation and textual criticism that was becoming standard with early modern texts—the new bibliography and textual criticism had made few forays into the eighteenth century. But Chapman was a textual critic at heart, and nothing thrilled him more than a well-chosen conjectural emendation. His copy of Johnson lacked the errata slip, but he took great pride in independently discovering and correcting every mistake the publisher had identified, as well as a few he had not. "The corrections were … exceedingly simple—child's play to trained performer. But I confess I was pleased to find that I had detected and corrected *all* the errata."[28] The posting was no sinecure. The Central Powers had around 600,000 men, the Allies more than 700,000, tightly packed into the Macedonian theater; together they suffered something on the order of 150,000 casualties. Chapman was stationed at an artillery position on the left bank of the Vardar next to a six-inch Mark XI gun, and that is where he had the first edition of Johnson's *Journey* and the first, second, and third editions of Boswell's *Journal* shipped to him. He describes his working conditions:

> I made a hut of sandbags, with a roof constructed of corrugated iron in layers, with large stones between … and here, in the long hot afternoons … a temporary gunner, in a khaki shirt and shorts, might have been found collating the three editions of the *Tour to the Hebrides*, or re-reading *A Journey to the Western Islands* in the hope of finding a corruption of the text. Ever and again, tiring of

collating and emendation, of tepid tea and endless cigarettes, I would go outside to look at the stricken landscape—the parched, yellow hills and ravines, the brown coils of the big snaky river at my feet, the mountains in the blue distance; until the scorching wind, which always blew down that valley, sent me back to the Hebrides.[29]

There is something remarkable about the thought of a scholar collating variants "in camps and dug-outs and troop-trains."[30] For him the books—books by and about Johnson—represented his only contact with the world he had left behind:

The graces of civilization and the delights of learning are far from me now. But my nomadic and semi-barbarous existence is still solaced by a few good books; and the best odes of Horace, the best things in Boswell or Elia, often awake memories of Attic nights.[31]

As Kathryn Sutherland points out,

he stands at his post in Macedonia at the outermost limits of an inheritance and ... the preservation of its threatened values is part of his patrol, too ... . In Macedonia civilization is conjured only in moments ... . In this remote region the decay of English syntax and thoughts on spelling reform assume a political resonance.[32]

## IV. The Dignity of Danger

For most readers the political resonance drowned out the obsession over textual minutiae. When readers in 1916 encountered Johnson, it was often Johnson the well-known advocate for British military intervention. In his early *Marmor Norfolciense* he attacks Sir Robert Walpole's pacifist policy toward Spain. "In conversation," Boswell records, Johnson "always exalted the profession of a soldier." He lectured Boswell: "the profession of soldiers and sailors has the dignity of danger. Mankind reverence those who have got over fear, which is so general a weakness."[33] He was particularly impressed with the excellence of his own nation's soldiers:

Our nation may boast, beyond any other people in the world, of a kind of epidemick bravery, diffused equally through all its ranks. We can shew a peasantry of heroes, and fill our armies with clowns, whose courage may vie with that of their general. (Yale *Works*, 10:281)

And so, Johnson was conscripted, at age 26, to serve in the war as a kind of recruiting officer.

We talked of war. Johnson. "Every man thinks meanly of himself for not having been a soldier, or not having been at sea … . were Socrates and Charles the Twelfth of Sweden both present in any company, and Socrates to say, 'Follow me, and hear a lecture in philosophy'; and Charles, laying his hand on his sword, to say, 'Follow me, and dethrone the Czar'; a man would be ashamed to follow Socrates. Sir, the impression is universal." (*Boswell's Life*, 3:265–66)

Johnson was now imagined laying his hand on his sword and crying "Follow me, and dethrone the Kaiser."

His putative nationalism and militarism sometimes involved some creative excision of Johnson's own language. In the aftermath of the war, for instance, *The Saturday Review* quoted "that sturdy Englishman Dr. Johnson" on the "epidemic bravery" of the English common soldier.[34] In fact Johnson in that essay goes on to criticize this desire for the military life, but the criticism was suppressed when passages like these were trotted out as propaganda. Selective quotation also informs a patriotic collection that came out in 1916. The Oxford archaeologist Alexander Montgomerie Bell, then in his seventies and unable to go to war himself, published *The Johnson Calendar; or, Samuel Johnson for Every Day in the Year: Being a Series of Sayings and Tales, Collected from His Life and Writings* and dedicated it to Asquith. The character of Bell's Johnson rested on four pillars: "loyalty to Church and King, obedience to Conscience, hatred of oppression, … [and] a hearty belief in England, and the sterling character of English men."[35] The Scottish-born Bell elides Johnson's notorious anti-Scottish prejudice—"He is commonly said to have been a hater of

Scotland and the Scotch, most untruthfully"—but regrets that America let Johnson, and Britain, down. America's failing was all the more poignant in 1916, when the Empire was standing up to the Bosch but the Americans were watching from a distance:

> At the present day, when we see the glorious stand which England, aided by Canada, Australia, New Zealand, South Africa, and India, has made in the cause of freedom, can fail to wish that our American kindred had still stood by our side, and fought for the same cause?[36]

The *Johnson Calendar* has a long section on war, covering the days through much of May, where the quotations are partial, many qualifications gone, most anti-war sentiments swept under the rug. So too was his openness to other nations. S. C. Roberts, writing in 1918, concludes his book on Johnson with a chapter titled "The True-Born Englishman," in which xenophobia is a Johnsonian virtue: "If London meant life to Johnson, it meant the life of England. His prejudice against foreigners was of the old-fashioned kind."[37]

All the icons of Britishness were deployed in war recruiting posters. I have not found a recruiting poster with an image of or a quotation from Johnson, but John Bull was all over them—and Johnson, of course, had long been John Bull. Boswell wrote that Johnson "was indeed, if I may be allowed the phrase, at bottom much of a *John Bull*" (*Boswell's Life*, 5:21). Archibald Primrose, 5th earl of Rosebery, former Liberal prime minister, echoed Boswell in 1909: speaking before the Johnson Society of Lichfield, he called Johnson "John Bull himself."[38] And Sir William Ryland Dent Adkins, another Liberal politician, toasted Johnson in Lichfield in 1916, calling him "one of the most typical Englishmen who ever lived. He was one of those Englishmen who were not only marked illustrations of the characteristics of the race, but he, as it were, hugged those characteristics."[39]

If Johnson represents Britishness—the distinction between British-ness and Englishness was almost completely elided—and if Britishness means standing up for brave Tommy against the murderous Hun, then Johnson could be recruited to support the war effort. In July 1918, for instance, the Johnson Club heard E. S. P. Haynes discuss "Dr. Johnson on

Liberty," in which he informed the gathered crowd that Johnson promoted liberty, "a characteristically British ideal on which reposes the solid fabric of the British Empire."[40] A few favorite quotations were trotted out repeatedly: "Every man thinks meanly of himself for not having been a soldier, or not having been at sea" ("Daddy, what did *YOU* do in the Great War?").

And, when Johnson does not oblige with a suitably bellicose quotation, why not simply make one up?—better still, make up a whole dialogue? That is what Archibald Rutledge, who would go on to be named South Carolina's poet laureate, did in September 1915, crafting an imaginary dialogue between "the chief of my heroes of literature ... the celebrated sage Dr. Samuel Johnson" and "Dr. Bernhard Dernburg, the unofficial spokesman of the German cause. ... That these two men ... were to speak on the great war I had no doubt."[41] The fantasized Johnson demands Dernburg's justification of "Germany's rape of Belgium"; he blames Germany for beginning the war: "If Germany had not wished to fight, the war would never have begun." And the Doctor's famous debating style ends the conversation on who was at fault for the war: "Have done, sir, have done! If your country is virtuous, your manner of talk has disgraced her; if she is not virtuous, you have disgraced yourself by defending her crimes. And that's an end on it, sir."[42]

## V. The Refuge of a Scoundrel

The bellicose recruiting officer was not the only Johnson on offer during the war. Just as his words could be pulled out of context to make him a militarist, he could also be presented as an anti-war campaigner.

John Richardson refers to "Johnson's deep-seated skepticism about war ... he disliked the excitement that accompanies wars, the elevation of soldiers into heroes, and the use of armed force to solve any but the most intractable of problems."[43] Donald Greene, too, refers to "Johnson's normal pacifism and his prejudice against soldiers."[44] There are undoubted criticisms of the military throughout Johnson's life. He included a number of Quakers among his acquaintance, such Thomas Cumming.[45] He also "denied that military men were always the best bred men" (*Boswell's Life*, 2:82). Sometimes he suggested things had declined from a golden past: "Being asked ... what was become of the gallantry and military spirit of the old English nobility, he replied, … 'it is gone into the city to look for a fortune'" (*Boswell's Life*, 2:126). During a time of patriotic enthusiasm for the Seven Years' War Johnson refused to join his friend David Garrick in celebrating the country's "Heart of Oak." Instead he published an *Idler* essay on September 9, 1758 in the *Universal Chronicle* in which two vultures look eagerly on human beings engaging in pointless combat:

> Two herds of men will often meet and shake the earth with noise, and fill the air with fire. When you hear noise and see fire which flashes along the ground … men are surely destroying one another; you will then find the ground smoking with blood and covered with carcasses, of which many are dismembered and mangled for the convenience of the vulture. (Yale *Works*, 2:319)

The essay was so shocking that it was removed from collected editions of the *Idler*; its number in the series, 22, was surrendered to the following essay, and all the others shifted back by one.

Writing like this no doubt led Donald Greene to discover a thread of "condemnation of the military" running through Johnson's writings.[46] As Richardson points out, "Johnson took the idea of extremity seriously, and did not call for war lightly."[47] In *Thoughts on the Late Transactions Respecting Falkland's Islands*, Boswell observes, Johnson "successfully endeavoured to persuade the nation that it was wise and laudable to suffer the question of right to remain undecided, rather than involve our country in another war" (*Boswell's Life*, 2:134). He had a grim conception of life during wartime, and thought that most of his contemporaries were too enthusiastic about military engagement:

> It is wonderful with what coolness and indifference the greater part of mankind see war commenced. Those that hear of it at a distance, or read of it in books, but have never presented its evils to their minds, consider it as little more than a splendid game; a proclamation, an army, a battle, and a triumph. Some indeed must perish in the most successful field, but they die upon the bed of honour, "resign their lives amidst the joys of conquest, and, filled with England's glory, smile in death." (Yale *Works*, 10:370)

Real-life military figures rarely come off well in his works. As Richardson notes, in *The Vanity of Human Wishes* Johnson's

> four examples of military greatness—Charles XII of Sweden, the fifth-century BCE Persian emperor Xerxes, the Elector Charles of Bavaria, and the Duke of Marlborough—have in common both a disappointing end to their ambitions and the flawed nature of the ambitions themselves.[48]

Paul Fussell has famously written at length about how the conditions of modern war overwhelmed the literary resources available to an entire generation, who found their inherited inventory of poetic diction and conceits wholly inadequate in the face of machine guns, damp trenches, dysentery, and gangrene. "The problem for the writer trying to describe the elements of the Great War," Fussell observes, "was its utter incredibility, and thus its incommunicability in its own terms."[49] Fussell supports these observations with evidence from the First World War, but he was no doubt influenced by Johnson's description of what was for him modern war:

> The life of a modern soldier is ill represented by heroick fiction. War has means of destruction more formidable than the cannon and the sword. Of the thousands and ten thousands that perished in our late contests with France and Spain, a very small part ever felt the stroke of an enemy; the rest languished in tents and ships, amidst damps and putrefaction; pale, torpid, spiritless, and helpless; gasping and groaning, unpitied among men made obdurate by long continuance of hopeless misery; and were at last whelmed in pits, or heaved into the ocean, without notice and without remembrance. By incommodious encampments and unwholesome stations, where courage is useless, and enterprise impracticable, fleets are silently dispeopled, and armies sluggishly melted away. (Yale *Works*, 10:370)

A few lexical archaisms aside, this could have been written in the Somme, or Ypres. The "damps and putrefaction," the "gasping and groaning"—all this could have come from a description of trench warfare.

During the First World War, therefore, when he was not being drafted to serve in the Allied war effort, Johnson was sometimes imagined as a pacifist. He pointedly refused "to vindicate the sanguinary projects of heroes and conquerors," preferring "to diminish the reputation of their success, than the infamy of their miscarriages." He could not "conceive, why he that has burnt cities, and wasted nations, and filled the world with horror and desolation, should be more kindly regarded by mankind, than he that died in the rudiments of wickedness."[50] The British public in the 1914–1918 war bore this pacifist sentiment in mind.

For pacifists, the nearly incomprehensible series of events that plunged Europe into war in 1914 did not call for what Johnson called "the last of remedies." Johnson had been used as a mouthpiece for pacifist views before the war: the *Advocate of Peace* for July 1879 published an anti-war selection from *Falkland's Islands* under the heading "Picture of the Miseries of War."[51] He shows up in that same pacifist publication in October 1915:

> Suffice it to say that the world is full of the tragedies of force; that these tragedies have been written in blood, and that they have left little or nothing behind them but memories of desolation … . In the *Vanity of Human Wishes* Doctor Johnson sums it all up in a couple of lines: … He left the name at which the world grew pale, | To point a moral or adorn a tale.[52]

And so, said William Kent in the *Socialist Review* in 1920, those who don't recognize the pacifist Johnson "do not properly know Samuel." Kent's Johnson "was no advocate of knock-out blows and bitter ends"; he was instead a pacifist whose writing "might surely melt the heart of the sternest War Minister." The pathetic fall of the projector who builds a flying machine in *Rasselas* shows that Johnson "contemplated the fearful possibilities of aerial warfare" even before the invention of the hot-air balloon. He concludes his article with a meditation on "Patriotism is the last refuge of a scoundrel" (*Boswell's Life*, 2:348), discovering that "Johnson was always suspicious of patriots" and arguing that his fellow socialists and pacifists "need not apologise for regarding ourselves as being in some respects in the apostolic succession of Samuel Johnson."[53]

Kent was far from the only pacifist fond of quoting Johnson's famous bon mot on patriotism. Here is a typical invocation:

> There's nothing cheaper, narrower or more dangerous than a good deal of the bunk that calls itself patriotism. It was crazy patriotism that got Germany into this war. The Turks thought they were patriotic, and so did the Austrians ... . Patriotism unchecked, and unmixed with justice, humaneness, chivalry and common sense, is an unmitigated curse, truly "the last refuge of a scoundrel."[54]

And Johnson's passage about the horrors of modern war from *Thoughts on Falkland's Islands*—"damps and putrefaction; pale, torpid, spiritless, and helpless; gasping and groaning"—was republished in *Blackwood's Magazine* in October 1915, just as the war that was supposed to be over by Christmas was turning into a nightmare from which everyone was struggling to awake. "There was no more than the exact truth," the article notes, "in Dr Johnson's sonorous enumeration of the evils of war."[55]

Shortly after the war, David Starr Jordan, the pacifist and eugenicist who had been the first president of Stanford, published an article in *Advocate of Peace through Justice* that somehow turned Johnson into an enemy of social subordination, because socialists were convinced that subordination leads to war:

> The marks which distinguish the aristocracies of today, love of display, titles, finery, and the sports of leisure, are not indicative of any real excellence ... . In the aristocratic castes, as with royalty, the law of primogeniture obtains, an excellent thing according to Dr. Samuel Johnson, "because it ensures that there will be but one fool in the family."[56]

Hugh Kingsmill, writing fifteen years after the end of the war, imagines a pacifist Johnson posthumously surveying the memoirs of its leaders:

> The literature of self-justification produced in the last ten years by all the chief figures in the Great War, whether statesmen, generals, or members of the Secret Service, lends a special force

to Johnson's remark that, if writers were as well acquainted with other professions as with their own, they would realize that the egotism of which they accuse one another is common to all mankind.[57]

## VI.  Universal Hope

Johnson never went to war, but he learned melancholy lessons about life by living through several wars, and perhaps those who lived through a war became better qualified to read him. E. S. Roscoe wrote in 1928 that "the present generation has more appreciation of his work than had their immediate forefathers; and it may be that his realism, sincerity, and intellectual honesty are appreciated by those who have passed through the period of the Great War."[58]

The American journalist Christopher Morley, writing only a few weeks after the conclusion of the war, imagines Johnson reconciling the Central Powers and the Allies, and even providing a post-hoc rationale that might have made sense of one of history's most senseless episodes:

> But we will never cease to pray that every honest man should study Boswell. There are many who have topped the rise of human felicity in that book: when reading it they feel the tide of intellect brim the mind with a unique fullness of satisfaction. It is not a mere commentary on life: it *is* life—it fills and floods every channel of the brain. It is a book that men make a hobby of, as golf or billiards. To know it is a liberal education. I could have understood Germany yearning to invade England in order to annex Boswell's Johnson. There would have been some sense in that.[59]

And yet the kind of realism Johnson embodied was in short supply after the Treaty of Versailles. "After the end of the World War of 1914," Winston Churchill wrote, "there was a deep conviction and almost universal hope that peace would reign in the world."[60]

For any reader of Johnson, though, the phrase "universal hope" necessarily calls to mind the *Vanity of Human Wishes*. Johnson knew too well that human beings are too deeply flawed ever to live in that utopia of perpetual peace. In using Johnson to advance their own positions, the people who lived through the war and the ensuing peace were more eager to speak through him than to listen to him. Had they read the *Vanity*, had they read *Rasselas*, had they read the original *Idler* 22, had they even read to the end all the passages they abridged to avoid the passages that made them uncomfortable—had they done any of this, they might have been less surprised by what happened less than twenty years later.

The early issues of the *Johnsonian News Letter* make for fascinating if often melancholy reports and queries on the whereabouts of young men who were stationed abroad and not heard from for months at a time—among those who survived are a list of names that every Johnsonian today will recognize. Not all, however, made it. An emblematic piece is H. R. Kilbourne's article "Johnson and War," written as Europe slid into another war. Kilbourne imagines Johnson as a military enthusiast: he quotes Johnson's declaration that "Every man thinks meanly of himself for not having been a soldier," and proclaims that this is Johnson "at his bow-wow best."[61] But Kilbourne himself never saw it in print: it appeared in *ELH* in June 1945 above the grim note "Captain Kilbourne died September 1, 1944."

Johnson, I venture to speculate, would be saddened by this but not at all surprised. The peace that left so many hopeful soon enough led to another war to end all wars—a war in which an exceptionally literate prime minister was fond of quoting Johnson, another war in which Johnson was recruited as both critic and booster, another war in which the Gough Square house was damaged by German bombs, and another war in which millions of people who never read a word of Johnson or Boswell were left dead. And yet, for Johnson, despair is never the appropriate course. Our own reading of Johnson will teach us that wars to end all wars are too much to hope for, but also that, while we should leave to heaven the measure and the choice, we can keep wishing—we must keep wishing—that some kind of salvation is not necessarily beyond our grasp.

# CHAPTER SIX

# Samuel Beckett and Samuel Johnson

## Like-minded Masters of Life's Limitations

*Thomas M. Curley*

## I. Beckett's Subversive and Formative Samuel Johnson

England's greatest moralist, Samuel Johnson, was a devout Christian, renowned for his loyalty to church and state, despite considerable reservations about abuses of power and privilege in the establishment. There was also a well-documented dark underside to his legitimate persona of orthodoxy, masking eccentricities of mind and body that reflected profound fears of insanity, death, damnation, and, worst of all, the possibility of an ultimate nothingness behind reality. Hints of such nihilistic anxieties lurk in favored moral–psychological assumptions: a human being hardly exists in the present but situates the self in the form of flashbacks and flash-forwards—that is, either in a remembered past as a bygone entity or in an imagined future as something in prospect but not yet possessed. As Imlac says in Johnson's *Rasselas*, "The truth is that no mind is much employed upon the present: recollection and anticipation fill up almost all our moments."[1] Johnson's overall philosophy of life was decidedly Christian in explaining the human predicament, but he was an uneasy believer, dreading mortality and existential emptiness. At times he perceived a black hole at the center of the here and now, in line with his conviction that life in the present is a void to be filled with past and future apprehensions of existing. No famous modern author was more fascinated by Johnson and his anxieties than was Samuel Beckett.

He turned a blind eye to the traditional magisterial figure of the Great Cham. Instead, he focused on a doubt-ridden and phobia-filled figure, a subversive Johnson, wrought in his own nihilistic image and serving as a formative influence on his canon. Such a fellow-feeling developed in the 1930s and after that he attempted to write a fascinating play about this intellectual soul-mate, entitled *Human Wishes*, which looked ahead to the work of his future fame, especially *Waiting for Godot* (1948–1949) and *Krapp's Last Tape* (1958).

## II.  Ontological Insecurity and Psychological Vacuity

The heart of Johnson's thinking is found in the magnificent *Ramblers* of the early 1750s. According to *Rambler* 2, time present is too often an escape into other temporal zones. Hence, there is little metaphysical being in lived life, which is more a ceaseless becoming: "The natural flights of the human mind are not from pleasure to pleasure, but from hope to hope" (Yale *Works*, 3:10). Static states of pleasure tend to be impossibilities; all that we have and all that we are verge on fleeting past experiences or unrealized future goals. Like *Ramblers* 203 and 207 at the end of the essay series, *Rambler* 41 stresses the basic emptiness of the present as a chaotic flux forcing us to find meaning in either remembered or anticipated apprehensions of existence. Essentially, we are only in recollection or expectation; in between, a terrible void can emerge in need of filling up, not in direct experience, but in internalized cognition of bygone or coming events:

> [W]e are forced to have recourse every moment to the past and future … and relieve the vacuities of our being, by recollection of former passages, or anticipation of events to come … . Indeed … the present is in perpetual motion, leaves us as soon as it arrives, ceases to be present before its presence is well perceived, and is only known to have existed by the effects which it leaves behind. (221, 223–24)

Sometimes, too, even gazing into the past offers no escape from psychological vacuity. According to *Rambler* 8,

> If the most active and industrious of mankind was able, at the close of life to recollect distinctly his past moments ... how many chasms he would find of wide and continued vacuity, and how many interstitial spaces unfilled, even in the most tumultuous hurries of business .... (41)

Analogously, near the end of his life, Beckett admitted that confronting the void was his own defining literary mission: "And the preposterous conviction formed long ago, that here in the end is the last & by far best chance for the writer. Gaping into his synaptic chasms."[2]

Johnson's earliest prose fiction, his *Vision of Theodore* of 1748, accentuates the emptiness and inscrutability of the world, albeit from a religious standpoint, by a vivid symbol of its insubstantiality in the form of an allegorical Mountain of Existence without fixity: "Thus I stood terrified and confused; above were tracts inscrutable, and below was total vacuity" (Yale *Works*, 16:198). Theodore's terror of formlessness found fresh expression a year later in Johnson's *Vanity of Human Wishes*, his classic poem about life's uncertainty as a "clouded Maze of Fate."[3] The poem's concluding affirmation of a spiritual righting of all temporal wrongs allays the poem's almost tragic message of universal unhappiness caused by a pervasive vacuity of life sending us in quest of elusive fulfillment. Although Beckett would name his play *Human Wishes* after this poem, he had little patience for religious consolations of any type. Johnson's most celebrated prose fiction, *Rasselas* (1759) substitutes a happy valley kingdom under Mount Amhara for Theodore's Mountain of Existence to demonstrate the emptiness of life inherent in our illusory "whispers of fancy, and ... phantoms of hope" (7) driving a tragi-comic quest for soul-satisfying happiness in our frustratingly limited world. Although there is a faint hint of a comforting choice of eternity in the penultimate chapter, the tale's inconclusive conclusion only reinforces an overall insistence on life's limitations. The four characters opt for final choices of life previously shown to be pointless: Pekuah wants an invariable state in the present that is impossible to find in the flux of life; Nekayah cherishes learning, blind to the lesson of so many foolish intellectuals populating her travels; Rasselas imagines utopia, even as he projects a dystopia fueled by his power-hungry ambition; and Imlac prefers to be rudderless and nescient, existing in a present without presence, despite all his previous advice for purposeful intellectual exploration. Concerning the much-debated question about the travelers' ultimate destination—whether they return to the boring happy valley or to the larger world of Abysinnia and beyond—there can be no upbeat answer. Wherever they go, they will exist in a temporal realm of never-ending disappointment, where the vanity of human wishes prevails. Not surprisingly, Beckett pronounced *Rasselas* "a grand book" and must have appreciated its thematic dead-end.[4]

The specter of metaphysical emptiness emerges in Johnson's astute attack against philosophical optimism and the Great Chain of Being in his mid-life review of Soame Jenyns' *A Free Inquiry into the Nature and Origin of Evil*:

> This scale of being I have demonstrated to be raised by presump-
> tuous imagination, to rest on nothing at the bottom, to lean on
> nothing at the top, and to have vacuities from step to step through
> which any order of being may sink into nihility … .[5]

This powerful statement of ontological non-entity bears comparison with Johnson's disconcerting experience of "naked nature" in the sublime sterile scenery of Scotland in 1773. Indeed, as Hester Thrale insisted, his distaste for vacuity of any kind was a lifelong obsession. He graphically captured the terrifying feeling of metaphysical nothingness in his concise biography of Thomas Browne. Without religious direction or a heavenly destination, humanity would sink into despairing nihilism, as Johnson stressed by citing Browne's Christian admonition "which can never be too frequently recollected … ."

> It is the heaviest stone that melancholy can throw at man, to
> tell him that he is at the end of his nature; or that there is no
> further state to come, unto which this seems … made in vain:
> …. unsatisfied considerators would quarrel at the justness of the
> constitution, and rest content that Adam had fallen [into a] lower
> form [of life without a mind or soul and, therefore, unable to
> recognize the meaninglessness of existence].[6]

Johnson's biographers noted how he liked to quote to himself from *Paradise Lost* the devil Belial's abhorrence of ending up in nothingness,

> swallowed up and lost
> In the wide womb of uncreated Night,
> Devoid of sense and motion?[7]

James Boswell more than once one confirmed his great friend's abiding dread ("he never had a moment in which death was not terrible to him"), and Beckett took careful note of the phobia, including Johnson's angry response to hearing that David Hume, the non-believer, died not fearing death and annihilation: "It was not so, Sir. He had a vanity in being thought easy."[8]

## III. The Johnson Project of the 1930s according to Beckett's Correspondence

All the anguish poured into Johnson's self-confessional *Prayers and Meditations* gripped Beckett's imagination, particularly self-loathing journal entries about an indolent wasting of time punctuated by recurrent bouts of disbelief. The weaknesses of this sincere but over-scrupulous Christian became a focal point of Beckett's interpretation of Johnson and provided the Irishman very welcome confirmation of his own pessimistic understanding of life. On the surface, no two men would seem more unlike. Epic and expansive in his thinking and writing, Johnson was deeply religious and respectful of the Christian–classical heritage of Western civilization, in all of which he was extraordinarily learned. Adhering to a bible-based, almost tragic vision of human unhappiness found in Ecclesiastes, he committed himself as an author to striving for moral and spiritual meaning for the sake of his readers, who needed, as Seamus Heaney said in his Nobel Address, "what Samuel Johnson once called with superb confidence 'the stability of truth' even as [the mind] recognizes the destabilizing nature of its own operations and enquiries."[9] Beckett forged a very different intellectual path. An understated and incredibly well-read atheist/agnostic with a Proustian sensibility and a Schopenhauerian pessimism, he was very much a minimalist nihilist, wary of the past, despairing of the future, and focused on the ordinary absurdity of the present with a highly developed taste for the grotesque, for irreverent comic irony, and for freewheeling literary experimentation. However, both men had some remarkable affinities: an acute sensitivity to words and to human psychology, a pervasive compassion for human misery complementing the world's ultimate inscrutability, and a philosophical insistence on the inevitable dissatisfactions of daily existence within a vast and lonely universe.

Under the overwhelming influence of James Joyce in early maturity, Beckett wanted to find his own literary voice, a new artistic identity with a very different emphasis on the fragility and/or emptiness of all foolish and broken mortal things.[10] Among many other influences on his development as an author, the force of Johnson's life and writings probably offered some much-needed liberation for redirecting his career. Seeking artistic distance from Joyce, Beckett immersed himself in a new authority figure, a reinvented Johnson who could serve as a like-minded everyman personification of life's absurdity and oddity, validating distinctive literary innovations to come in his writings. His interest in Johnson probably began as a Trinity College undergraduate, surely continued into his formative years as an author in the 1930s and 1940s, and lasted through his achievement of mature celebrity until his death on December 22, 1989. Research notebooks for his early prose fiction, kept roughly from 1932 to 1935, testify to his consulting *Rasselas*, the Lives of Ascham and Dryden, his own two-volume eighth (1799) corrected and revised edition of Johnson's *Dictionary of the English Language*, George Birkbeck Hill's landmark edition of Boswell's classic *Life of Samuel Johnson* (1887), and Thomas Carlyle's *On Heroes and Hero-Worship, and the Heroic in History* (1840), with its Lecture V focused on Johnson as Heroic Man of Letters.[11] In the summer of 1935, after his mother returned to Ireland following their tour of English towns, he made sure to make a pilgrimage on his own to the Johnson Birthplace Museum in Lichfield.

As Beckett removed himself and his writing from Joyce's powerful hold, a new project of composing a play about Johnson would soon usher in an ambitious program of study centered on the late-life friendship and highly speculative romantic attachment with Mrs. Hester Thrale-Piozzi.

Beginning as an academic, Beckett enjoyed his serious long-term research and gave shape to a daringly iconoclastic view of Johnson for the stage. In late May of 1936 he mentioned working at a library, perhaps in the Trinity College and/or National Library archives in Dublin, and then on July 7 alluded to James Barry's stark painting of a dying Johnson by way of hinting at a bold reimagining of the moralist as an insecure oddity at a loss with himself and his world: "Do you know Barry's portrait of Dr Johnson or where it is? Looked at in the reproduction beside the various [Sir Joshua] Reynoldses it is very impressive, the mad terrified face that I feel was the truth a very little below the adipose."[12] A month later he included in his journal a German translation of Johnson's famous letter to Lord Chesterfield.

Evidence of intensive scholarship under way is strikingly clear in three octavo Notebooks of about two hundred pages (*circa* spring 1936 to August 1937), with several additional notes on members of Johnson's London household, along with both a handwritten ink draft and a type-script of a fragment of a play, entitled *Human Wishes*, which is barely half a first act in length. All these valuable materials were, on April 27, 1966, personally delivered to the distinguished Beckett scholar the late Ruby Cohn, who in 1989 donated them to the Department of Special Collections at the University of Reading, England.[13] The notations consist primarily of haphazard quotations, interspersed with a few source summaries and evolving plot outlines but with relatively little commentary by Beckett himself. For the actual developing conception of Johnson, scholars fortunately have ready access to Beckett's correspondence, collected and edited comprehensively for publication in four volumes from 2009 to 2016. His letters on the project are indispensable; they corroborate the variety of sources consulted in the Notebooks and paint a more defined picture of the shadowy protagonist, who is, in fact, totally absent in the short extant unfinished play. Like the elusive Godot later on, Johnson never materialized on stage, but his ghost haunts the correspondence, sometimes in memorably graphic form.

Beckett depended upon a large number of works about Johnson during the intricate creative process of shaping the story intended for the stage. The key texts were G. B. Hill's edition of the *Boswell's Life* (1887) and the first four volumes of L. F. Powell's revised edition of the same biography (1934); Hill's two-volume *Johnsonian Miscellanies* (1897) (especially *Prayers and Meditations, Annals,* Hester Lynch Piozzi's *Anecdotes* of 1786; Arthur Murphy's *Essay on Samuel Johnson*; *Extracts from Sir John Hawkins's Life of Johnson*; John Hoole's *Narrative of Johnson's End*, and William Windham's *Narrative of the Last Week of Johnson's Life*); possibly Hill's edition of the *Letters of Samuel Johnson, LL.D.* (1892); C. E. Vulliamy's *Mrs. Thrale of Streatham* (1936); Thomas Seccombe's *Essay Introductory* for Alexander M. Broadley's *Dr. Johnson and Mrs Thrale* (1910); Leslie Stephen's *Samuel Johnson* (1878, 1891); Sir John Hawkins's *The Life of Samuel Johnson, LL.D.* (1787), including the Globe edition of Hawkins in 1893; and possibly Thomas Carlyle's *On Heroes and Hero-Worship, and the Heroic in History* (1840). The research also entailed recourse to Abraham Hayward's edition of the *Autobiography, Letters and Literary Remains of Mrs. Piozzi (Thrale)* (1861); *Thraliana* (1784, 1809) (perhaps also extracts edited by C. Hughes, 1913); the Marquis of Lansdowne's edition of *The Queeney Letters* (1934); Joseph D. Wright's edition of *Some Unpublished Letters to and from Dr. Johnson* (1932); Frederick A. Pottle's edition of *The Private Papers of James Boswell from Malahide Castle* (1937); A. Edward Newton's *Dr. Johnson: A Play* (1923); Sir Humphry David Rolleston's "Medical Aspects of Samuel Johnson," in *Glasgow Medical Journal* (1924); Llewelyn Powys's "Dr. Johnson—Idler, Rambler and Straggler" in *Dublin Magazine* (1937); the *Dictionary of National Biography*; and the *Encyclopedia Britannica*.[14]

In his research, Beckett made occasional use of Johnson's own writings but, more than anything else, was fixated on the pathological personality of the man in old age. According to Ruby Cohn, he confessed to committing himself to this systematic research only after seizing the "kernel" of an idea about Johnson being madly, if ineffectually, in love with Mrs. Thrale, especially after her husband's death in 1781 and before her scandalous marriage to her daughters' Italian music teacher, Gabriel Piozzi, in 1784.[15] One of the principal texts feeding into this extravagant thesis was Thomas Seccombe's mildly provocative biography of seventy-two pages introducing A. M. Broadley's *Doctor Johnson and Mrs Thrale* (1910).[16] A few snippets of Seccombe's account suggest some of the impetus for Beckett's image of a lovelorn Johnson:

Now ... the time has come for the bride-elect of the great Doctor's intellect to receive a rather more equitable share of study and appreciation [3] ... . He became the Socrates of Streatham Park ... . Had he not called her "angel" and dearest, his heavenly Urania, the pattern of her sex? Was she not his honoured mistress ... his lovely Hetty? ... But when the master of the house died, his wild nature broke out; he was untamed after all [15–16] ... . [Anna] Seward ... says that his most enduring love, that "for Mrs. Thrale, was composed of ... Platonic love ..." [19–20].

Adding to Seccombe's heated conjectures was detailed medical commentary in so many of the sources about Johnson's physical ailments—his hydrocele in the swollen right testicle, a stroke of palsy, asthma, and dropsy—all of which played into Beckett's fixed idea of a thwarted romance with Mrs. Thrale.

An important letter of December 13, 1936 to a confidante in Boston, Mary Manning Howe, demonstrates Seccombe's impact on Beckett's work in progress. The intention at this point is to compose only a one-act play set at Streatham or at Bolt Court in London, concentrating on Johnson in love but frustrated by impotence from bad health, from guilt over desiring an old friend's wife, and from insecurity about sexually satisfying her in her now unmarried state. The attitude in the letter is noticeably irreverent, bawdy, and bemused. There is impish, even unsavory, enjoyment in his conjuring a grotesque, sexed-up dirty old man, dancing awkwardly home, broken by diseases of body and mind. The humorous conflation of a failed erection with mortality—"*rigor mortis*"—is clever but callous. So, he writes exuberantly and a bit unfeelingly:

I am also very interested in the Johnson-Thrale-Piozzi arrangement, and often thought what a good subject was there, perhaps only one long act. What interested me especially was the breakdown of Johnson as soon as Thrale disappeared. I do not think Piozzi enters Johnson's psychological situation at all. I think that his abuse of Piozzi is a blind. Piozzi was the pretext that he needed, to get away with an appearance of justification. What interests me above all is the condition of the Platonic gigolo or house friend, with not a testicle, auricle or ventricle to stand on when the bluff is called. His impotence was mollified by Mrs Thrale so long as Thrale was there, then suddenly exasperated when the licensed mentula was in the connubial position for the first time for years, thanks to *rigor mortis*. Think of a film opening with Johnson dancing home to his den in Fleet Street after the last visit to Mrs Thrale, forgetting a lamppost & hurrying back. Can't think why there hasn't been film of Johnson, with [Charles] Laughton. But I think one act, with something like the psychology above, in an outburst to Mrs Thrale, or in his house in confidence to the mysterious servant, would be worth doing. There are 50 plays in his life. (*LSB*, 1:396–97)

An intermediary actually contacted the famous Charles Laughton about a screenplay—"It was kind of Miss Vernon to mention me to Laughton. I am trying to think of something"—and Beckett was advised to send the actor some stories "Irish and decently indecent" (*LSB*, 1:455 and n.6). Nothing came of the proposal, but the ribald cast of the requested stories for Laughton was in keeping with Beckett's comic caricature of a sexualized Johnson.

## IV.  Beckett's Wild Impotence Theory for a Sexualized Samuel Johnson

Where did this outrageous impotence theory originate? The most probable single stimulus was a recent pseudo-scholarly study claiming to shed stunning new light on the relationship with Mrs. Thrale but actually capitalizing on a wildly sensationalized interpretation of events. This over-heated text was Colwyn E. Vulliamy's *Mrs. Thrale of Streatham* (1936).[17] The book makes for an irritating read. Vulliamy was insufferably patronizing toward all parties, a snobbish and snarky know-it-all pretending to divulge shocking new truths: "No serious attempt has ever been made to examine the sexual character of Dr. Johnson" (243). Drawn to the grotesque underside of things, Beckett in the above letter to Mary Manning Howe let himself subscribe to baseless revelations of Johnsonian passion and to faint hints of impotence, as the following excerpts from Vulliamy make clear:

> It should be remembered that Johnson ... was a curiosity, an exhibition—not so much a prodigy as an oddity [57–58] ... What were the actual relations between Mrs. Thrale and Dr. Johnson at this period? ... [W]e are not mistaken in supposing a definite emotional quality in the situation, at least on the side of the Doctor [98] ... . We have to go back ... to a very odd letter, written in French by Johnson [copied from Vulliamy in Beckett's Notebooks] ... . He refers ominously and mysteriously, to the possible advantages of being locked up in actual confinement ... . Dr. Johnson, this rugged and philosophical Dr. Johnson, this huge perambulating and vociferating Dr. Johnson, with all his methodical immensity of common sense, was more than a little in love [101–103] ... . Poor Thrale was hardly in his grave, before people were speculating ... on the possibility of his widow marrying Dr. Johnson. It is almost unquestionable that Johnson speculated on the same possibility [202] ... . Anna Seward ... says "His ... long-enduring passion ... was composed ... of ... Platonick love ... ." Where she is wrong is using a term so tepid and unsuitable as "Platonick love." [252]

Beckett's weird diagnosis of impotence may also reflect personal health concerns, along with two issues examined by Vulliamy: specifically, Johnson's operation for a hydrocele in his testicle in 1783 and old womanizing Henry Thrale's sterile flirtation with a winsome Sophia Streatfield: "As for Thrale, poor man ... he was desperately though impotently in love with his dear Sophia" (181). All this lurid biographical information offered Beckett salacious cues for his pet impotence theory, which motivated him to work on the Johnson project in fits and starts well into the next year of 1937. On April 13, 1937, for example, he reported (*LSB*, 1:484) that "Pomposo continues to occupy me" (as Vulliamy noted [58] Charles Churchill "satirized the moralist in the ridiculous figure of Pomposo"). Beckett had just returned home from Germany in an ambivalent mood and soon, on April 26, wrote his close friend, the poet and critic Thomas MacGreevy, about his current thoughts on Johnson: "A foul article by Llwelyn Powys [*for*

Llewelyn] on Dr Johnson, making him out a John Bull, the orthodox balls in fact" (*LSB*, 1:488 and n. 18). Beckett here rejected the stereotypical Johnson of conservative legend but began to see that his own tragi-comic caricature put him in the contradictory position of having to concede a lack of proof for impotence, even as he firmly clung to the preposterous idea. What has changed by the time of this noteworthy letter of April 26 is his plan for the still unwritten play, no longer apparently to be one act but a longer drama, perhaps roughly corresponding to a more ambitious plot outline sketched in the Notebooks: "Act I Mrs Thrale in Bath. April 1784 Act 2 [Mrs Thrale] & J. In London May 1784 Act 3 J. in London July."[18] At times thinking of enlarging the scenario to embrace many events of Johnson's old age, Beckett at other times imagined squeezing the action of the longer play into the last year of his protagonist's life in 1784. So, he intimated to MacGreevy:

I have been working, in so far as I have been working at all, at the Johnson thing, to find my petition of principle, after many disap-pointments, more strikingly confirmed than I had dared hope. It seems now quite certain that he was rather absurdly in love with her, all the 15 years he was at Streatham, though there is no text for the impotence. It becomes more interesting—the fake rage to cover his retreat from her, then the real rage when he realizes no retreat was necessary, and beneath both the despair of the lover with nothing to love with—and much more difficult. It explains what never has been explained, i.e. his esteem for the imbecile Mr Thrale. The last meeting in 1783, about 6 months before her marriage to Piozzi, a year before his death, has always remained nebulous. He has a brief reference to it in his *Meditations*. I think that is an interview that must be written, though I should have wished to keep it all in 1784 or spread it out to catch the scene where the Thrales find him on his knees before Dr Delap, praying for a continuance of his reason. Arthur Murphy is important, the only one, not excluding Fanny Burney, of the Streatham Circle who stuck to Mrs Thrale through the scandal. I think we will have a very quiet Dr Johnson. Perhaps his nigger Frank Barber was the only person he never bellowed at. (*LSB*, 1:489)

This letter points to Beckett's repeated reliance on his old research standbys, Vulliamy and Seccombe, mixed with information gleaned from G. B. Hill's *Johnsonian Miscellanies*—namely, *Prayers and Meditations*, Arthur Murphy's *Essay on the Life and Genius of Samuel Johnson*, and Mrs. Thrale's *Anecdotes*. Seccombe confirmed the time at Streatham ("fifteen years" [15]), the date of the last meeting ("5th April 1783" [25]), and Murphy's "staunch" loyalty (83 and 130). Vulliamy documented Johnson's mental relapse ("on his knees with Delap, praying for the continued use of his understanding" [63]), which Arthur Murphy previously recorded: "Mr. and Mrs. Thrale ... found him on his knees, with Dr. Delap, ... beseeching God to continue to him the use of his understanding" (1:423). Mrs. Thrale's *Anecdotes* noted the special favor enjoyed by the black servant, Francis Barber: "whenever disputes arose in the household, [Johnson] always sided with Francis against the others, whom he suspected (not unjustly, I believe) of greater malignity" (1:292). Finally, Johnson's *Prayers and Meditations* preserved his poignant farewell to Streatham: "I took leave of Mrs. Thrale. I was much moved. I had some expostulations with her. She said that she was likewise affected. I commended the Thrales with great good will to God; may my petition have been heard" (1:111). In his first Notebook, Beckett reiterated his determination to expand this brief parting scene into compelling drama: "*What happened at interview impossible to say* (I shall say it)."[19]

Any excitement about his evolving scenario did not prevent more delay in the project that spring and into the mid-summer of 1937. On June 5 he confided to Mac Greevy that he was practically at a standstill: "The only thing resembling work has been in the library on Johnson. I know the whole thing pretty well now and could start anytime" (*LSB*, 1:504). But he did not put pen to paper; his obsessive source-hunting was becoming an excuse for not writing. An incomplete letter to another literary friend, Joseph Hone, on July 3 indicates that more research occurred for a slightly changed conception of the play, less focused on a romance with Mrs. Thrale and now stressing Johnson and his phobias about death, damnation, and annihilation in the finale:

Still there is a mass of marginalia that would be useful, e.g. in the *Annals* his recollection of the first time the Heaven-Hell dichotomy was brought to his notice, when he was in bed with his mother aged 18 months [?]. Heaven she described as the happy place where some people went, hell as the *sad* place where the lost went. She does not seem to have been at all High Church. The following morning, so that he might impress the information on his mind, she required him to repeat it to Thomas Jackson, their serving man. But he would not. All this would come in quite naturally in the last act, ie. the fear of death, when he was being reproached by his clerical friend [Rev. John] Taylor for holding the opinion that an eternity of torment was preferable to annihilation. He must have had the notion of *positive* annihilation. Of how many can as much be said. (*LSB*, 1:508–9)

Here Beckett reveals his debt to the *Annals* in *Johnsonian Miscellanies* for the traumatic early childhood memory of an afterlife (1:135). The *Annals* also contained an equally arresting opening sentence conflating birth and death, "I was born almost dead, and could not cry for some time" (1:129), which Beckett made sure to transcribe twice, in his second and in his third Notebooks. The same morbid interest in his subject's dread of mortality ensured his close attention to a frightening dialogue, along with its disturbing footnote, in *Boswell's Life*. Johnson, like Boswell, had a horror of death and said so to the resolutely pious Lichfield poetess Anna Seward in 1778:

MISS SEWARD. "There is one mode of the fear of death, which is certainly absurd, and that is the fear of annihilation, which is only a pleasing sleep without a dream."
JOHNSON. "It is neither pleasing, nor sleep; it is nothing. Now mere existence is so much better than nothing, that one would rather exist even in pain, than not exist."
BOSWELL. "If annihilation be nothing, then existing in pain is … a positive evil … ."
JOHNSON. "The lady confounds annihilation, which is nothing, with the apprehension of it, which is dreadful." (*Boswell's Life*, 3:295–96 and n.2)

G. B. Hill's footnote for this exchange left a lasting imprint on Beckett's mind: Rev. John Taylor, although a very dear friend, publicly criticized such talk in a *Letter to Samuel Johnson on the Subject of a Future State* (1787) because the implications of the conversation were terrifying. The Johnsonian sense of nothingness and of comprehending it simultaneously made for a concept that was truly worse than even the almost unimaginable idea of experiencing eternal damnation. Poor Johnson. Beckett understandably registered the shocking thought in his Notebooks: "Much as he dreaded the next world he dreaded annihilation still more" (*LSB*, 1:511 n.9).

A week later, on July 11, 1937, he mentioned his usual discouragement about "the Johnson play if it is ever written" to Mary Manning Howe and indicated again some distancing from the impotence theory to concentrate on the many neuroses and ailments surrounding his protagonist's attraction for Mrs. Thrale. The scoffing catalog of unwanted afflictions and genuine religious scruples comes close to qualifying as an off-putting attempt at surreptitiously cruel humor. Johnson remains very much a comic caricature in his creator's mind, but with a little less of the clinical sexual baggage weighing down the original reimagined portrait of a bumbling lusty lover. Despite professions to the contrary, Beckett indulges in a "wisecracky" mood below:

> There won't be anything snappy or wisecracky about the Johnson play if it is ever written. It isn't Boswell's wit and wisdom machine that means anything to me, but the miseries that he never talked of, being unwilling or unable to do so. The horror of annihilation, the horror of madness, the horrified love of Mrs Thrale, the whole mental monster ridden swamp that after hours of silence could only give some ghastly bubble like "Lord have mercy upon us." The background of the *Prayers and Meditations*. The opium eating, dreading-to-go to bed, praying-for-the-dead, past living, terrified of dying, terrified deadness, panting on to 75 bag of water, with a hydrocele on his right testis. How jolly.[20]

Proud of possessing a 1799 edition of the monumental *Dictionary of the English Language* (1755), Beckett always loved quaint words and inventive phrases. The above passage directly borrows the verb "panted on" from

Johnson's letter in the *Boswell's Life* (4:267), and multiple variations of the usage, suggestive of morbidity and mortality, would reappear in Beckett's later publications as a telling sign of a Johnsonian signature involved in the creative process.[21]

Again, on July 27, he acknowledged continuing research with the same misplaced enthusiasm for an unprovable impotence theory, which rightly caused him to label his imagined play "my Johnson fantasy":

> My efforts to document my Johnson fantasy have not ceased. The evidence for it is overwhelming. It explains what has never been explained (e.g. his grotesque attitute [*for* attitude] towards his wife & Mr Thrale). It is hard to put across, he being so old at the crisis, i.e. she could hardly have expected much from him. We will make him younger & madder even than he was.[22]

Little more than a week later, on August 4, he sent MacGreevy his last extensive commentary on the Johnson project, this time stressing a radical reading of the entire eighteenth century, not as a so-called Age of Reason but as a period of disturbing skepticism reflected in the anxiety-ridden romance with Mrs. Thrale:

> Dr. J.'s dogmatisme was the façade of consternation. The 18th century was full of ahuris [bewildered people]—perhaps that is why it looked like age of "reason"—but there can hardly have been many so completely at sea in their solitude as he was or so horrifiedly aware of it—not even [William] Cowper. Read the *Prayers & Meditations* if you don't believe me. (*LSB*, 1:529)

This comment recalls Thomas Carlyle's indictment of the Age of Johnson in *On Heroes, Hero-Worship, and the Heroic in History* (1840):

> Johnson's fatal misery was the *spiritual paralysis*, so we may name it, of the Age in which his life lay; whereby his life too, do what we might, was half-paralyzed! The Eighteenth was a *Sceptical* Century; in which little word there is a whole Pandora's Box of miseries.[23]

The rest of Beckett's remarks to MacGreevy points to a broadened conception of the play. Focused more on an angst-ridden rather than a lovelorn
Johnson, the plot would make room for the full story—now more tragic
than comic—of his dealings with widowed Mrs. Thrale, from 1781 to
1784, in line with a scenario, found in the Notebooks, for a four-act drama
ending "with J. panting in silence [N.B. Beckett's favorite Johnsonian
usage] after 'sent to hell, Sir, etc.' curtain falls."[24]

Years later, Beckett confirmed intending *Human Wishes* to be in four
acts, one for each year from the time of Henry Thrale's death to Mrs.
Thrale's marriage to Piozzi, with Johnson first appearing near the end of
Act I.[25] Such a play, as he wrote to MacGreevy, was now in contemplation
by early August of 1937:

> Mrs Thrale was nee Salusbury-Hester (!) Lynch(!!) Salusbury.
> There is no question of being partisan in the matter, one way
> or another. He made her Salon & she made him comfortable.
> When he wrote her the famous rough letter he didn't know
> what he was doing. Probably it was the only overt cruelty in the
> "friendship never infringed by one harsh expression during 20
> years of familiar talk," as she herself expressed in her admirably
> dignified last letter to him. And of the covert she had certainly
> no more to suffer than he, indeed certainly a great deal less,
> because she had none of that need to suffer, or necessity of
> suffering that he had, and never found in him the peg to hang
> her pain on that he did in her. His horror of loving her I take it
> was a mode or paradigm of his horror at ultimate annihilation,
> to which he declared in the fear of his own death that he would
> prefer an eternity of torment. And if the play is about him and
> not about her, it does not mean that he was in the right, or
> any nonsense like that, but simply that he being spiritually self
> conscious was a tragic figure, i.e. worth putting down as part of
> the whole of which oneself is a part, & that she, being merely
> physically self conscious is less interesting to me personally. She
> of course didn't get what she wanted either. Piozzi being a poor
> performer. "*Human Wishes*" (*LSB*, 1:529–30)

The main inspiration for this revealing passage was an amalgam of memories from his attentive reading of Seccombe and Vulliamy. The chapter heading immediately after Seccombe's compact biography— "HESTER LYNCH THRALE [NEE SALUSBURY, AFTERWARDS PIOZZI], 1740–1821."—precedes coverage of the Streatham salon with its climactic Johnson–Mrs.Thrale correspondence about "a friendship never infringed by one harsh expression … during twenty years of familiar talk" (28–29). Seccombe also mentions Mrs. Thrale's comparative shallowness, befitting "a nature planted in a light dry soil, incapable … of appreciating the fundamental qualities of Johnson's profound character" (40). Vulliamy seconded this insight: "while Johnson's affection … [smacked] of passionate devotion, Mrs. Thrale's … was only the limited concern of an egotist" (256). He also insinuated Piozzi's romantic deficiencies: "Mrs. Thrale was in love with Piozzi, but Piozzi was disappointing, respectful, tepid, and apparently unaware of his conquest" (211).

Despite all the energy poured into his research for the play, Beckett was badly stalled. On the very same day, August 4, when he wrote buoyantly to MacGreevy about his expanding plot and evolving interest in a broken rather than a lovelorn Johnson, he let another correspondent know of his mounting weariness with his work: "The Johnson thing has gone away to be dyed. I mean the idea of it. For nothing has been degraded to paper. I have been too tired."[26] The writer's block persisted, because, ten days later, MacGreevy himself heard the same bad news. "I had the Johnson thing fairly clear in my mind but with thinking about it has gone obscure again. Perhaps it gets clearer elsewhere."[27] But, far from losing faith in the project, at the end of 1937, when he took up permanent residence in France, he hinted to Mary Manning Howe that the still unwritten play was intended to be an integral part of his finding a distinctive artistic vision for his future career. Any Joycean literary apprenticeship lay mostly in the past, even though his friendship with the Joyces continued unabated. *Human Wishes*, if he could bring it to fruition, would stand with his other experimental writings, including his newest novel, as a formidable benchmark attempt at reshaping himself into a new kind of twentieth-century author:

I have not written a word of the Johnson blasphemy. I trust that acts of intellection are going on about it somewhere.

Which will enable me eventually to see how it coincides with the Pricks [*More Pricks than Kicks*, 1933], Bones [*Echo's Bones, and Other Precipitates*, 1935] and Murphy, fundamentally, and fundamentally with all I should ever write or want to write. (*LSB*, 1:569)

Never a man given to hyperbole, he should here be taken at his word about his long-term literary ambitions for the play. Significantly, labelling the projected drama a "Johnson blasphemy" is an implicit acknowledgement that he treated his protagonist reductively, inventing a slightly ridiculous imitation of a classic English author.

The new year of 1938 did not signal any new start for the play. His stagnant existence in Paris "is the kind of life that filled Dr Johnson with horror. Nothing but the days passing over. It suits me all right" (*LSB*, 1:606). By August 4 a renewed appetite for writing surfaced, but only momentarily: "Dr Johnson is back on my consciousness & I hope to settle down to it when I get back to Paris" (1:637). This resolve also fizzled within a month or two: "No work. I read on average an hour a day, after an hour the illusion of comprehension ceases, Kant, Descartes, Johnson, Ronsard ... " (1:643). The next year of 1939 witnessed more false promises to himself, "then it will be Johnson at last" (1:669), following a French translation of his novel *Murphy*. At long last, as he twice reported, *Human Wishes* came into being in its present short and incomplete state during the winter or by the early spring of 1940: "And I wrote half of a first act of Johnson."[28] This statement marked a very considerable stretch of time wasted since his almost year and a half of research begun in the spring of 1936.

## V. Beckett's *Human Wishes* (1940) and *Waiting for Godot* (1948–1949)

What caused the paralysis behind the creation of less than half a single act of a projected four-act play? In 1965 he confided to Ruby Cohn his problems with reproducing authentic eighteenth-century English speech for the protagonist while Irish actors in other roles discoursed in their modern idiom:

> I was fascinated for years by the idea of a play on Dr J & Mrs
> Thrale (1781–1784) and accumulated a mass of notes which I
> still have. Actually started first act. Then gave up—chiefly but not
> only because of language difficulty.[29]

Certainly something more than a language problem discouraged him. All
the prolonged and scrupulous source-hunting must have overwhelmed
his imagination, even though he had more than enough dramatic incident to compose a gripping play—far more action, in fact, than he ever
cared to incorporate in the stark inventive drama of his later fame. Then,
too, he was entrapped dangerously behind the lines in a demoralized
Nazi–Vichy France as an unregistered alien and resistance fighter under
German occupation for the duration of World War II. This war-torn environment would have exacerbated his constitutional nihilism and probably
disheartened him from further playwriting. Finally, putting on display
such a distorted version of a protagonist as an impotent lover or as an
anxiety-riddled eccentric old fool must have proven an awkward, perhaps
even distasteful, outcome for this playwright, and properly so. At the start
of 1959 he confessed to realizing that his long-ago impotence hypothesis
had no basis in fact and was sorry for all the lost time spent on trying to
validate a specious theory. He simply lost interest in the play as he moved
away from a sexualized image of Johnson toward a death-obsessed and
depressive figure more congenial to his own evolving literary vision. He
knew the greatness of Johnson and, if he evidently missed imagining
anything like the authentic persona, he nonetheless might well have
bridled at the thought of dramatizing a spurious parody. No completed
play ever appeared, and no Johnsonian protagonist ever became a public
spectacle.

The little-known fragment of *Human Wishes* that has survived is well
worth close examination. It looks forward to the future and particularly
anticipates unique features of his well-regarded dramaturgy: a tragi-comic
preoccupation with death, unhappiness, loneliness, immobility, and stag-
nation; punning word-play and ironic irritable banter leading nowhere;
and ominous silences interrupting disconnected dialogue symptomatic
of a distressing failure of communication and lack of meaning within a
vast surrounding universe of nothingness. Doubtless, scholars should

take care not to exaggerate the long-range literary impact of the Johnson project in the latter 1930s. Along with his wide-ranging learning, Beckett's own difficult life experiences, especially in World War II France, molded his pessimistic outlook massively. His literary allegiances were many and profoundly influential, from the bible to Joyce, Dante, Shakespeare, Proust, and Schopenhauer, to name a few. Johnson definitely belonged to this group, but few readers would easily detect his faint signature, unless in search of it, in novels such as *Watt, Molloy, Malone Dies*, and *The Unnameable* or in plays such as *Endgame* and *Happy Days*.

What is clear is that, in composing the existing fragment of *Human Wishes*, he depended upon his three Notebooks, especially about thirty-five additional sheets of notes on the members of the Johnson household, including Frank Barber (who does not appear in the extant fragment). But so many haphazard notations from multiple sources would have disoriented the struggling playwright, and he needed a narrative blueprint to create a plot. He turned to a specific source, mentioned in his third Notebook, for help in organizing his miscellaneous information. This was Chapter V of Leslie Stephen's *Samuel Johnson* (1878, 1891), namely, "The Closing Years of Johnson's Life," which offered perhaps a ready template for plotting.[30]

Although, like most Victorians, Stephen could be deplorably dismissive of his subject, he would have caught Beckett's attention by remarking on Johnson's affinity with Schopenhauer and by offering a concise story of the relationship with Mrs. Thrale, replete with stagey promptings useful for shaping a play. Here are some suggestive excerpts of Stephen's narrative:

> The year 1781 brought with it a catastrophe which profoundly affected the brief remainder of Johnson's life. Mr. Thrale ... died suddenly on the 4th of April ... . The change did not follow at once, but as the catastrophe of a little social drama, upon the rights and wrongs of which a good deal of controversy has been expended. (150)

Such dramatic heightening, along with Sir John Hawkins's mention of Anna Williams's skills with a needle, combined with the following summary of

Johnson's household in Stephen's biography to provide Beckett key cues for starting *Human Wishes*:

> The head of his household was Miss Williams ... . She was a [blind] woman of some sense and cultivation ... . [But she] was peevish ... . The next inmate of this queer household was [a drunkard physician] Robert Levett ... . [T]here was a Mrs. Desmoulins ... . [A]nd we have a dim vision of a Miss Carmichael [of low reputation] who completed ... his "seraglio." It was anything but a happy family. He summed up their relations in a letter to Mrs. Thrale. "Williams hates ... everybody. Levett hates Desmoulins, and does not love Williams. Desmoulins hates them both; Poll (Miss Carmichael) loves none of them." ... His cat, Hodge, should be famous ... . Bozzy remarked that he was a fine cat. "Why, yes, sir," said Johnson; "... he is a very fine cat, a very fine cat indeed." (146–50)

The opening of *Human Wishes* makes creative use of Stephen's chapter, from the initial stage direction and repetitious dialogue about "fine" Hodge, "fine" perceptions, and Poll Carmichael's "fine" writing, down to the general crankiness of the odd family. Beckett did echo the first lines of A. Edward Newton's stodgy *Dr. Johnson: A Play* (1923): "Mr. *Stewart*. Dr. Johnson is late this morning. Mr. *Maitland*. Dr. Johnson is always late." But Stephen seems largely responsible for outlining the overall scene:

*A room in Bolt Court. Wednesday April 14, 1781. Evening*
Mrs Williams *(meditating)*.
Mrs Desmoulins *(knitting)*.
Miss Carmichael *(reading)*.
The cat Hodge *(sleeping—if possible)*.

Mrs D. He is late.
*Silence.*
Mrs D. God grant all is well.
*Silence.*
Mrs D. Puss puss puss puss puss.

*Silence.*
Mrs W. What are you reading, young woman?
Miss C. A book, Madam.
Mrs W. Ha!
*Silence.*
Mrs D. Hodge is a very fine cat, a very fine cat indeed.[31]

This initial phase of the drama attempts to capture Johnsonese language playfully, sometimes with the author's trademark dramatic mode of repetitious inconsequentiality. It also makes much of the lack of humor at Bolt Court in an ironic tragi-comic manner suited to the women's dreary but amusingly competitive situation. Intermittent silences and pervasive stasis haunt the entire household scenario of depressing decrepitude, loneliness, and looming mortality, which directly reflects key concerns in Beckett's background reading for the play.

Most noteworthy is his insertion of an elaborate doodle in the bottom half of a sheet containing his handwritten draft of a portion of the opening dialogue. Perhaps his research for the Johnson project, with its morbid stress on death and damnation ("my Redeemer has said that he will set some on his right hand and some on his left," *Boswell's Life*, 4:300), evoked this irreverent doodle. It is a cartoon depiction of Christ's crucifixion between two crucified thieves, the good one on the right hand and the bad one on the left, just above a bowler-clad smirking man with his left arm around a petite woman wearing a wedding gown, while his right hand holds a suitcase marked with a capital "J."[32] The two tiny individuals watching the crucifixion could be anybody, but, given the context of their appearance in the manuscript of *Human Wishes*, could they very well be stick-figures of Johnson and Mrs. Thrale? If so, does such an identification, weighted with possible associations of Johnson's fear of death and hell, have anything in common with the memorable banter in *Waiting for Godot* about death and damnation surrounding Christ's crucifixion between two thieves? That conversation also highlights a lack of humor among comparably lonely and cranky characters:

One of the thieves was saved. (*Pause.*) ... *Vladimir breaks into a hearty laugh which he immediately stifles* ... . VLADIMIR: One daren't even laugh any more. ESTRAGON: Dreadful privation. VLADIMIR: Merely smile …. It's not the same thing. Nothing to be done. (*Pause.*) … Ah yes, the two thieves … . One is supposed to have been saved and the other … damned … . One out of the four [Evangelists tells the story of a good and bad thief crucified beside Jesus] … . [A]nd the third says that both of them abused him … . ESTRAGON: Why? VLADIMIR: Because he wouldn't save them … . From death … . ESTRAGON: I thought you said hell. VLADIMIR: From death, from death … . Then the two of them must have been damned."[33]

The next movement of *Human Wishes* revolves around the absence of merriment in the Johnson household. A possible inspiration for some of this dialogue can be found in the Notebooks, in a quotation from Johnson's *Idler* 58 on abortive schemes of merriment involving a group of witty gentlemen made angry and unhappy by their unappreciative audience:

Nothing is more hopeless than a scheme of merriment. Wits and humorists are brought together … . [T]hey gaze a-while on each other, ashamed to be silent, and afraid to speak; every man is discontented with himself, grows angry with those that give him pain and resolves that he will contribute nothing to the merriment of such worthless company.[34]

This essay may have prompted Beckett to transpose the male-oriented situation into a female-oriented scenario of comparably disgusted and mutually contemptuous household members. The women's desultory and eerily repetitive talk, like jazz, riffs on the theme of missing merriment in their humorless lives:

Mrs. W. (*at the top of her voice*). IS SHE MERRY?
Miss C. (*softly*). She is not.
Mrs. W. (*softly*). Nobody in this house is merry.
Mrs. D. I hope you are satisfied, Madam.
*Silence.*

Miss C. And the doctor, is the doctor … .
*Silence.*
Mrs D. He is late.

*Human Wishes* next introduces Robert Levett briefly to the stage, emitting "*a single hiccup of such force that he is almost thrown off his feet*" in a drunken pantomime that anticipates later dramatic techniques. Then there is an extended death-obsessed conversation centered on two deceased Irish playwrights, "Dr." Oliver Goldsmith and Hugh Kelly. This section of the play elaborates creatively on information mined from many sources, including biographies by Hawkins and Boswell. Levett, the bumbling and burping physician to the poor, recalls Hawkins's portrait of the alcoholic: "Had (said Johnson) all his patients … [rewarded] him with meat and strong liquors instead of money, he would … have burst, like the dragon in the Apocrypha … " (*JM*, 2:111). The "dead and damned" Hugh Kelly relates to Johnson's charitable activities on behalf of the then dead pensioner–playwright, whose failed drama "in the playhouse phrase, was *damned* (*Boswell's Life*, 3:113–14 and n.3). Significantly, another link between *Human Wishes* and *Waiting for Godot* lurks in this dialogue. When the women speak respectfully of the dead dramatists in an almost Brecht-like direct address to the audience ("Let us not speak unkindly of the dead"), they prepare for the sad indictment of modernity in the later famous play: "Let us not then speak ill of our generation … . Let us not speak well of it either … . Let us not speak of it at all" (*Waiting for Godot*, 22a). Perhaps too, Johnson's opening comment in his *Annals* ("I was born almost dead" which haunted Beckett) filtered into Pozzo's final statement about life's meaninglessness: "one day we were born, one day we shall die …. They give birth astride of a grave, the light gleams an instant, then it's night once more" (*Waiting for Godot*, 57b). Although Beckett refused to say what or whom Godot represented, one possible identification might tentatively be connected to the making of *Human Wishes*: The never-appearing Godot may subconsciously reflect the never-created character of Samuel Johnson for the stage. Beckett's own artistic frustrations in this regard might just have some bearing on the vision of human frustration in his dramatic masterpiece.

The final extant portion of *Human Wishes* intensifies the gloomy Johnsonian theme of human mortality and borrows directly from Jeremy Taylor's devotional work, *Holy Living and Holy Dying* (1650–1651), to underline the message that death rules all. When Beckett read the Anglican treatise late in 1933, he sardonically remarked about its title that living and dying were one and the same.[35] In this section of the play, Beckett resorts again to Boswell and Hawkins for Anna Williams's death-obsessed account of her father (*Boswell's Life*, 1:302 n.3, 1:247 n.2, 1:232 and n.1; Hawkins, *Life of Samuel Johnson, LL.D.*, 135–36), and Hawkins also verified Johnson's admiration for Jeremy Taylor and Thomas Browne (116, 143). As the women debate the authorship of quotations about ever-present human mortality, whether by Taylor or by Browne, the comically mindless banter brings *Human Wishes* to an abrupt halt, at the word "Taylor," and perhaps appropriately so. This name, which points to Jeremy Taylor, may also faintly hint at Rev. John Taylor, who, as Beckett carefully noted in his research, criticized Johnson in print for talk of dreading death and annihilation. Any such possibility of a subliminal reference to a John-sonian fear of death and nothingness would have been in keeping with the play's overriding theme and its abrupt termination into the nothingness of incompletion.

## VI. The Ghost of Samuel Johnson Incarnated in *Krapp's Last Tape* (1958)

From Beckett's nihilistic perspective, *Human Wishes* ends like life itself: There is no more to it. But there is more. His fascination with Johnson continued and possibly induced him eventually to make good on the unmet promise of this fragment of a play. Returning to *Boswell's Life* with unabated pleasure on August 17, 1951, he did not miss probably the most important discovery in modern eighteenth-century scholarship, the publication of Boswell's voluminous, often spicy, journals:

> I am re-reading Boswell in the handsome Birkbeck Hill edition. Calming effect, as always. They have found some unpub-lished manuscripts of Boswell, scandalous apparently, in Malahide Castle, near Dublin. A first volume has been published

by Heinemann, the *London Journal*. Toned down for sure … . The whole of the English eighteenth century is there.[36]

A postcard attached to page forty-nine of the *London Journal* invited his correspondent to regale herself on a salacious passage about Boswell living it up with prostitutes. On the following December 29 he sent his American director, Alan Schneider, hearty "Congratulations on TV Great Cham" in the CBS *Omnibus* production of *The Life of Johnson*, played by Emmy Award-winning Peter Ustinov.[37] Knowing his enthusiasm for any Johnsoniana in print, friends made sure to send him welcome gifts of books, including the recent first volume of the authoritative Yale edition of the *Diaries, Prayers, and Annals* (1958): "It will not be among the vast number that I intend to scrap" from his large personal library.[38] A few months later, he expressed thanks again for the cherished "Yale Johnson if it's not too expensive. I find it hard to resist anything to do with that old blusterer, especially his last years."[39] He then "finished the Johnson with relish, when I got out of the Welsh hills and into the *Aegri Ephemeris*"— that is, the "Sick Man's Journal" in the Yale edition. His early fixation on the private pathological Johnson had diminished not at all.

The closest that Beckett ever came to bringing something like *Human Wishes* to the stage was perhaps his highly regarded one-act play, the semi-autobiographical *Krapp's Last Tape*, first performed on October 28, 1958.[40] Although the protagonist, an old worn-out author reviewing his life by way of a tape recorder, bears only the vaguest resemblance to Johnson at first glance, a few plausible clues exist to suggest their fitful identification. Krapp is morbidly introspective and faintly analogous to the soul-searching Johnson of the *Prayers and Meditations* (Beckett's receipt of the Yale edition actually *postdated* the play's creation by several months). Comparable Johnsonian anxieties over decay and death hover over Krapp's often self-loathing, stream-of consciousness musings. Krapp too seems a seedy contemporary personification of Beckett's weird impo-tence hypothesis about Johnson two decades ago. Lonely and lusty, he has sterile relationships with Bianca in his youth ("Hopeless business … . Plans for a less … engrossing sexual life … . Flagging pursuit of happi-ness"), with a nameless woman in middle age ("I said again I thought it was hopeless … and she agreed"), and, in senility, with a "Bony old ghost of a whore. Couldn't do much … . How do you manage it, she said, at your age." His midlife epiphany of artistic vision for creating a magnum opus fades, with the aging process, into literary failure. Compare Krapp sadly "drowned in dreams and burning to be gone" with the ambitious scholar in *The Vanity of Human Wishes*: "Through all his Veins the Fever of Renown / Burns from the strong Contagion of the Gown" (ll.137–38; Fleeman, *Poems*, 86).

The tip-off for Johnson's presence in the creation of the play surfaces in the scene where Krapp must consult "*an enormous dictionary*," alluding to Johnson's huge, folio-sized *Dictionary*, for the meaning of "viduity, that is, 'widowhood.'"[41] Beckett's own playbook prompt substantiates this inference: "Comes back with volume of the Concise Oxford" or "Johnson's Dictionary and quotes example."[42] Krapp then plays with several *OED* definitions, one of which, bearing on the related term "viduate," is tellingly illustrated in this dictionary by Boswell's pornographic poem about Johnson's nuptials with Mrs. Thrale (see also *Boswell's Life*, 4:387: "*Cervisial coctor's viduate* dame/ … A captive in thy *ambient* arms"). In a final ironic fit of empty bravado, Krapp denies defiantly any wish to return to the "best years" of his better past. "But I wouldn't want them back. Not with the fire in me now. But I wouldn't want them back" (*Krapp's Last Tape*, 28). His concluding resolve is reminiscent of Johnson's conviction that life is so generally miserable as to discourage most people from ever wanting to relive it. As Boswell stated in the *Life of Johnson* (4:300–302), "no man would choose to lead over again the life which he had experienced. Johnson acceded to that opinion in the strongest terms."

The clinching piece of evidence for establishing Krapp's ties to Johnson has gone completely unnoticed previously but would seem to be right in front of the reader at the very beginning of the play. The opening stage directions, including the reference to a lair-like "den" and "rusty" clothes, may well bring to mind a famous source for Beckett's description of a decrepit Krapp:

> *Krapp's den … . Sitting at the table, facing front … a wearish old man: Krapp. Rusty black narrow trousers too short for him. Rusty black sleeveless waistcoat, four capacious pockets. Heavy silver watch and chain. Grimy white shirt open at neck, no collar.*

*Surprising pair of dirty white boots … . Disordered grey hair. Unshaven. Very near-sighted (but unspectacled). Hard of hearing. Cracked voice. Distinctive intonation. Laborious walk.* (9–10)

Later, the audience hears a tape recording of Krapp in his desolate quarters: "Good to be back in my den, in my old rags" (14). This description of Krapp would, on careful analysis, seem an updated adaptation of Boswell's endearing, hero-worshipping portrayal of Johnson during their first meeting and first days together. That encounter is the most celebrated and beloved example of Boswell's scene-painting in all the many hundreds of pages of the *Life of Johnson*. Fascinated by all portraits of Johnson, Beckett would understandably not have forgotten this key episode. As Boswell memorably recorded,

> I found that I had a very perfect idea of Johnson's figure from the portrait of him painted by Sir Joshua Reynolds … sitting in his easy chair in deep meditation … . "People (he remarked) may be taken in once, who imagine that an author is greater in private life than other men." … I … 'found the Giant in his den:' … [I]t must be confessed, that his apartment and furnishings, and morning dress were sufficiently uncouth. His brown suit of cloaths looked very rusty. He had on a little old shriveled and powdered wig, which was too small for him; his shirt-neck and knees of his breeches were loose; his black worsted stockings ill drawn up; and he had a pair of unbuckled shoes by way of slippers. But all these slovenly particularities were forgotten the moment he began to talk. (*Boswell's Life*, 1:392–93, 396)

By comparison with Boswell's description, Krapp is Beckett's anti-Johnson. Even if the two figures are similarly unkempt, near-sighted, hard-of-hearing, and ensconced on a chair in a dingy den on the verge of speaking, the slovenly subject of the *Boswell's Life* is at the peak of his fame and powers, whereas Krapp is at a physical and intellectual endpoint, as he really was in lowly "private life." Johnson is a great man for all ages, and Krapp is all but kaput. One collects orange peels in his bulging pocket for their nutritious and medicinal value (*Boswell's Life*, 2:330–31, 4:205), and the other fingers banana peels as sterile penis symbols of sexual inadequacy and unsatisfying romantic encounters. Krapp, it may very well be, incarnates the ghost of Johnson and, from that perspective, might have evolved directly out of the tragi-comic caricature envisaged for *Human Wishes*. As such, he was transformed into a broken old everyman embodiment of modernity in shambles, with a tenuous hold on life, not by living it but only by remembering it, until the oblivion of death takes over and ends in nothingness. Perhaps as a sign of linkage between Johnson and Krapp, Beckett extended the very same affectionate epithet to both. Of the first, he affirmed in 1957, "Yes, I always had a passion for that old ruffian," of the second, he expressed satisfaction in 1960 that the play bearing his name would have a longer run: "Pleased to hear that *Krapp* has been extended *in extremis*, looks as if the old ruffian might pant on to 1961."[43] That favorite Johnsonian borrowing, "panted on," reappears in the latter letter as possibly a hint of Johnson's presence lingering faintly in the playwright's subconscious even here. With the success of *Krapp's Last Tape*, Beckett may virtually have fulfilled his long-ago expectations for the Johnson project behind *Human Wishes*.[44] Any such accomplishment might help to explain his disinclination to permit the unfinished early play an actual performance: "I'll never do the Johnson in this or in any other century," he observed, not a month after he composed the heavily revised draft of *Krapp's Last Tape* in March of 1958.[45] However, since that date, *Human Wishes* has so far enjoyed at least three separate one-day amateur productions into the twenty-first century.[46]

### VII.  "Yes, I always had a passion for that old ruffian."

At Beckett's death his substantial private library testified to his lifelong admiration for Johnson. The fourteen extant holdings constitute a very respectable amateur scholar's worth of Johnsoniana: Walter Jackson Bate's Pulitzer Prize-winning *Samuel Johnson* (1979, a gift from Ruby Cohn), the six-volume *Boswell's Life* (1887, purchased in 1966), *Boswell's London Journal* (1951), James L. Clifford's *Young Samuel Johnson* (1955), *The Poetical Works of Samuel Johnson, LL.D* (1785), the two-volume eighth edition of *The Dictionary of the English Language by Samuel Johnson, LL.D.* (1799), Walter Raleigh's second edition of *Johnson on Shakespeare* (1957, a gift from Barbara Bray), the Yale *Diaries, Prayers, and Annals* (1958, a gift from Barbara Bray), a two-volume edition of *Johnsonian Miscellanies* (1966), J. D. Fleeman's edition of *Samuel Johnson: The Complete English Poems* (1971), Christopher Hibbert's *The Personal History of Samuel Johnson* (1971), *Dr. Johnson by Mrs. Thrale: the Anecdotes of Mrs. Piozzi in Their Original Form* (1984), Richard Ingram's edition of Robert Lynd's *Dr. Johnson and Company* (1946), and C. E. Vulliamy's *Mrs. Thrale of Streatham* (1936).[47] As all these works make abundantly clear, Beckett remained true to his lifelong fondness for the like-minded master of the vanity of human wishes. If he tended to transform Johnson into his own nihilistic image, his allegiance to this classic English moralist and critic was nonetheless unquestionable and rich in consequences for the Irishman's developing canon. Responding to scholars asking about his deepest literary affiliations, whether perhaps to Fielding or to Sterne, he responded emphatically and sincerely: "They can put me wherever they want, but it's Johnson, always Johnson, who is with me. And if I follow any tradition, it is his."[48] And, by an ironic but happy twist of fate, with all their stark differences and with all their mutual doubts about life, these two brilliant authors died peacefully at the last.

CHAPTER SEVEN

# The "Plexed Artistry" of Nabokov and Johnson

*Carrie D. Shanafelt*

## I. Introduction

Beginning in the epigraph of his 1962 experimental novel *Pale Fire*, Vladimir Nabokov repeatedly invokes Samuel Johnson as a figure of powerful fascination and literary envy. The metanarrative of *Pale Fire*, throughout John Shade's poem and Charles Kinbote's commentary, is a painful search for meaning in the seemingly random coincidences produced in the depressive or paranoid mind. The poet, devoted to the search for Enlightenment-style objectivity, is tortured by his irrepressibly sublime imagination, while the commentator grafts his own mad certainties into the rootstock of Shade's hard-won epiphanies. This tension, between induction and deduction, between skepticism and zeal, is central to Nabokov's fiction, but it also serves as a crucial commentary on the literary, critical, and linguistic inquiries of Samuel Johnson.

Analytical comparisons of Nabokov and Johnson tend to begin with the surface dissimilarities between them in terms of content and reputation. As Jeffrey Meyers puts it, Johnson was a didactic moralist and patriot, while Nabokov is "the embodiment of the witty, urbane, and cosmopolitan modern writer."[1] It strikes literary critics as strange that Nabokov, the author of several novels about pedophilia, incest, suicide, and murder, would invoke the morally conservative Johnson not just as an influence on a character but as an influence on his own ideas about language, poetry, and meaning.

Just as Samuel Johnson seems simultaneously to be an avatar for eighteenth-century British aesthetics, ideas, and values, while having explicitly resisted most of the Enlightenment's core ideas and principles, Vladimir Nabokov wrote several quintessentially twentieth-century American novels, though he did not identify as American, a novelist by vocation,[2] or even a person sharing an era with his contemporaries.[3] Both writers were irascible eccentrics who, after living much of their lives working in obscurity, nevertheless found themselves suddenly identified as cultural insiders, icons of literary wisdom to readers of popular fiction and the educated elite alike.

Johnson and Nabokov both wrote in styles that struck readers as old-fashioned in their own times, resistant to the tremendous aesthetic shifts that their contemporaries had embraced. Yet their works ultimately demonstrate not sentimentality about idealized times past but a kind of bruised wariness about trends in intellectual innovation. Nowhere in Nabokov's fictional work is this wariness more apparent than in *Pale Fire*, a novel about creative and critical work at an American liberal arts college, written in part as an explicit homage to Johnson and his biographer James Boswell.

Quoting from James Boswell's *The Life of Samuel Johnson, LL.D.* (1791), Nabokov opens *Pale Fire* with an epigraph of Boswell recounting Johnson telling his friend Bennet Langton a story about a young man they knew:

> This reminds me of the ludicrous account he gave Mr. Langton, of the despicable state of a young gentleman of good family, "Sir, when I heard of him last, he was running about town shooting cats." And then in a sort of kindly reverie, he bethought himself of his own favorite cat, and said, "But Hodge shan't be shot: no, no, Hodge shall not be shot."[4]

In this excerpt from the *Life*, Boswell is, as usual, listening in on the conversation and revealing Johnson's peculiar obsessions. Boswell, who loathed cats, represents Johnson's tenderness for Hodge with revulsion and surprise.

Seeming to catch Johnson here in a moment of narcissism—thinking more of his own cat than of the young gentleman—Boswell reveals something intensely endearing about his titanic subject, who is never such an abstract moralist that he would forget to dote on his furry friend.

Likewise, throughout *Pale Fire*, Kinbote attempts to undermine John Shade's grand poetic reputation by revealing his potentially embarrassing personal secrets—his affinity for forbidden alcohol, a rumored affair with a student, his obsequiousness to his headstrong wife—all in ways that only serve to vivify the self-portrait offered by Shade in the poem as a shy, too-fond, private mystic "distributed through space and time" (38). The intimacy of the account Kinbote provides, like Boswell's account of Johnson's private feelings, paradoxically elevates the poet, whose real personal struggles are the substance of his finest art and speculation.

For both Johnson and Nabokov, poetry is the means by which a mortal human being can transcend mere empirical reality. The pragmatic philosophies of language that were prevalent in the mid-eighteenth century and in the mid-twentieth century took for granted that language is a socially constructed tool for representing a shared reality. For Johnson and Nabokov, artistic language has the potential to transform reality into something sublime and otherworldly, and to discover non-empirical truth through poetic inquiry. Although Samuel Johnson's poetic discoveries adhered to a roughly Anglican divine imaginary, while Nabokov's ventured into something perhaps more heretical,[5] both authors felt that their experiences of the sublime had unmoored them from the fashionable empiricism of their own intellectual cultures.

In this chapter, I compare how Johnson and Nabokov each describe linguistic and aesthetic meaning in ways that resist the pragmatic empiricism of their intellectual contemporaries. Samuel Johnson's understanding of meaning serves as a direct criticism of David Hume's theory of language, while Nabokov seems to be responding to the language philosophy of Willard Van Orman Quine (the latter of whom makes a brief appearance as "Quine the Swine" in *Lolita*[6]). The literary authors, in each case, insist that poetic language is not merely description, rhetoric, or representation; it can also achieve sublime discovery, creation, or transformation.

In Canto Three of the poem in *Pale Fire*, John Shade erupts in an epiphany that the work of poetry is to make peace with the maddeningly meaningless resemblances offered by empirical experience, and to learn to take pleasure in the mental shell game offered by creative language:

> Yes! It sufficed that I in life could find
> Some kind of link-and-bobolink, some kind
> Of correlated pattern in the game,
> Plexed artistry, and something of the same
> Pleasure in it as they who played it found. (63)

For Nabokov, poetic language has a demon-summoning magic; it is like a spell—untranslatable, idiosyncratic, and semiotically haunted by the author's personal collection of etymologies, anagrams, false cognates, acquired and invented languages, and experiences of desire and trauma. As Kinbote muses in an uncommonly lucid passage near the end of the commentary, "I wish you to gasp not only at what you read but at the miracle of its being readable" (289). The miracle of artistic language is that it is legible despite being contingent on so many private variables both in its usage and in its reception. Poetry is successful insofar as it can transcend subjective contingency, and thus the marginal, strange, lonely poet finds himself the object of admiration and sympathetic sentiment.

Samuel Johnson's aesthetic theory of poetry is similar to Nabokov's in its ambition. Like Nabokov, Johnson also wrote a novel about a flawed but earnest older poet and his protégé-turned-critic: *The History of Rasselas, Prince of Abissinia*. In this 1759 work, Johnson stages a discussion about the role of poetry; Imlac expounds at length on the superhuman virtue of the true poet, who must try to understand all of human life and existence, but then goes beyond human understanding to reveal sublime truths. Rasselas interrupts Imlac's self-aggrandizing reverie: "Enough! Thou hast convinced me, that no human being can ever be a poet. Proceed with thy narration," to which Imlac slyly replies: "To be a poet … is indeed very difficult."[7] Like Nabokov, Johnson uses a fictional dialogue simultaneously to satirize the extraordinary ambition of his own aesthetic ideal and to undermine the excessive skepticism of his contemporaries. For a poem to merely record what is plainly apparent to everyone in the normal course of life would be poor poetry indeed.

During the mid-eighteenth century in London and the mid-twentieth century in the United States, philosophical empiricism formed the basis of most philosophy of language and aesthetics, and writers who worked in non-empiricist aesthetics were largely criticized as sentimental, old-fashioned, or foolish, while gritty realism and comic satire became ubiquitous. That Johnson and Nabokov nevertheless garnered the admiration of both popular and intellectual readers in their own lifetimes seems hardly possible, except for the force and pleasure of their linguistic and aesthetic genius. Both writers would ultimately come to seem prophetic, anticipating new developments that would emerge both in philosophy and in the arts, in the forms of Romanticism and Postmodernism, each of which constituted what the philosopher Charles Taylor would call "the massive subjective turn of modern culture"[8] that has, in two distinct waves in the late eighteenth and late twentieth centuries, centralized extra-empirical conceptions of trauma, desire, and moral purpose.

## II. Johnson and the Communal Eye

The problem of objective perspective in the works of Samuel Johnson haunts nearly every critical approach to his work. As a lexicographer, social commentator, literary critic, poet, and narrative author held in broad esteem throughout his later years, Johnson has often been assumed to provide one of the most objective perspectives on life in mid-eighteenth century England. He openly despised prejudice, cruelty, greed, opportunism, snobbery, violence, and fashion—all common vices among a rising middle class profiting from slavery and colonialism abroad. Both his contemporaries and ours have tended to assume that Johnson did not hold fundamentally different ideas about epistemology or aesthetics from the leading empiricist philosophers or artists of his own time. Adam Potkay has argued at length that there is much to be gained from reading Hume's moral philosophy alongside the works of Johnson, who shared some of Hume's optimism about the worldly happiness that may come from developing a moral life.[9] However, when he was directly confronted with the ideas of prominent empiricist philosophers or authors who justified their work as based on objective observations of nature, Johnson responded with hostility and derision.

According to James Boswell, who in his *Life* often lamented his biographical subject's low opinions of so many great thinkers of their time, Johnson was dismissive of George Berkeley,[10] scornful of Henry Fielding,[11] and contemptuous of David Hume. He did not address his objections to these three authors by name in his written work, but in conversation Johnson aligns each of them with an absurd kind of fashionable modern skepticism, oblivious to some apparently simple truth about reality or morality. Boswell evaluates Johnson's hasty dismissal as the product of "politicks" in the case of Berkeley (1:471–72), and "prejudice" against Fielding (2:49), which prevented Johnson from giving either his full intellectual attention or a calmly engaged explanation of their failures.

This hostility is most acutely apparent in Johnson's response to the work of David Hume. In the *Life*, Boswell frequently expresses confusion that an intellect of Johnson's stature is unable even to abide conversation about the work or ideas of a variety of intellectual figures, especially those of Boswell's fellow Scotsman Hume. During a conversation about attitudes toward death, Boswell offered Hume as an example of someone who claimed not to fear death, which aroused such a passionate argument that Johnson angrily sent Boswell away, calling out, "Don't let us meet to-morrow" (2:106–7). Boswell's insistence on soliciting agreement from Johnson on matters related to secularist empiricism uniformly end in resentment and apologies from the younger man.

Although he did not write an explicit public response to David Hume (or any of the empiricists he reportedly disdained in conversation), Johnson is clear throughout his written work that true knowledge is not to be gained solely through the collation of verifiable sensory observation. Hume proposes in *A Treatise of Human Nature* (1739–1740) that the importance or relevance of a particular object of observation is a quality inherent to the object, or to the socially determined value of the object as communicated in language, rather than in the personal preferences or values of the individual observer. For example, in explaining why it is just that women should not be allowed to inherit or manage property, Hume concludes that it is simply obvious to everyone that women are inferior to men:

'Tis a quality of human nature, which we shall consider afterwards, that the imagination naturally turns to whatever is
important and considerable; and where two objects are presented
to it, a small and a great one, usually leaves the former, and dwells
entirely on the latter.[12]

He goes on to explain that if women were obviously equals to men, they
too could inherit property, but everyone can plainly observe that they are
not. Hume uses the first-person plural throughout his work as a way of
universalizing observation and rendering objective the judgments that he
derives from those observations. It is not that Hume finds women to be
plainly inferior to men; it is that "we" find them inferior.

Hume repeatedly ascribes moral and aesthetic values not to individual taste, preference, prejudice, desire, or antipathy but to objective
standards of value that pre-exist any individual act of observation either
in the nature of the object itself or in the social meaning that object has
for a particular community or era. We do not approach the world with a
personal system of values or meaning and apply it; rather, Hume writes, we
derive all of our values from the objects of our observation and our social
conversation about the proper meanings of those objects. The observation
and evaluation performed by an individual is therefore more correct when
verified by others. For Hume, there is no personal identity or "self" at
all—merely a receptacle of a set of observations and the conclusions that
those observations produce. He writes, "I may venture to affirm of the rest
of mankind, that they are nothing but a bundle or collection of different
perceptions, which succeed each other with an inconceivable rapidity, and
are in a perpetual flux and movement."[13] Without a self to which moral or
value judgments could be ascribed, the individual, for Hume, is a kind of
machine that dutifully collates the accurate but limited data collected by
the senses. Prejudice against women or foreigners, then, would not be a
personal failure, but an accurate assessment of the values of one's society.
Cruelty and greed would not be moral flaws among like-minded persons,
but practical values gleaned from living in a cruel society.

The reason Hume offers that vice is not more widespread lies in his
philosophy of language, best articulated in his later work, *An Enquiry*

*Concerning the Principles of Morals* (1752), where he declares, "The very nature of language guides us almost infallibly in forming a judgment of [a moral] nature."[14] Hume concludes that, because language must be shared within a society in order to be of any use in communication, it is also the best means of discovering the objective sense of value or morality that has been ascribed to a particular object or behavior by that society. "General language, therefore, being formed for general use, must be moulded on some more general views, and must affix the epithets of praise or blame, in conformity to sentiments, which arise from the general interests of the community."[15] Although individual persons may, from their own idiosyncratic experience, derive values that do not adhere to the terms of praise or blame ascribed by general society, they will find, Hume argues, that it is simply too difficult to communicate meaningfully with others unless they adopt the objective sense of values and morals shared by other people and inscribed into language. For an example, Hume points out that chastity is a virtue praised in women, but less so in men, because, he insists, the social and economic utility of female chastity is higher for women owing to the objective social utility of controlling female reproduction.[16] Hume argues that this is why poetry and narrative that praises virtue and denigrates vice is so much more universally lauded than literature that explores criminal or prurient pleasures—not because moral art pleases the individual more, but because it conforms to shared objective values.[17]

With respect to linguistics and rhetoric, Johnson's skepticism far outstrips Hume's. While Hume takes for granted the social utility of language and its purpose of inculcating moral sentiment, Johnson describes English language usage as naturally tending toward disorder, confusion, and rhetorical manipulation. In his preface to the *Dictionary*, he laments the lack of order or reason he finds in the language:

> When I took the first survey of my undertaking, I found our speech copious without order, and energetick without rules: wherever I turned my view, there was perplexity to be disentangled, and confusion to be regulated; choice was to be made out of boundless variety, without any established principle of selection; adulterations were to be detected, without a settled test of purity; and modes of expression to be rejected or received, without the

suffrages of any writers of classical reputation or acknowledged
authority. (Yale *Works*, 18:74)

This description of language as an ever-growing and ever-changing enormous collection of signifiers with no authoritative sense of logic or order
is quite different from Hume's sense of language as a self-regulating tool
for creating social order. For Johnson, nothing must be taken for granted
by the author of literature, who must energetically apply himself to use
this imperfect tool in representing an imperfect world to readers who may
be willing to accept him at his every word.

Johnson's quarrel with Hume is not merely that Hume lacks respect for
God or religion; Johnson is consistently disturbed by empiricist descrip-
tions of morality and value that ascribe the source of value to "society" or
to the objective qualities inherent in the thing, person, or behavior under
observation. If there could be something like a "communal eye," to use
a term from Nabokov,[18] an objective perspective that houses the aggregate judgments of social utility and approbation, it would necessarily and
obviously be evil, according to Johnson. Hume assumes that the linguistic
terms for praise and blame that affix to objects and behaviors are inher-
ently correct because they necessarily represent shared values; Johnson
is far more skeptical about the ever-changing, ironic, easily manipulated
nature of linguistic meaning and value, especially in a literary context.
Johnson asserts in *Rambler* 4 that much of the popular literature written
and enjoyed in the early eighteenth century has little interest in praising
virtue, as Hume seems to think all true art must do, but instead serves to
titillate readers with vicarious pleasures and dangers that might arise from
immoral and hazardous behavior (Yale *Works*, 3:21–22). For Johnson, the
mind is not simply an impartial receptacle of information and objective
values gained through aggregate observation, but is driven by individual
desire, expectation, fear, and attention.

Ian Donaldson points out that in *The Vanity of Human Wishes*,
Johnson's subject, "Observation" itself, is pointedly excluded from any
particular subjective eye or even a divine perspective, but is intended
as a kind of satirical response to the empiricist fantasy of an objective
perspective against which human observation could be compared. Rather
than finding that "Observation" would conveniently validate the typical

normative values of English society, "Observation" in the poem reveals that human endeavor is universally delusional, and that an empiricist "common sense" of praiseworthy behavior encompasses a vast range of conflicting subjective self-deceptions. Donaldson writes, "*The Vanity of Human Wishes* might thus be described as a poem about the nature of human myopia: not a literal, physical myopia, but one that is spiritual and psychological."[19] For Johnson, moral failure is not caused by the limitations of one's empirical experience, but by the failure to develop moral clarity and purpose within oneself before engaging with the moral confusion of worldly values.

Johnson continually argues that subjective interest distorts observation through prejudice, perversity, and selfishness; however, without personal interest, there would be little motivation to gain experience among society at all. In *Idler* 80, he writes, "To know the world is necessary, since we were born for the help of one another; and to know it early is convenient, if it be only that we may learn early to despise it" (Yale *Works*, 2:251). In the space of one sentence, Johnson argues that observation is the only way to inspire compassion for humanity, and then that observation of humanity can only end in disgust for the society we observe. Although both of these impulses seem to have driven Johnson to write, often with apparently paradoxical results, neither is an impulse that arises from passively developing an objective sense of human nature.

In his critical writing, Johnson insists that literature must not simply represent an observation of nature that is recognizable to the worldly reader; rather, a true artist is one whose subjective representation changes the nature of the world for the reader. The eye of the poet is not best when it is most like the reader's own eye, or like some imagined communal eye, but when it clearly presents its own unique perspective, judgments, and meanings. For example, Johnson's praise for the poet James Thomson, qualified though it is, concentrates on Thomson's ability to employ observation and experience in the service of his subjective poetic vision:

> He thinks in a peculiar train, and he thinks always as a man
> of genius; he looks round on Nature and on Life, with the eye
> which Nature bestows only on a poet; the eye that distinguishes,
> in every thing presented to its view, whatever there is on which

imagination can delight to be detained, and with a mind that at once comprehends the vast, and attends to the minute. The reader of the *Seasons* wonders that he never saw before what Thomson shews him, and that he never yet has felt what Thomson impresses.[20]

The eye of the poet, according to Johnson, should change what the reader is capable of seeing by introducing a plausible alternate perspective, not by merely validating the reader's own perception or literary expectation. As long as the representation of the sensible world in the poem is deemed sufficiently accurate according to his own experience, then the reader will be likely to adopt, perhaps without even realizing it, the moral and aesthetic judgments inherent to the author's unique vision.

The potential failures of observation and subsequent representation are many, and Johnson shares much of Hume's concern about the limitations of empirical observation. The organs of perception may be impaired. One's field of observation may be limited by age, society, gender, education, and place. The conclusions drawn from observation may be unwittingly influenced by self-interest, or by a misguided sense that one has a clear understanding of God's will. Johnson's skepticism outstrips Hume's, however, in the matter of the mediation of experience through language. Rather than bringing experience closer to shared common sense, Johnson insists that the transformation of observation into language will warp the evidence of experience through the inaccuracies of the medium, no matter how perfectly employed. He is also far more skeptical about the role of the literary market, which may follow fashion or vice rather than wisdom or aesthetic quality. For Johnson, unlike Hume, the art of pleasing the reader has a dubious relationship with social and moral utility.

Johnson expresses particular concern about the rise of realistic fiction in the 1730s and 1740s. Unlike more formal art forms such as song or poetry, fiction may give a young reader the illusion of being somehow unmediated, as if it is an objective account of real events. Authors of realistic fiction in this period often embraced this deception, and used claims of veracity (or at least verisimilitude) as advertisements for their stories. The various "histories" and "lives" that appeared to have been written by their protagonists, and only edited by their authors, offered a metafictional pleasure, in that these stories were not only compelling and entertaining but also, possibly, in some sense, "true." Even those realistic fictions of the 1740s that do not claim to be actual memoirs offer something far more potentially tantalizing than romances and fantastic tales; they offer the promise of vicarious experience of human nature without the risks of immediate observation.

Johnson finds it unnerving that realistic fiction may be read for the purpose of gaining evidence about the real world. The conflation of fiction and reality was not, as for Hume, a reasonable means of gathering evidence about social values and judgments, but a kind of epistemic crisis, in that a reader could come to feel familiar with danger or pain without experiencing an aversive reaction. The epistemic irony of fiction is that it offers vicarious empirical knowledge without the wisdom one gains from real experience, unless the author has represented a clear subjective perspective. Rather, realistic fiction should call attention to the aesthetic intervention of the author, and thus allow the reader to participate in critical interpretation of the text. In *Rambler* 3, he writes:

> The task of an author is, either to teach what is not known, or to recommend known truths, by his manner of adorning them; either to let new light in upon the mind, and open new scenes to the prospect, or to vary the dress and situation of common objects, so as to give them fresh grace and more powerful attractions, to spread such flowers over the regions through which the intellect has already made its progress, as may tempt it to return, and take a second view of things too hastily passed over, or too negligently regarded. (Yale *Works*, 3:14–15)

Although Johnson clearly values the realistic object of art—that is, the representation of situations and experiences within the scope of life as it is lived by the average reader—he sees potential value only in a consciously transformative representational style, an active aesthetic intervention in the world, rather than an apparently naïve passivity of style.

In his clearest defense of consciously transformational representative aesthetics, *Rambler* 4, Johnson attacks the idea that any work of art that represents realistic objects can ever be truly passive in its representation of reality, or, even if it could be, that it would be worth reading at all. "If the world be promiscuously described, I cannot see of what use it can be to read the account; or why it may not be as safe to turn the eye immediately upon mankind, as upon a mirror which shows all that presents itself without discrimination" (Yale *Works*, 3:22). If literature were, in some sense, exactly like the fallen, morally confused world it describes, it would be entirely useless to the reader who already lives in and experiences the world first-hand. He goes on:

> It is therefore not a sufficient vindication of a character, that it is drawn as it appears, for many characters ought never to be drawn; nor of a narrative, that the train of events is agreeable to observation and experience, for that observation which is called knowledge of the world, will be found much more frequently to make men cunning than good. (Yale *Works*, 3:21)

When an author seeks to represent the world without clearly providing a moral perspective that mediates the events, the result may be that the events that please the reader most will be those that seem most attractive. Although Johnson seems here not to see the aesthetic value of realistic representation, he admits that it is exactly the pretense that there is no aesthetic intervention that allows for this disturbing moral confusion.

In a literary genre consumed largely by those who lack the moral certitude and experience of life to judge the world itself, this moral absence may even produce a kind of delusional false knowledge. Of novels, Johnson writes,

> They are the entertainments of minds unfurnished with ideas, and therefore easily susceptible of impressions; not fixed by principles, and therefore easily following the current of fancy; not informed by experience, and consequently open to every false suggestion and partial account. (Yale *Works*, 3:21)

Without first-hand knowledge of the world, young readers may, Johnson fears, fill their minds with false observations of human nature. This young reader with whom Johnson is particularly concerned in *Rambler*

4 is highly susceptible to narrative fiction that represents common life experiences because they have not yet had these experiences and look to literature as a sort of conduct book, telling him what to expect from life and how to behave.

> When an adventurer is levelled with the rest of the world, and acts in such scenes of the universal drama, as may be the lot of any other man; young spectators fix their eyes upon him with closer attention, and hope by observing his behavior and success to regulate their own practices, when they shall be engaged in the like part. (Yale *Works*, 3:21)

The pretense of writers who represent common life as outside the jurisdiction of divine law is often that the world itself is apparently not subject to any such law. The wicked often go unpunished, the corrupt may be charming, the innocent suffer, and the benevolent languish for want of recognition or earthly reward. In respect to the nature of the world, Johnson and the author of this kind are in clear agreement.

Yet his belief in the power of aesthetic language causes Johnson to censure such authors because, to the young and inexperienced reader, if not all readers, fiction contains within it the power of moral instruction. Fictions of this morally confused kind, though more representationally "realistic," fail, in Johnson's account, to take advantage of the morally instructive potential of literature, instead falling prey to moral cynicism. The emergent aesthetic of realism threatens to become the pornography of moral poverty.

In *Samuel Johnson and the Impact of Print*, Alvin Kernan argues that Johnson's literary criticism is so demanding in part because of his peculiar conception of the "reader," a necessarily fictional person whose perspective must be imagined in order to construct a coherent understanding of the potential relationship of influence that published texts create between authors and readers. He writes:

> When seen in the long tradition of literary audience-making, Johnson's common reader is not just a reflection of an actual historical audience of readers, nor merely an attempt to control

the interpretation of books, nor only a way of overcoming the isolation of reader and author. The reader is all of these things, but ultimately he is also a way of attributing to letters, as if its nature were a prior fact, a certain kind of existence and worth that in part corresponds to the realities of print culture, and in part realizes a conception of what letters at its best might be.[21]

Johnson's imagined reader is active in response to texts, not merely praising or rejecting their aesthetic qualities, but also learning from them in morally significant ways that demand critical attention. As Kernan asserts, Johnson was keenly aware of the reach and effects of the medium of print, and he devoted as much attention to imagining the possible responses of readers as to describing the purposes and perspectives of authors. Rather than envisioning the author–reader relationship as a one-sided exchange in which the author fills the passive reader with the information in the text, Johnson depicts the relationship of authors and readers as a complicated web of aesthetic, hermeneutic, and moral questions.

Unlike Hume, who takes for granted that writing is necessarily a socialized representation of experience, Johnson is critical of the Augustan movement toward realistic representation, which, in its quest to destroy the sentimental abstractions that deform perception, often eschews moral prudence. Poetry and fiction, Johnson argues, must not be seen as passive media through which unscrupulous representation yields perverse moral instruction. Rather, he argues that authors have the duty to offer mediation between worldly experience and moral truth. Johnson suggests that this may only be possible if the author relinquishes the claim to know the objective truth about the world.

## III. Nabokov's Subjective Language

In 1959, Vladimir Nabokov contributed an essay titled "The Servile Path" to *On Translation*, a collection edited by Reuben Arthur Brower.[22] During this time, Nabokov was in the midst of several years spent on an experimental translation of Alexander Pushkin's *Eugene Onegin*. In a later poem addressed to Pushkin, Nabokov would describe his *Onegin* as "Dovedroppings on your monument."[23] He became convinced in the process of this work that to forcibly render the rhyming Russian tetrameter into English verse would commit unforgivable violence against the original work—all the more so if the resulting poem was functionally poetic in a language that had little influence on its author. Many of the essays in Brower's volume begin with bold declarations of epistemological commitments; Nabokov's begins with an account of the literary and pedagogical fashions of Russia during Pushkin's childhood.

To translate, Nabokov insists, is not to strip the language away to reveal the reality that may then be hidden behind another language, but to understand what it meant for the author to use a language, and what it means for readers to use another. Nabokov rejects the possibility of an empirical reality that exists outside of the subjective linguistic experiences the author and the reader each have. In his essay on translation, he includes an anecdote about wondering what Americans know about the English words for plant life, and asking his college students if they can identify a common tree outside the window (an American elm). "[O]ne, a girl, said she guessed it was a shade tree" (103). The difficulty with translation is not merely discovering whether the word for a "real" thing is extant in the target language, but whether words that describe a particular category of things have any immediate meaning for the typical reader in that language. In Pushkin's Russian, Nabokov suggests, naming a tree has an aesthetic purpose and immediacy for the reader that naming even a familiar tree would not have for most twentieth-century Americans.

Likewise, he wants the reader to know that Pushkin's seeming familiarity with English authors such as Byron or Sterne was almost certainly through very poor French translations, or even Russian translations of French translations of English. Here one finds the basis for many of Nabokov's most humorous passages in *Pale Fire*, such as the absurd semi-English response of the fictional Zemblan Shakespeare translator Conmal to one of his critics:

> I am not slave! Let be my critic slave.
> I cannot be. And Shakespeare would not want thus.
> Let drawing students copy the acanthus,
> I work with Master on the architrave! (*Pale Fire*, 286)

Like Nabokov's students, unable to name the elm, the reader of Conmal in English would be unlikely to be able to identify the features of Greek architecture enough to justify using them as a metaphor. Yet the architectural metaphor is precisely apt for what Nabokov ultimately chose to do in his translation of *Eugene Onegin*, sacrificing poetic wit and loveliness (the acanthus, the decorative plant represented on the frieze) to focus on the structural narrative (the architrave, the base of the entablature supported by the columns). The translation, published in 1964 with the subtitle "A Novel in Verse," abandoned rhyme, line length, and idiomatic ease while preserving the fundamental iambic meter shared by Russian and English poetry.

Edmund Wilson's famously exasperated review of Nabokov's Pushkin would put an end to their personal friendship; Wilson could not understand why a writer of Nabokov's towering intellect and ethereal beauty would render a poem they both loved into flat-footed literalism. Wilson writes, "It would be more to the point for the student to look up the Russian word than to have to have recourse to the *OED* for an English word he has never seen and which he will never have occasion to use."[24] But sending the reader to the dictionary (or even to the original Russian)— demanding that the reader struggle to read a text beautifully constructed in a very different language—was Nabokov's intent. The translation is self-consciously, rhetorically unaesthetic. The "Servile Path" he describes is one in which the translation never rivals the original, but instead teaches the reader how to become a fellow servant.

Just a few pages after Nabokov's essay in *On Translation*, Willard Van Orman Quine's very different essay, "Meaning and Translation," begins: "Empirical meaning is what remains when, given discourse together with all its stimulatory conditions, we peel away the verbiage. It is what the sentences of one language and their firm translations in a completely alien language have in common."[25] Quine's philosophy of language is in precise contrast to Nabokov's. For Quine, words are arbitrary sounds used within a society to signify a particular object or idea about objects. This empiricist understanding of language, which was first articulated by John Locke in 1689 in *An Essay Concerning Human Understanding*, assumes that, were the object itself present, interlocutors who speak very different languages could "mean" the same thing by gesturing at it.

In his 1960 book *Word and Object,* Quine equates several very different conceptions of pragmatism and empiricism as a warrant for the project he is undertaking. He interprets Samuel Johnson's reported stone-kicking refutation of George Berkeley as intellectual kin to Ludwig Wittgenstein's pragmatist injunction in the preface of the *Tractatus Logico-Philosophicus*: "[W]hat can be said at all can be said clearly, and what we cannot talk about, we must pass over in silence."[26] Clear speech, Quine argues, is based in empirical verifiability, reducible even in abstract terms to recognizable elements from sensory information. He writes, "The mistake comes only in seeking an implicit sub-basement of conceptualization, or of language."[27] But even eighteenth-century empiricists quarreled about what constituted the conceptualization of ideas, especially through language, or whether objects themselves have a material existence beyond our sensory perception of them. Quine assumes throughout his work that the truth "behind" language is in the reality of things themselves, and that truth is not constituted in any way by the language we use to conceptualize those things.

To Nabokov, this model of linguistic meaning is based on a naïve and potentially dangerous error. An empiricist theory of language ignores that the semiotic signification even of sensible objects occurs within a framework of meaning that is complicated by accidents of language, personal experience, cultural signification, humor, trauma, desire, loss, and pleasure. Nabokov's frustration that his students cannot identify an elm tree is illustrative. They are young (making him feel old), they are Americans (making him feel foreign), they are uninterested in nature and uneducated about natural science, and they lack an immediate, emotional, romantic, linguistic history with any particular trees. How could they understand him at all, unless they do the work of trying to understand what trees mean to him?

In Nabokov's fiction, trees are intimate instruments of signification. The transplanted Iraqi "shattal tree" where Ada and Van first make sexual contact in *Ada, or Ardor* is a Nabokovian invention, but its name evokes the Shatt al-Arab River that marks the confluence of the Tigris and the Euphrates near the Persian Gulf. There is some intratextual editorial disagreement between Ada and Van about whether there were apples (an apple falls "with a thud" at the moment of contact, but Van insists "no apple trees grow in Iraq") or caterpillars (what thread did Van pull from his lip?), or whether there was an "Eden National Park" in Iraq at the time the tree was supposedly transplanted.[28] As we are constantly reminded throughout *Ada*, Nabokov's most intertextual and emotional novel, the banal fact of the diegetic reality of a particular item or specimen is laughably irrelevant in the face of the web of signification offered by the text—an intersubjective, speculative, shimmering account of two entire lives, written and edited by themselves as now-elderly incestuous lovers to whom only a little time remains. The invention of a semiotically infinite tree to house their first contact seems far more appropriate than a reference to one that could be found on the reader's own street, even if it is less empirically convenient.

Likewise, in *Pale Fire*, trees are sites of wordplay, evocations of pain or love, metaphors, and markers of personal time. At the beginning of Canto Three, John Shade's dazzling opening line and a half introduce the account of semi-academic studies of death at I. P. H., the Institute of Preparation for the Hereafter where he had served as a visiting lecturer. "*L'if*, lifeless tree! Your great Maybe, Rabelais:/The grand potato" (52). *L'if*, French for the yew, is a poisonous, long-lived conifer whose name sounds like "life," "if," and "I. P. H.," and, translated, "you," to whom the poem is addressed. The form of a tree suggests choices or chance, fate, and limitation. "The grand potato" is Shade's Anglicization of Rabelais's purported last words: "Je m'en vais chercher un grand peut-être"—the grand potato being, in this case, life after death. In this case, it matters somewhat that the reader knows, or is willing to learn, something about trees, and the possible ways that trees can convey meaning as words. The reader for whom the elm was indistinguishable from the oak is suddenly ushered into a semiotic orchard in which every tree contains a world of meaning in itself.

Unpacking all of the significations made by even a single word in Nabokov's fiction is ultimately tedious, and probably impossible. In Edmund Wilson's damning review of Nabokov's Pushkin, he seems to have suddenly discovered that his erstwhile friend is a boring, narcissistic snob, because he uses words, images, and phrases in his translation that are inconveniently obscure to the average reader:

> Mr. Nabokov is in the habit of introducing any job of this kind which he undertakes by an announcement that he is unique and

incomparable and that everybody else who has attempted it is an oaf and an ignoramus, incompetent as a linguist and scholar, usually with the implication that he is also a low-class person and a ridiculous personality.[29]

From an empiricist linguistic perspective, that could be the only possible conclusion; the author has chosen not to share a social, empirically relevant language with the reader, but instead insists that we research all of the author's own private meanings in order to get even a basic understanding of the text.

This roughly corresponds to the task as it has generally been undertaken by the narrow field of scholars who have chosen Nabokov's oeuvre for analysis. *Pale Fire: The Magic of Artistic Discovery* is only one volume of Brian Boyd's scholarly endeavors to explicate one slim fictional text through the lens of Nabokov's biography, intellectual interests, and linguistic associations.[30] Paul J. Thibault's *Social Semiotics as Praxis* develops an entire system of semiotic analysis based on a comparison of two short passages from *Ada* and *Lolita*.[31] Readers who wish to engage with Nabokov in any kind of "good faith" find themselves taking what Nabokov himself called "the servile path," treading obsequiously within the footsteps left by the author in order to guide others in that narrow way. Perhaps Nabokov would argue that even the bad faith critic, like his own Kinbote, or like Wilson, cannot help but display his own ignorance and hubris when refusing to take that servile path behind the author who has gone ahead.

Literary writing that demands servility on the part of the good reader must, in turn, offer something that typical empiricist realism cannot. At its best, realistic literature offers what Alexander Pope (who is also repeatedly invoked in *Pale Fire*) declared to be the highest end of wit: "*True Wit* is *Nature* to Advantage drest, / What oft was *Thought*, but ne'er so well *Exprest*."[32] The revelations provided by empiricist literature offer us new ways of thinking about the world that we recognize as this one. The possibility of subjective literature, such as Nabokov's, is that it might construct a new world about which we might have revelations of our own. In her article "Playing a Game of Worlds in Nabokov's *Pale Fire*," Martine Hennard writes, "Nabokov invites the reader to travel in the imaginary 'new worlds' of his fictions and, by defamiliarizing it, enables us to recover the sense of marvel and wonder which characterizes the reading experience."[33] Inviting the reader to perform the laborious tasks required by his strange, inimitable, subjective fictions, Nabokov also offers that reader a momentary escape from common-sense, pragmatic empiricism, and from the interpretive limitations of our own minds.

In *Pale Fire*, Kinbote criticizes the trompe l'oeil art of a Zemblan master named Eystein who inserts panels of real material near their painted imitations; Kinbote firmly states that, as talented as Eystein is, accurate mimesis alone is not true art. "'[R]eality' is neither the subject nor the object of true art which creates its own special reality having nothing to do with the average 'reality' perceived by the communal eye" (130). Although this passage, like the entire work, is so rife with irony that it is impossible to unravel fully, it seems likely that Kinbote is representing something of Nabokov's aesthetic theory whenever he approaches the topic of artistic purpose. Like Kinbote, Nabokov finds it disturbing when an author or artist attempts to represent "the world" as if from an objective or common perspective. To be human is to see the world as an individual, and to be an artist is to invite the audience to try to see out of one's own particular eyes.

After the climax of Canto Three in *Pale Fire*, John Shade has made peace with the fact that his mind will continually seek out patterns and meanings ("Some kind of link-and-bobolink" [l.812]) in the random evidence gleaned through sensory experience. Canto Four, then, is largely a description of the poet attempting to shave in the bathtub, cutting himself badly while composing lines in his mind.[34] As he composes, he loses track of where he is and what he is doing, unable to see, hear, or feel what is happening as he thinks through private images and ideas before settling them into words for others to read. A true artist, in Nabokov's sense, Shade is not a copier of nature, but a magician, inventing a new reality for our consideration.

The later literary works of Vladimir Nabokov grow increasingly resistant to the empiricist aesthetics of the mid-twentieth century, and even to empiricist philosophies of language, which attempted to reconcile all representation to the communication of common, shared, verifiable experience. Completing the endnote for *Lolita*, written a year after the novel was published, Nabokov writes:

> My private tragedy, which cannot, and indeed should not, be anybody's concern, is that I had to abandon my natural idiom, my untrammeled, rich, and infinitely docile Russian tongue for a second-rate brand of English, devoid of any of those apparatuses—the baffling mirror, the black velvet backdrop, the implied associations and traditions—which the native illusionist, fractails flying, can magically use to transcend the heritage in his own way. (*Lolita*, 316–17)

Even in the language itself, these works were the product of intellectual, cultural, aesthetic exile, in addition to the more literal national kind. Nabokov's fondness for Samuel Johnson may have been because he, unlike Quine, read Johnson as similarly exiled from the dominant empiricism and shared experience of his contemporary literary and intellectual culture. Reserving a category of the truly subjective in art and language would prove to be prescient in the case of both writers, who lived just long enough to witness the rise of aesthetic cultures that became newly invested in private experiences of trauma, desire, pleasure, and anxiety.

## IV. Conclusion

In drawing this comparison between the subjective aesthetics of Samuel Johnson and Vladimir Nabokov, I do not mean to suggest that either author would share the other's sense of what, precisely, exists or matters outside of a strictly empiricist epistemology. However, the similarities in their frustrations with their contemporaries' empiricist aesthetics and philosophies of language are striking. Especially as Johnson and Nabokov entered into the later years of their long and productive literary and critical careers, they each seemed to disengage more completely from the expectation that their work would reflect the dominant intellectual cultures that had elevated them as unwitting avatars.

At the time of Samuel Johnson's death in 1784, Immanuel Kant had recently published his *Prolegomena to Any Future Metaphysics* (1783), in which he describes the failure of Hume's empiricism as his unwillingness to do the difficult work of analyzing the web of paradoxes created by subjective cognition: "If our intuition had to be of the kind that represented things *as they are in themselves*, then absolutely no intuition *a priori* would take place, but it would always be empirical."[35] He goes on to demonstrate throughout the text that pure empiricism, which identifies knowledge only in the world as verified through the senses, leaves out a vast range of human thought and endeavor—in mathematics, in natural science, and in the study of the mind or soul. Kant's development of analytical methods for metaphysical analysis marked a shift in philosophical discourse from the study of objects to the study of subjects, not isolated from the world, but participating in society as individuals.

Likewise, in 1977 Nabokov died just as philosophical consensus was turning away from the empiricist linguistic pragmatism of Bertrand Russell, Ludwig Wittgenstein, and W.V.O. Quine. The influence of French theorists, including psychoanalyst Jacques Lacan and semioticians Roland Barthes and Jacques Derrida, helped to unsettle the intellectual consensus for empiricist meaning-making. In 1989, Charles Taylor published *Sources of the Self*, a history of the modern era told through the expanding and contracting role played by subjectivity in philosophy and art. Taylor is primarily concerned that the periodic return of Enlightenment-era empiricist pragmatism, as in the early nineteenth century and the mid-twentieth century, has been linked to periods of political extremism, censorship, industrialization, and the dehumanization of political subjects throughout the modern era. He writes, "The concept of an inexhaustible inner domain is the correlative of the power of expressive self-articulation."[36] Without recourse both to knowledge of the world and knowledge of the self, the artist is either limited to an already-interpreted world with its own ready-made meanings or trapped in the limitless abyss of private signification. Both Samuel Johnson and Vladimir Nabokov negotiated the terms of their artistry as reconciliations between their own subjective systems of meaning and value and the worlds where they invited their worldly readers to play.

# CHAPTER EIGHT

# Johnson and Borges

## Some Reflections

*Greg Clingham*

Da tomar un solo autor yo habría tomado a Johnson,
que permite meterse en *The Lives of the Poets*, en el prólogo
a Shakespeare, en el prólogo al *Diccionario*.[1]

[If I had to single out an author, I would choose Johnson, because
he engages the reader imaginatively in the *Lives of the Poets*, and in
the Preface to Shakespeare, and in the Preface to the *Dictionary*.]

Borges in conversation with Adolfo Bioy Casares

## 1

What are we to make of Juan Luis Borges' comment? What are the implications of not just anyone, but of Borges specifically saying that Johnson's writing engages the reader imaginatively? What qualities in these works appealed to Borges? What makes Johnson *the* author for Borges? What new appreciation of Johnson might become possible by taking Borges' interest seriously? Indeed, what can Johnson have to do with Borges—fiction writer, essayist, reviewer, poet, translator, lecturer, and conversationalist whose name is synonymous with fantasy, dream, and postmodern playfulness? This essay is a report on knowledge and traces a brief history of illumination.

2

Borges was famously cosmopolitan; he had an English grandmother (Frances Anne Haslam); he lived in Europe as a young man, and grew up speaking Spanish, English, French, and German. As Norman di Giovanni notes, "Borges's feeling for English prose often amounted to a preference for the English language over his own as a writing medium."[2] He wrote some of his works—such as his autobiography—in English, and only later translated them into Spanish. He read *Don Quixote* first in English (and when he read it in Spanish, thought it sounded like a translation).[3] He learned and loved Old Norse and Celtic, and proffered his knowledge as Professor of English and American Literature at the University of Buenos Aires from 1955 until 1970. He had visiting appointments at Texas, Harvard, Oklahoma, and New York universities, and gave lectures in Britain and Europe on English literature. Making no formal distinction between prose and verse, Borges' writings engage variously with Shakespeare, Donne, Milton, Joyce, Whitman, Emerson, Cervantes, Dante, Kafka, and Hugo. He frequently singles out Chatterton, Stevenson, and Wells, on whom—di Giovanni notes—he modelled his own prose (*Lesson*, 56).

I had come across references by Borges to Johnson; initially these suggested no remarkable interest nor offered any critical insight. In 2000, Martín Arias and Martín Hadis published the transcript of twenty-five classes Borges conducted in 1966, on works from Anglo-Saxon texts to Robert Louis Stevenson, at the University of Buenos Aires, including two classes on Johnson and one on Boswell's *Life of Johnson*.[4] The transcript of these classes are notes taken by students in class as a study aid rather than an attempt to capture the views or sayings of a celebrity. As Arias and Hadis point out, a few factual and grammatical corrections were made to the notes for publication, but no attempt was made to "modify Borges's spoken language, nor edit his sentences, which have reached us intact with their repetitions and their platitudes" (*Professor Borges*, xi).

This extraordinary opportunity to gain insight into the views and to hear the *voice* of one of the great twentieth-century writers was particularly piquant. Alas! Platitudes prevail. The observations seldom rise above the commonplace, if not the trivial. We hear about Johnson's interest in ghosts, his violent temper, his gluttonous appetite, his untidiness, his hatred of the Scots, his dislike of Milton, and the fortunate advent of Boswell, who made not only Johnson's reputation but his identity as well. The class on *Rasselas* offers little more. Imlac *is* Johnson, and there is little sense of the tale's artifice, narrative purpose, fictional perspective, or philosophical depth. We are told it is written in a "slow, musical style … in which all the sentences are perfectly balanced," and that it is filled with Johnson's melancholy, a "rejection of man's happiness" (*Professor Borges*, 82, 84). Borges is reported as saying, "Johnson's works have literary value, but as is often the case, knowing the person and appreciating him gives one much more desire to read his work. That's why it is a good idea to read Boswell's biography before reading Johnson's work" (96).

Whether or not Borges' students had stripped the intelligence and the nuance out of his words in their reportage, or whether (as Hadis notes) Borges chose to interest his students by opting for plot summary and biography, very little criticism can be salvaged from these documents. It was not, then, a surprise to me, when I asked a senior professor of Latin American studies at Yale about Borges' possible interest in Johnson, that the answer was categorical: "No, there is nothing there."

3

Yet, one occasionally had glimpses of something deeper. For example, Borges singles out a Johnsonian retort as an example of great verbal abuse: "Your wife, sir, under pretense of keeping a bawdy house, receives stolen goods."[5] To his students, Borges gave the following advice:

> If a book bores you, leave it; don't read it because it is famous, don't read it because it is modern, don't read a book because it is old. If a book is tedious to you, leave it, even if that book is *Paradise Lost*—which is not tedious to me—or *Don Quixote*—which is also not tedious to me … . Reading should be a form of happiness. (*Professor Borges*, 252)

This is essentially the Johnson who was easily bored with books, who seldom finished a book he began, and who said, memorably, in reviewing Soame Jenyns, "The only end of writing is to enable readers better to enjoy life, or better to endure it."[6] In 1963 Bioy reports Borges saying that Johnson was more English than Shakespeare:

> When I said that Johnson is much more English than Shake-speare, the English listened to me with an open mind and they said, "Alright," but it was an idea to which they had to accustom themselves, this had not occurred to them, but if it was fair they had to get accustomed to it. (Casares, 947)

Borges was given to making provocative critical statements, yet he returns to this idea of Johnson's quintessential Englishness. In 1960, for example, we have: "Which writers are essentially English? Samuel Butler, Johnson, Wordsworth, perhaps" (Casares, 663). What might this have meant for Borges? In a seminar on translation at New York University in 1971, in response to di Giovanni's remark that "Borges' spoken English is unbelievably good, but when he writes English he becomes stiff and formal," Borges said, "We all want to be Dr. Johnson, I dare say" (Lesson, 108). When "purity of language" came up in the same seminar, Borges declared, "If I could write eighteenth-century English, that would be my best performance. But I can't. One can't be Addison or Johnson at will" (Lesson, 108).

These Borgesian remarks suggest that "Englishness" lay in style, even if the Addisonian and the Johnsonian prose styles propose quite different characteristics as models. Still, there is an urgency to Borges' observation about Johnson and, without knowing what to make of it, I thought the interest in Johnson by Borges, a writer with wide comparative global associations and modernist and postmodernist appeal, was worth pondering.

Willis Barnstone recounts the following scene with Borges in his apartment in Buenos Aires:

> Borges felt his way to his library and pulled out a heavy volume of the first half of Samuel Johnson's dictionary.
> "A friend gave this to me. Not the first edition, but from that time. They haven't reprinted it, they should you know." Borges

took my arm and we went out for the elevator, about ten steps from the door.

It took us a very long time to reach the elevator because he was speaking avidly about Samuel Johnson. Finally, we were in the street, on the way to the newspaper offices of *La Nación*. (Burgin *Conversations*, 142)

What strikes me about this vignette—beyond Borges' glee in possessing an early edition of the *Dictionary*—is that his avid *speech* about Johnson is of no interest to Barnstone. It goes unrecorded. It is one thing to want to make one's way to the elevator; it is another to miss the opportunity for reflection later on. Only a few, perfunctory references to Johnson occur in Barnstone's other, more extensive Borges memoirs.[7] This deafness to Borges' enthusiasm is perhaps typical of critics and biographers, who usually expect him to adhere to certain interests. One wonders if this is not the case with Norman Di Giovanni, Borges' distinguished American translator, who, like Barnstone, spent years in Borges' company, and who collaborated with Borges on "An Autobiographical Essay" (1969).[8] In the essay, Borges describes his reading of many English, American, French, Spanish, and Argentinian writers, yet there is only one mention of Johnson, about a visit to his birthplace in Lichfield. Could Borges' silence in the autobiographical essay have at least partly been the influence of his American collaborator?

## 4

Quite serendipitously, one day I spotted a 1,800-page volume in Spanish on the new acquisitions table in the Bertrand Library at Bucknell—a tome entitled *Borges*, edited by Daniel Martino and published in 2006 by Destino.[9] These conversations between Borges and Adolfo Bioy Casares (1914–1999) span the years 1947 to 1986. There was no index, so I dipped in, trusting to my modicum of Spanish without great expectation, but discovering to my astonishment that Johnson's name often cropped up. Reading at random, I learned within a few minutes that Borges and Bioy had edited and translated works by Johnson (and by Thomas Browne). In July 1954 Bioy notes, "Con Borges enumeramos libros nuestros que esperan en editorials. En Emecé: *Suma* de Johnson, con notas mías; *Suma* de sir Thomas Browne, com notas de los dos." ["We made a list of our books that are awaiting publication at various presses. At Emecé, the works of Johnson with my notes; works by Sir Thomas Browne with notes by both of us"].[10] However, in May 1955, he remarks, "Como la busca da trabajo, siento que soy yo el que debe disculparse, pero la verdad es que nos han extraviado el libro; recupero las *Sumas* de Browne y Johnson (comentadas por nosotros)" ["We talked about the works of Browne and Johnson, written and annotated by us, retrieved from Emecé because never published"] (Casares, 130). These manuscripts and notes remain unpublished. According to Alberto Manguel, the former director of the National Library of Argentina (2016–2018), they were acquired from the Bioy estate in 2016, and are still to be catalogued.[11]

Reading more systematically in the volume of Borges–Bioy conversations, I realized how enmeshed Johnson was in their thinking. The pervasiveness of their references to Johnson's writings and to Boswell's *Life* suggested more than a passing acquaintance. The spontaneity with which they turned to Johnson in discussing literary topics, as well as educational, social, and political issues, suggested more than a *pro forma* approval or a cursory knowledge. In these conversations we find no plot summary, as in the 1966 class notes, but lively intellectual engagement and general critical statements, such as that in the epigraph quoted above, from 1956. At the same time, we also have minute knowledge, as in the following from 1959:

> Bioy: We talked about Jan de Panonia—or Vitalis—a Hungarian writer who passed on to Joachim du Bellay, Quevedo, and Spenser the idea that the only eternal thing in Rome was the transient Tiber. Borges: "It is interesting that Boswell quotes the verses by Quevedo with inaccurate punctuation, and Johnson attributes them to Vitalis." (Casares, 533)

The point about this cryptic exchange is not obvious. Not only do Bioy and Borges *know* Palermo (or Vitalis), du Bellay, and Quevedo, but Borges knows the *punctuation* of the poem by Quevedo, *knows* that Boswell got it wrong, and *knows* that Johnson attributed the lines to another in their discussion as recorded by Boswell. We learn from the Hill–Powell edition of the *Life* that it was Owen Cambridge who quotes a "Spanish writer's" lines on the eternal nature of the Tiber,[12] and that Boswell's editors, citing H. Gordon Ward in *Notes and Queries* (1929), identify the writer as Quevedo (*Boswell's Life*, 3:518). Johnson, however, informs Cambridge that the writer is not Quevedo, but Janus Vitalis (or Giano Vitale), and quotes two lines from Vitalis' poem *De Roma* (*Boswell's Life*, 3, 251). Hill and Powell, for their part, note the perpetuation of a spelling error in Johnson's quotation (*Boswell's Life*, 3:251n3). The intertextual knot under consideration here reveals Borges' interest in European humanism, his retentive memory, and his extraordinary knowledge of Johnsonian scholia. Indeed, Bioy Casares' volume of conversations with Borges makes it clear that, for Borges, Johnson was a kind of *"point de repere,"* in Matthew Arnold's words about the *Lives of the Poets*, "points which stand as so many natural centres, and by returning to which we can always find our way again, if we are embarrassed."[13]

The scenes conjured up by these conversations are fascinating: Borges and Bioy turning to Dr. Johnson—of all people—to open a door to European humanism and to English literature, while also helping them to formulate responses to social, political, and educational problems during the Peron era. Talking about the stultifying effect on the minds of young people of the system of public examination in Argentina in 1959, Borges said, "In contrast to us, Johnson thought that people have become too uncritical, too respectful of almost any ideas on offer, that not all knowledge is useful knowledge, and, indeed, that some knowledge is downright frivolous" (Casares, 488–89).

These conversations, from which I have quoted sparsely, suggest that Borges saw much *in* and perhaps much of *himself* in Johnson.

What *did* Borges see?

## 5

One thing Borges saw was a near-blind man, like himself, using his imagination, his rhetorical and creative grasp of language, and his deep and broad humanistic learning to engage with intellectual life, to create a mythic persona for himself as writer and as *character*. Blindness is a variable physical and mental state of consciousness for both Borges and

Johnson, in the sense that the degree of their sightlessness varied and changed over time. Chris Mounsey draws attention to the need to triangulate our understanding of one's physical abilities, and the perceptions and experience that accompany them: "Capacity, capability, and encounter ... can help to guide the analysis of experience, and highlight the relationship between body mind and other people."[14] *Some* degree of sightlessness is a lived experience for both Borges and Johnson, and blindness as a trope for the human condition operates strongly in the writings and conversation of both men. Borges often referred to his blindness, and Johnson never discussed his, though it was lifelong and, presumably, formative. Lennard Davis remarks that Boswell and others were strikingly blind to the clear physical traces in Johnson's eyes and face of his variable sight. Rather, they invested rhetorical skills in *not* seeing and explaining those traits: "How false and contemptible then are all the remarks which have been made to the prejudice either of his candour or of his philosophy, founded upon a supposition that he was almost blind" (*Boswell's Life*, 1:42).[15] For Davis, "the evolving interest in disability, and the paradoxical aestheticizing of it in Johnson's life, is actually part of a historical and cultural transition in which the modern discourse of disability became consolidated" (56). In the course of the eighteenth century, "disabilities" moved from being unremarkable, if not invisible, to a modality commanding scientific and medical languages that signified widely, as witness the historiography of Foucault. To wit, recent scholarship has historicized and theorized "disabilities" in the eighteenth century, but not Johnson's blindness.[16]

In the *Dictionary* Johnson defines "blindness" as "want of sight" and "ignorance; intellectual darkness," and his writings, and Borges', move constantly between the poles of insight and blindness. This attention to "blindness" in its various manifestations produces—or at least accompanies—a powerful *inwardness* in both men.[17] This makes for a powerful, radiant, seductive *eudemonia* that others notice and revere, to which friends gravitate, that biographers seek to capture, that carries over into their everyday lives, and that informs their evaluation of literature and their views of literary creation. In consequence, the shape and meaning of their lives of writing have been the subject of debate, recollection, and elaboration by biographers, critics, cultural appropriators, and friends and acquaintances. (This chapter is no exception.) Indeed, their lives were and their afterlives have likewise been governed by terms more readily associated with modern celebrity. Just as Johnson had Boswell, Hawkins, Thrale, Murphy, Shaw, Reed, Cooke, Steevens, Tyers, and Towers, so Borges had Bioy Cesares, di Giovanni, Barnstone, Richard Burgin, Richard Stern, Selden Rodman, Donald Yates, Alastair Reid, Rita Guibert, L. S. Dembo, Ronald Christ, Alexander Coleman, and Miguel Enguídanos. Their celebrity, though not my subject *per se*, does describe a discourse I touch on. This is a transparent mechanism for producing images of cultural and personal significance, in which the subject of representation—Borges or Johnson—is disclosed as an *invisible* sign, but one with a *real effect* on others and on cultural formation.[18] The iconic status of Borges or Johnson is thus inseparable from their language and their physical appearance, the latter of which was *visually* striking—Johnson's ungainly size and rolling gait, Borges' stark eyes, blank face and bumbling movement—yet also oddly *invisible* in critical and artistic representations of the two men.

Boswell-as-trope looms large in Borges' life, just as Boswell the friend and mentee does in Johnson's. Various biographers half-consciously play Boswell to Borges' Johnson. In Martino's edition of the Bioy–Borges conversations, Bioy is explicitly Boswell—responding, explicating, elaborating, implementing, suggesting, challenging, and collaborating with Borges, and often referring to Boswell's book in the act of doing so. Like Boswell, Bioy came under attack for venality, indulgence, and a perverse misrepresentation of the hero (the illuminated yet soiled object of desire). In reviewing the Bioy–Borges conversations in the *Times Literary Supplement*, Daniel Waissbein, for example, saw Bioy's Borges "not as Borges as he was, but a diminished, malevolent, repetitive, silly and arrogant Borges, as seen through Bioy's capricious perception of humanity in general, and, in this instance, Borges in particular."[19] Borges himself made no such complaint. Having met Bioy, fifteen years his junior, in 1930, in 1969 Borges celebrated their many collaborative projects, and acknowledged how much he had learned from Bioy:

> It is always taken for granted in these cases that the elder man is the master and the younger his disciple. This may have been true at the outset, but several years later, when we began to work together, Bioy was really and secretly the master ... . Opposing

my taste for the pathetic, the sententious, and the baroque, Bioy
made me feel that quietness and restraint are more desirable. If I
may be allowed a sweeping statement, Bioy led me gradually to
classicism. ("Autobiographical Essay," 245–46)

Others were would-be Boswells to Borges-as-Johnson. For biographer James Woodall this role was played by Néstor Ibarra, a young
television, radio, and sports personality (1938–2005), a longtime friend of
Borges.[20] For di Giovanni (1933–2017), Borges' Boswell was di Giovanni
himself—though he does not say so openly. His fresh, audacious accounts
of his five-year literary collaboration with Borges are self-serving, but
energetic, intelligent, illuminating, and commercially successful. He is a
worthy Boswell, though quite different from Bioy or Barnstone, both of
whom had successful careers independent of Borges, while di Giovanni's
reputation rests largely on his translations of Borges' essays and stories.
Eventually the jealousy and vindictiveness of di Giovanni's competitors,
vying for possession of Borges' archive and, as it were, of his textual body
after his death, overwhelmed di Giovanni.[21] Similar battles among Johnson's biographers are well known, and the battles have come down to our
own time as individuals and groups strive to control how we interpret
Johnson's writings and life.

Bioy and Borges both thought highly of Boswell's biographical enter-
prise. They imagined the relation between biographer and subject as
dynamic and *collaborative*, distinguishing Boswell's *Life* from the more
two-dimensional Johann Eckermann's conversations with Goethe.[22]

Boswell solved the problem of showing the manners, absurd
traits, and even unpleasant characteristics of Johnson and at the
same time persuaded us that Johnson was a great man—a great,
admirable and lovable man. (Casares, 499)

Something that no one has thought about until now is the
possibility—and it seems to me very probable—of Johnson's
collaboration with Boswell [in writing the *Life*] ... . At a certain
point people say that Johnson ceased writing; it is very clear to me
he did not have a reason to write because he knew that Boswell

was writing his Life in which he [Johnson] could "write" whatever he wanted to. (Casares, 339–40)

The notion of Boswell and Johnson's "collaboration" in the making
of Johnson's persona (and celebrity) via the *Life* has taken many forms,
including Alvin Kernan's argument (adapting Macaulay's) that "for all
Johnson's power as a maker of poets, his own reality as a poetic type
is finally the work of Boswell. Johnson himself suffered a surprising
deficiency in regard to himself in this kind of reality-making,"[23] and
culminating recently in John Radner's celebration of the intricacies of
their friendship.[24]

For Borges, however, the point of entry into the question lies in the
creative dynamic of his conversations with Bioy Casares. Conversation,
and the natural impulses to a conversational style—a fluid, flexible, skeptical, natural manner of writing that is responsive to the nature and tone
of particular experience and to the particulars of the human voice—was
a vital form for Borges' literary imagination and sensibility, just as it was
for Johnson's.[25] Johnson's conversation may have had a wider register than
Borges', extending from polite to aggressive, from pleasing to punishing,
but for both it was a vital form. As Stephen Miller suggests, a culture of
conversation and the possibilities of conversation as a genre depend on a
rich and substantial sense of social reality, of the enduring, external idea
of society as a natural and sustaining home for the individual.[26] Borges
is most like his eighteenth-century models in his conversation, and
both Borges and Johnson's commitment to these forms and realities are
significant in the light of their partial blindness.

## 6

Both Borges and Johnson use language not only to cut pretentiousness
down to size but also to elicit moral and intellectual truth. Johnson's words
on true wit in the *Life of Cowley* speak to the suppleness and readiness
with which he—and Borges—could uncannily find the right words to
say surprising, illuminating, and truthful things about human experience, past and present, and about literature. True wit is, in "a noble and
more adequate conception ... [that] which is at once natural and new, that

which, though not obvious, is, upon its first production, acknowledged to be just."[27] This may have been what Borges had in mind when saying, "The main merit of Johnson was his capacity to speak the truth" (Casares, 1056), understanding, of course, that "truth" lies in the "happy" and "just" coincidence of style and content, as much as it does in the correspondence between text and "facts" or events that lie outside of the text.

Of Thomas Browne, Borges notes, "Johnson remarks on [Browne's] tendency to reason strangely and associates that with his use of strange vocabulary" (Casares, 213–14); and, in his *Life of Sir Thomas Browne*, Johnson elaborates on Browne's "exuberance of knowledge, and plenitude of ideas," which "sometimes obstruct the tendency of his reasoning, and the clearness of his of decisions" (Yale *Works*, 19:336–37). In their early years both Borges and Johnson were fascinated by Browne's arcane, neo-Latin baroque imagination and prose style—they wrote about, translated, edited, and imitated Browne. This interest in alternative worlds gave way in the course of developing the conversational, natural styles with which we associate their mature thought.[28] In an interview with Alexander Coleman at New York University in 1971, Borges links his mature, simpler style with his blindness: "living in a colorless world ... also stands for a simplification in my vision of the world in a metaphysical sense, and in my style also" (Burgin *Conversations*, 134). This style, as I have suggested, is one in which formal, social and moral qualities are made one, in which, as Pope says in the *Essay on Criticism*, true wit cannot be defined, but can only be exemplified:

> True Wit is Nature to advantage dress'd,
> What oft was thought, but ne'r so well express'd;
> Something, whose truth convinc'd at sight we find,
> That gives us back the image of our mind.[29]

As Johnson puts it in writing of Dryden's prose, "delight is mingled with instruction, and ... the author proves his right to judgment, by his power of performance" (*Lives*, 2:120).

This holistic proposition is widely exemplified by both Johnson's and Borges' writing. Homer, for Borges, is not only the exemplum, with Milton, of the blind creator, but also an example of the dynamic idea of poetic identity that animates the *Lives of the Poets*. "The only certainty" in talking of Homer's poetic identity, says Borges, "is the impossibility of separating what pertains to the author from what pertains to the language" ("The Homeric Versions," *On Writing*, 59). Just such an organic principle informs Johnson's criticism. Dryden, in his translations (and in his writing generally) is "always another and the same, he does not exhibit a second time the same elegances in the same form, nor appears to have any art other than that of expressing with clearness what he thinks with vigour" (*Lives*, 2:123). The force—and the beauty—of this passage lies in its saying something true of Dryden, while also *exemplifying* something true of Johnson. In such instances, truth is inseparable from the language, form, and harmony of Johnson's own sentences. Many other examples of this critical manner link Borges with Johnson. For example, in conversation with Bioy in June 1958, Borges summarizes Johnson on Socrates from the *Life of Milton*: "The most important thing is to teach how to distinguish between good and bad. We are perpetually moralists but rarely astronomers or botanists" (Casares, 446). Bioy and Borges are talking about the intellectual dangers of over-specialization—particular manners rather than general nature, in Johnsonian terminology—and their moral interest is inseparable from considerations of literary pleasure.

About literary pleasure, Borges writes of "this terrifying and almost inexpressible truth": that "beauty in literature is almost incidental, depending on the harmony or discord of the words manipulated by the writer, and is not tied to eternity."[30] Almost but not quite incidental— because, as Pope and Johnson remind us, the truth of the representation is inseparable from the form and the choice of words. It is these aligned variables that make wit—whether in prose or verse—"at once natural and new" and "though not obvious ... upon its first production, acknowledged to be just" (*Lives*, 1:200). An essential aspect of this critical orientation—as we recognize Borges and Johnson both commanding a fluid, flexible, and playful grasp of language in relation to form and meaning—informs their idea of dictionaries.

It is one of the paradoxes (and pleasures) of Johnson's *Dictionary* that his commitment to defining and "fixing" the language exists in proportion to his understanding of how *impossible* the task is—because of the changeableness of words and their usage over time. The tension Johnson sustains between those two principles—fixity and change—and his sure handling and embodiment of the fluidity of language, like the fluidity of nature, in both the Preface and the *Dictionary* itself, make for a poetic meditation on writing and speaking that fascinated Borges. To Bioy, Borges said of the Johnson of the *Dictionary*: "What a consciousness he had of total forgetfulness, and how he saw himself as insane, as a crazy man. One has to see oneself as insane. The life of each of us, each day of our lives is stranger than that of Ulysses" (Casares, 639). Yet, furthermore, "there is nothing more human ... than grammar," and "the doctrine of every grammar I have consulted ... maintains that each individual word is a sign and denotes an autonomous idea. This doctrine is upheld by common consensus and fortified by the dictionaries" ("An Investigation of the Word," *On Writing*, 23, 25).

The slightest understanding, however, of how words operate to make meaning contradicts this commonplace, for, as Borges subsequently says, "words are not the reality of language: words—by themselves—do not exist" (25–26). This view leads in one direction to the language theories of Croce and Saussure, yet in another to the poetic use of language as the *form* of meaning. Such a praxis links the fantasy of a Borges to the lexicography of a Johnson.

## 7

Both Borges and Johnson sustain an identification of mind with language by a skeptical, yet sure grasp of their own authorial identities. Formally and stylistically Borges' writing—whether fiction or non-fiction—records social and historical realities as having very porous and flexible boundaries, and his approach to his own identity as a writer is commensurate. The author is very much alive, but the author *is* the text. With Bioy, Borges created two works he attributes to completely fictitious and pseudonymous "authors," Honorio Bustos Domecq—*Six Problems* (1942) and *Two Memorable Fantasies* (1946) ("Autobiographical Essay," 239, 246–47). His collaboration with di Giovanni on the writing of his own "life" may have something of the parody or pastiche about it, eliding insight into his life and mind, as V. S. Naipaul suggests, even as it promises, by virtue of its genre, to open it.[31] The ability to borrow and imitate various stylistic conventions, in hoax, parody, and pastiche, and in simple imitativeness, and to use these stylistic features with playful, sometimes irresponsible inventiveness, runs deep in Borges' writing. For Paul de Man, "all the stories have a similar mirror-like structure," and

> the least inadequate literary analogy would be with the eighteenth-century *conte philosophique*: their world is the representation, not of an actual experience, but of an intellectual proposition ... . [Borges] differs, however, from his eighteenth-century antecedents in that the subject of the stories is the creation of style itself.[32]

That the subject of Borges' style is Borges' style itself is a de Manian commonplace (all language being necessarily about language for the deconstructionists), and obviously in need of nuancing, as Borges' frequent recourse to Johnson's stylistic ability to render truth attests. Borges' relativity may look like the antithesis of Johnson's principled stance—"he that thinks reasonably must think morally" (Yale *Works*, 7:71)—but his language points to the same meaningfulness as Johnson's idea:

> if the reader wants to read something moral into the text, that's all to the good. When I'm writing a story, I'm not thinking in terms, let's say, of political or ethical opinions: I'm merely trying to be true, let's say, to the plot, to the dream, perhaps. Of course, if my writing is any good, then I suppose many purposes should be creeping in; but that's up to them, not to me. (Burgin *Conversations*, 121)

Johnson's ghost writing for friends and supplicants—most obviously Sir Robert Chambers (lectures on the law), Rev. John Taylor (sermons), and Rev. William Dodd (legal advocacy)—is widespread and a deep part of his identity. As a person, he is driven by a moral imperative to human decency; as a writer, that purpose is fictionalized by a powerful rhetorical imagination. Johnson's social commitments stand in contrast to a writer such as Swift, portrayed in the *Life of Swift* as descending into madness as a result of isolation from the social world:

> Having thus excluded conversation, and desisted from study,
> he had neither business nor amusement ... his ideas, therefore,
> being neither renovated by discourse, nor increased by reading,
> wore gradually away, and left his mind vacant to the vexations of
> the hour, till at last his anger was heightened into madness. (*Lives*,
> 3:207)

There is more of Swift in Borges' stylistic machinations, but Borges' benign
hermeneutic and social vision separates him—with Johnson—from Swift's
darker irony and madness. Paul Fussell has written about Johnson's ability
to use generic formalities to rise above the merely personal in being deeply
serious,[33] and Alvin Kernan has written about Johnson's "power to make
not just an individual literary identity ... for himself, but a poetic role of
the first magnitude that blazes in the cultural sky."[34] Yet we seldom, if ever,
notice one stylistic feature that Johnson shares with Borges, the *invisibility*
that comes with a certain kind of seriousness.

Successful writing of a certain kind—of a kind that Johnson finds
very appealing and pleasurable—produces a certain invisibility; as he
says of Dryden's translations, "a writer who obtains his full purpose
loses himself in his own lustre" (*Lives*, 2:119).[35] This perspective and the
kind of writing it acknowledges look towards Borges, for whom collaboration "requires a joint abandoning of the ego, of vanity, and maybe
of common politeness" ("Autobiographical Essay," 247). In Borges'
writing, this inclination commonly finds expression in the paradoxical
open-occluded effect of such a work as "Pierre Menard, Author of the
Quixote" (1939), an apparently serious account of an *imaginary* writer
by a devoted, but fictitious biographer. Menard is an imaginary author
who recreates excerpts from *Don Quixote* that are identical to the original, but which signify something quite different from what Cervantes
intended. In this vein, Borges draws attention to the translational nature
of all literary meaning.

This is where blindness, invisibility, and translation run into the same
channel in the practice of both Johnson and Borges and underpin their
shared interest in memory (and forgetfulness). Discussing Borges' essay
"Blindness" (1977), Jacques Derrida sketches Borges' lineage in blindness
and poetic seeing:

Among the blind ancestors whom [Borges] identifies or claims in the gallery of Western literature, it is clearly Milton who is his rival; it is with Milton that he would like to identify himself, and it is from Milton that he awaits, with or without modesty, the noble lineage of his own blindness. For this wound is also a sign of being chosen, a sign that one must know how to recognize oneself, the privilege of a destination, an assigned mission: in the night, by the night itself. To call upon the great tradition of blind writers, Borges thus turns round an invisible mirror. He sketches at once a celebration of memory and a self-portrait. But he describes himself by pointing to the other blind man, to Milton, especially to the Milton who authored that other self-portrait, *Samson Agonistes*.[36]

This is to emphasize the romantic side of Borges, and to make blindness and poetry heroic and pathetic. However, there is nothing invisible about Milton, as there is for Homer, the other great blind, mythic presence in "Blindness."

Attractive (and representative) as Milton is for Borges, he is not seduced by the pathos (*Samson*) or the greatness (*Paradise Lost*) of poetic achievement. "Milton's blindness was voluntary," says Borges ("Blindness," *Total Library*, 479). The shock of this statement is only partly ameliorated by the qualification that follows, "He destroyed his sight writing pamphlets in support of the execution of the king by Parliament" (479). This is to place Milton's blindness in the context of a moral—and political—universe that Milton himself had called into being, and to identify Milton as a subject, if not the victim thereof. Johnson invokes the same moral universe when implicitly naming Milton's blindness as the *consequence* of his attack on monarchy. In describing Milton's heroic solitariness and the imaginative greatness of *Paradise Lost* in the *Life of Milton*, Johnson draws a number of parallels between Milton's advocacy of regicide and his complaint, after the Restoration, of being "with darkness and danger compass'd round" (*Paradise Lost*, 7, 1.27). Johnson writes, "This darkness, had his eyes been better employ'd, had undoubtedly deserved compassion" (*Lives*, 1:268). Unlike Salmasius, who "reproached Milton with losing his eyes" in writing *Defensio pro Populo Anglicano* (1651) (*Lives*, 1:255), Johnson eschews a direct cause-and-effect link between blindness and moral turpitude, but he does repeatedly place political action in a moral universe, as in the following paragraph:

> Nothing can be more just than that rebellion should end in slavery: that he, who had justified the murder of his king ... should now sell his services and his flatteries to a tyrant [Cromwell], of whom it was evident that he could do nothing lawful. He had now been blind for some years. (*Lives*, 1:256)[37]

The syntactical conjunction of murder, slavery, tyranny, and blindness speaks volumes. While there is little if any direct comment by Johnson on his own near-blindness, he was severe on what he considered to be his spiritual blindness, seen most clearly in the anguish of the Prayers and Meditations and in conversations about self-knowledge, action, and responsibility recorded in Boswell's *Life*. These utterances are versions of the vanity of human wishes and explorations of the universal structure of human suffering in relation to human folly, as we indulge fantasies of having and doing more than is humanly possible. However, Johnson's self-castigation and the moral gloom that runs through the writings of the 1750s and 1760s are balanced by the comprehensive comic vision and style, with its deep feeling for the multiplicity, leavened, and imperfect nature of life, that exists alongside the melancholy. This makes for a more bearable lightness of being with which to oppose the monumentality of a Milton. We see it in Johnson's love for Shakespeare's mingled drama and for Dryden's *Fables* and translations, the antithesis of the unified, transcendent vision that he admires in *Paradise Lost*. We see it in the beautiful, skeptical vision of life in *Rasselas*, where a natural and thus forgivable blindness transcends the Miltonic, heroic solitariness, articulated by Imlac as he counsels the deluded though well-meaning astronomer:

> Do not let the suggestions of timidity overpower your better reason; the danger of neglect can be but as the probability of the obligation, which, when you consider it with freedom, you find very little, and that little growing every day less. Open your heart to the influence of the light, which from time to time breaks in

upon you; when scruples importune you, which you in your lucid moments know to be vain, do not stand to parley, but fly to business or to Pekuah; and keep this thought always prevalent, that you are only one atom of the mass of humanity, and have neither such virtue nor vice as that you should be singled out for supernatural favours or afflictions. (Yale *Works*, 16:162–63)

The sense of the beneficence of life as it exists *beyond* the will and beyond direct human control or definitive choice is the deep ground-note of Johnson's mature style, characteristic not only of the *Lives of the Poets* and the Shakespeare criticism but also of earlier writings, *Rasselas*, and the moral essays. How Borges could have told his students that *Rasselas* "is really a rejection of man's happiness" (*Professor Borges*, 84) is a mystery, for the pleasure Johnson takes in experience in *Rasselas* is manifestly an embrace of the possibilities, if not the easy possession, of human happiness.[38] Perhaps Borges here was unable to see past himself, for, as James Woodall suggests,

Borges resembles most closely those eighteenth-century men of sensibility—such as one of his favourites, Johnson—whose learning and intellectual ebullience, and the rigour of their professional writing lives, somehow weighed heavily against their success in love. Melancholy is endemic in Johnson; so it is, perhaps better concealed, in Borges.[39]

For Nekayah's reflection on the impossibility of absolute choice could have been uttered by many of Borges' characters:

Of the blessings set before you make your choice, and be content. No man can taste the fruits of autumn while he is delighting his scent with the flowers of the spring; no man can at the same time fill his cup from the source and from the mouth of the Nile. (Yale *Works*, 16:110)

Notwithstanding the prominence of Milton in Borges' mythology of blindness, he is more forgiving, if paradoxical, about his own blindness.

"Blindness has not been for me a total misfortune; it should not be seen in a pathetic way. It should be seen as a way of life: one of the styles of living" ("Blindness," *Total Library*, 478). It is odd to think of a physical condition as a *style*, yet the substitution of this term for *experience* points to the meshing of life and writing that is central to both Johnson's and Borges' thought, which Borges exemplifies by quoting lines by what he calls "the greatest Spanish poet," Fray Luis de León:

> Vivir quiero conmigo,
> gozar quiero del bien que debo al cielo,
> a solas sin testigo
> libre de amor, de celo
> de odio, de esperanza, de reclo.
> [I want to live with myself,
> I want to enjoy the good that I owe to heaven,
> Alone, without witnesses,
> Free of love, of jealousy,
> Of hate, of hope, of fear.] (*Total Library*, 482)

## 8

The master trope for the invisibility that comes with poetic success is translation, which, as I have suggested, both Borges and Johnson saw as the quintessence of literary creativity. In recent decades, invisibility has been a contentious issue in translation theory. As Lawrence Venuti (among others) argues, Western notions of the *necessary* invisibility of the translator have been part of an ideology that undervalued translation as a literary mode, was blind to the intrinsic interests and characteristics of other languages and literatures, and assumed the universality of the values associated with the target language, usually English or French.[40] For Venuti, to "foreignize" translation and to resist or to creolize the culture of the target language is to introduce heterogeneous cultural and historical experiences into English (39–42). It is precisely in this fissure that both Borges and Johnson, in their different ways, embrace translation as the literary means of renewing and energizing their own language and culture by opening them to the force of poetry from elsewhere. In Borges' essays on translation—"Two Ways to Translate" (1926), "The Homeric Versions" (1932), "The Translators of *The Thousand and One Nights*" (1936), and "The Enigma of Edward FitzGerald" (1951)—and in Johnson's *Lives of the Poets* (1779–1781) (especially the *Lives* of Dryden and Pope), we have two unsystematic bodies of thought, separated by time and language, yet articulating a similar understanding of translation as necessary and creative. There is no *a priori*, no formal, no qualitative distinction between originals and translations for either writer. For them, a particular translation always exists dialectically between the "spirit" and the "letter" of the original—to use the terms already current in Dryden's prefaces and still pertinent in the debate between Arnold and Newman about the nature of translation two hundred years later—and is always nimbly responsive to both past and present, to both "source" and "target" language. Given the long history of translation in the continuous renovation of national literatures, both Borges and Johnson know that there is always more than one way to translate, and yet always only one way for the moment.

If for Borges the only difference between the "original" and the version is that the version can be measured against a visible text,[41] then in writing of Pope's versions of Homer Johnson is clear that the "gain" and "loss" are dynamically, inextricably interrelated when placing Pope's versions against the Greek texts. If Pope's Homer is sometimes found to lack Homer's "awful simplicity, his artless grandeur, his unaffected majesty," yet "it must be remembered that *necessitas quod cogit defendit*; that may be lawfully done which cannot be forborn. Time and place will always enforce regard" (*Lives*, 4:73). This situation is inseparable from the great strengths of the poem. Pope

> Cultivated our language with so much diligence and art, that he has left in his Homer a treasure of poetical elegances to posterity. His version may be said to have tuned the English tongue; for since its appearance no writer ... has wanted melody. Such a series of lines so elaborately corrected, and so sweetly modulated, took possession of the publick ear; the vulgar was enamoured of the poem, and the learned wondered at the translation. (*Lives*, 4:73)

Likewise, in taking Dryden's translations as the measure of the creative embodiment of the past in the present, Johnson draws together all of the threads about style, conversation, literary form, and aesthetic pleasure that resonate for Borges, for here the poetic self is entirely lost—lost to sight if not to experience and history—in the finished poem. Of Dryden's translations, Johnson writes:

> The affluence and comprehension of our language is very illustri-
> ously displayed in our poetical translations of Ancient Writers .... .
> It was reserved for Dryden to fix the limits of poetical liberty,
> and give us just rules *and examples* of translation ... . It is not by
> comparing line with line that the merit of great works is to be esti-
> mated, but their general effects and ultimate result ... . Works of
> imagination excel by their allurement and delight; by their power
> of attracting and detaining the attention. That book is good in
> vain, which the reader throws away. He only is the master, who
> keeps the mind in pleasing captivity; whose pages are perused
> with eagerness, and in hope of new pleasure are perused again;
> and whose conclusion is perceived with an eye of sorrow, such as
> the traveller casts upon the departing day.[42]

## 9

Even more than Shakespeare, Cervantes is the Renaissance writer who opens up and inhabits the space between languages, cultures, and time most appealingly for Johnson and for Borges. They both love Cervantes. In Foucault's archaeology, Cervantes witnesses—and perhaps helps bring about—an epistemic change that divides language from things and the world; *Don Quixote* introduces an awareness into language of its own fictive nature. In *Don Quixote*, says Foucault,

> writing has ceased to be the prose of the world; resemblances
> and signs have dissolved their former alliance; similarities have
> become deceptive and verge upon the visionary or madness; ... .
> The erudition that once read nature and books alike as parts of
> a single text has been relegated to the same category as its own

chimeras: lodged in the yellowed pages of books, the signs of language no longer have any value apart from the slender fiction which they represent. The written word and things no longer resemble one another. And between them, Don Quixote wanders off on his own.[43]

Alongside Johnson, in Borges' essays, stories, and conversations Cervantes is the constant touchstone, the writer who created a text that could not be killed either by translation or linguistic change ("The Superstitious Ethics of the Reader," *Total Library*, 54). He who created a character who exists in time, but remains beyond the representations by which we know him. Quixote forever asks to be translated, while he remains beyond full representation. Borges' response to the epistemic disjunction—the overturning of the ontological privilege of the real over the fictive that *is* the Renaissance—is his grand narrative of the universe as a library, to be written and to be read. For his part, Johnson's appreciation of Quixote fuels the comedy and, perhaps, also the pathos of *his* grand narrative of the vanity of human wishes. As he says in *Rambler* 2:

> We are all like the Knight of La Mancha, Don Quixote, who aspires beyond his reach, who loses himself in dreams of greatness and heroism; but even while we are laughing at Quixote, very few readers ... can deny that they have admitted visions of the same kind ... . When we pity him, we reflect on our own disappointments; and when we laugh, our hearts inform us that he is not more ridiculous than ourselves. (Yale *Works*, 3:11)

Johnson's readiness to embrace Quixote as an avatar of his engagement with all kinds of human endeavor, achievement, and disappointment may be his most appealing feature to Borges—though it is still not clear how this made Johnson more English than Shakespeare.[44] Perhaps what Borges meant was that it made Johnson more *Borgesian*!

CHAPTER NINE

# Ernest Borneman's
# *Tomorrow Is Now* (1959)
## Thoughts about a Lost Novel,
## with Glances toward
## Samuel Johnson and other Modernists

*Robert G. Walker*

M y title is partly serious, partly facetious, as is the subtitle of
Borneman's novel—*The Adventures of Welfare Willy in Search
of a Soul.* Among the most useful definitions of literary
modernism is one that sees it as a reaction against (as well as a successor
to) nineteenth-century realism. The limits of labels, of course, become
apparent in attempts to trace the roots of the seemingly more straightforward term realism. Ignoring the collateral branch of naturalism, we still
find ourselves expanding the term when we trace realistic prose fiction
back through Jane Austen to Samuel Richardson to Daniel Defoe—the
differences among those three seem far more important than their similarities except within this critical exercise. How, then, can we profitably
apply the more slippery term modernist to someone like Samuel Johnson,
who falls so far outside the chronological limits? One answer is to see how
the attitudes and approaches to literature and life that Johnson exhibited
lead us to insights about a twentieth-century writer largely unknown to
mainstream criticism, one who is undoubtedly a modernist at his best

and perhaps betrayed by his realism. This essay attempts to triangulate on Borneman from the seemingly disparate points of Johnson on the one hand and modernism on the other. The choice of Johnson is not arbitrary, for he would have been at once a sympathetic and harsh critic of Ernest Borneman. Both showed themselves to be comfortable with mixing compositional conventions and defying narrative expectations, while simultaneously aiming at popular trends in order to realize commercial success.

**I**

It always gratifies curiosity to trace a sentiment.

Samuel Johnson, "The Life of Waller"[1]

In 1959 very few people read the first paragraph of Borneman's *Tomorrow Is Now: The Adventures of Welfare Willy in Search of a Soul* and even fewer have read it since—more about that later—but those who did may have been reminded of the opening of a novel published four decades earlier. Borneman's work begins,

> Once upon a time Monica Moss, 5, was walking down a dirt track in Missouri. From the other side came a bearded farmer with a beardless goat. At the crossroads they met up with a stew bum. The stew bum looked at the goat, then at the farmer, then at Monica. Then he got mad and said to the farmer: "Hey, give that goat back his beard."
>
> "Who says so," said the farmer.
>
> "I say so," said the stew bum.
>
> "And who are you?" asked the farmer.
>
> "I'm a friend of the goat," said the bum.[2]

Monica awakens from what turns out to be a dream as her plane lands in England, and realistic memories of time spent there with her two friends, Willy and Jean, enter her mind—"We were very young then. Did we ever sleep that summer?"(9). Borneman's fairy-tale opening is surely meant to echo the opening paragraphs of James Joyce's *Portrait of the Artist as a Young Man* (1916):

> Once upon a time and a very good time it was there was a moocow coming down along the road and this moocow that was coming down the road met a nicens little boy named baby tuckoo ... .
> His father told him that story: his father looked at him through a glass: he had a hairy face.
> He was baby tuckoo. The moocow came down the road where Betty Byrne lived: she sold lemon platt.[3]

But the echo is discordant. The little boy has become a little girl, the cow a goat, and the hairy-faced father a bearded farmer, with his beard, Borneman implies, taken from the goat. Unpacking Borneman's opening requires skills very similar to those necessary to read the Joyce of *A Portrait* and *Ulysses*, and Borneman's most enduring profession as an academic sexologist may suggest that in his fiction a goat is never merely a goat, nor a beard merely a beard.

To begin our unpacking, the opening first shows Borneman providing readers with pleasure—gratifying them by inclusion within a group that recognizes allusions—and deliberately placing the author himself in a literary tradition, much as T. S. Eliot did when he referenced Chaucer's *Canterbury Tales* with the opening lines of *The Wasteland*:

> April is the cruellest month, breeding
> Lilacs out of the dead land, mixing
> Memory with desire, stirring
> Dull roots with spring rain.

When Monica arrives for an unexpected visit with two former lovers, Willy Proctor and Willy's wife Jean, the month is an even more despair-inducing October, but the theme, introduced in the fractured fairytale dream, of mixing memory with desire, is never far to seek. The remainder of the chapter shows Borneman's prose at its best, as Monica recalls both the summer in New England eighteen years earlier, when as Radcliffe girls she and Jean had formed a ménage à trois with Willy, and subsequent times when they were together:

> So here I am ... back in London with the morning rain ... . That was how I saw London first, in the brown light, in October. The days are getting shorter now, the autumns longer, spring is a muted ache. I am old. (12)

Even in these final two short sentences one can see how Borneman has mastered the rhythm of English, no small achievement for someone who fled Berlin for England in 1933 at the age of eighteen hardly knowing a word of its language. It is inadvisable, perhaps even impossible, to discuss Borneman's work while ignoring his interesting life.

## II

> Nothing detains the reader's attention more powerfully than deep involutions of distress or sudden vicissitudes of fortune, and these might be abundantly afforded by memoirs of the sons of literature ... . The gradations of a hero's life are from battle to battle, and of an author's from book to book.
>
> Samuel Johnson, Idler 102[4]

Borneman lacks a Boswell and is unlikely ever to have one. But he is a prime example of the attraction of using biography as a part of literary criticism, as Tim Parks has argued recently in general terms:

> Throughout the twentieth century, as the practice of literary criticism developed, there was much talk of the virtues of eliminating the personality of the author from the work. Yet when we return now to the writers who were presumed to have achieved this—Eliot and Joyce and Beckett—we find their work drenched with their personalities, supreme expressions of their manner and character and behaviour, each absolutely recognizable, triumphantly unmistakable, thanks to their creative powers.[5]

Parks is pushing back, of course, against those who urge vigilance against the dangers of the biographical fallacy, and in the early twenty-first century he may be jousting at windmills that time has largely laid waste, but it is useful to observe that students of Johnson have never been tempted to adopt this particular tenet of New Criticism, for various reasons. Some of us may share the self-professed prejudice in favor of biography that Johnson expressed when commenting on Bayle: "Bayle's Dictionary is a very useful work for those to consult who love the biographical part of literature, which is what I love most."[6] Moreover, Johnson is the subject of the best literary biography ever written in English, and, as Jack Lynch has pointed out recently, "Boswell opens his famous book by hailing Johnson specifically as a biographer: in the first paragraph of the *Life* he is not the great lexicographer, not the author of *Rasselas*, not the great essayist, not the great critic, not the great moralist, but the man 'who excelled all mankind in writing the lives of others'" ("Johnson's Lives," 6). His last major work, *Critical and Biographical Prefaces to the Works of the English Poets*, soon became known as *The Lives of the Poets*, both because its afterlife was independent of the anthology in which it originally appeared and because the "lives" of literary people were logically assumed to incorporate both biography and literary criticism, as Johnson had done. But none of Johnson's subjects, it is safe to say, had lives as diverse as Ernest Borneman's.

Following the author Borneman from book to book is not so easy as it might seem. I was led to *Tomorrow Is Now* from Cameron McCabe's *Face on the Cutting-Room Floor* (1937), a review of which by David Collard in the *Times Literary Supplement* piqued my interest.[7] Collard explained that the credited author—not to be confused with the protagonist of the same name—was

> the pseudonym of the prodigiously gifted Ernst Wilhelm Julius Bornemann (1915–95) .... As well as writing crime fiction he was a filmmaker, psychoanalyst, ethnomusicologist, musician (piano, double bass and drums) and jazz critic (writing a 600-page study of Swing).[8]

Encouraged by Collard's comments that "the novel is deeply precocious and experimental and reflects the author's admiration for Proust,

Joyce, John Dos Passos, Dashiell Hammett, Aldous Huxley and, especially, Ernest Hemingway," I bought the just published edition and
discovered that it was indeed "a cut above other Golden Age detective
fiction."[9] Borneman had mined hard-boiled crime fiction for language
and his own vocation—he was working as a film editor in a London
studio at the time—for plot (a movie actress is found murdered on the
floor of the cutting room the same day the director has cut her entirely
out of the picture). In a *Guardian* review of the new edition Jonathan
Coe describes *FOCF* as postmodern: "only two years separate [it] from
that true masterpiece of early postmodernism, Flann O'Brien's *At Swim-
Two-Birds*." Unlike Coe, I see Borneman as a late modernist rather than
an early postmodernist, based on the streaks of realism that coexist with
avant-garde tendencies in his novels; regardless, his undermining of
literary conventions in a Borges-like fashion is indisputably present in
*FOCF*. Characters spill out of the narrative: is the first-person narrator
Cameron McCabe, who is also one of the murder suspects, distinct from
the author Cameron McCabe, a pseudonym for Borneman, who is a film
editor "in real life," as was the character McCabe in *FOCF*? Similarly, the
final quarter of the work, written, we are told, by a minor character from
the murder plot, is titled "An Epilogue by A. B. C. Müller as Epitaph for
Cameron McCabe" and is composed in part of "quotations from actual
contemporary reviews rewritten to apply to the novel we have just read"
(Collard).

   This recent edition pulls together most of the information we have
about Borneman available in English; however, it is not always easy to
credit the information, for two reasons: first, Borneman's playful treatment of the truth, apparent in his use and abuse of literary conventions;
second, the occasional tendency of a critic, editor, or publisher to make
a good story even better. Borneman's dedication, with its journalistic
overtone, suggests that what follows is more a work of true crime literature than fiction: "To pay back a debt to Jim Harris and his camp in
Archirondel Bay, for the long nights of that summer of 1935 when
Mr. McCabe's story broke." Next comes a tables-turning disclaimer, a
"Warning to Débutants In The Libel Business," who would ignore the
author's statement that no identification with actual people is intended
by any character in the book:

> Any person who doubts the author's word for this, and accuses
> him … of having committed a libel by portraying any actual
> person … will therefore himself commit a libel, namely, that of
> accusing the author of telling lies, and will thus himself be sued
> for libelling the author instead of the author being sued for libel-
> ling him.

The final item of front matter is a "Sentimental Exegesis" that quotes from a film encyclopedia a contemporary definition of the expression "face on the cutting-room floor," ending "Thus are dreams and hopes felled with one snip of the scissors" (*FOCF*, front matter).

The back matter provided by the publisher of this latest edition, relying as it does on material that appeared in previous editions or reprints, is almost as confusing as Borneman's novel itself. "A Dossier on a Vanished Author, and a Vanished Book by the Editors" is annotated "A version of this Afterword first appeared in the edition of *The Face on the Cutting-Room Floor* published by Gregg Press (a division of G. K. Hall & Co), Boston, 1981." This Afterword cites reviewers of an earlier edition (Gollancz, 1974), who were either uncertain about or ignorant of the true name of the author. But after five pages "we, the editors of Penguin Books" break in with assurances that they have certainly identified the author and discovered him alive and well, "teaching sexology at Salzburg University and living on a huge farm in Upper Austria" (*FOCF*, 301, 306). Since the Penguin edition was published in 1986, this seems to be when the true author of the 1937 novel was firmly established to the literary world. The Penguin edition also includes a partial transcript of an interview that Borneman gave to Reinhold Aman in 1979, as well as copies of letters to Borneman from critics Julian Symons and Frederic Raphael (provided by Borneman to Penguin), and a letter to Penguin from Borneman himself. These documents raise further questions.

We are told, for example, that in 1974 Gollancz was unaware of the true author when it published a facsimile reprint of the 1937 edition, and therefore "advertised for his heirs and placed the royalties in a trust fund for them" (*FOCF*, 304). But this now appears to be merely a pro forma search. The used copy of *Tomorrow Is Now* (1959) I recently purchased came with a torn but intact dust jacket, the flap copy of which reads, "Ernest Borneman is a Canadian who has written three previous novels, *The Face on the Cutting Room Floor*, *Love Story* and *Tremolo*." The dust jacket clearly shows that Borneman was known as the author of the first work, despite what may be a howler about his nationality: Coe's introduction explains, "As a German national living in the United Kingdom, not long after the outbreak of war he was apprehended and shipped off to an internment camp in northern Ontario" (*FOCF*, ix). He was released a year later to work for the National Film Board of Canada, and returned to England in the 1950s, where he wrote film and television scripts as well as novels. How many novels, however, is an open question.[10]

## III

> Several of us got round Dr. Johnson, and complained that he would not give us an exact catalogue of his works, that there might be a complete edition. He smiled, and evaded our entreaties ... . I once got from one of his friends a list ... written down in his presence by this friend, who enumerated each article aloud ... . Johnson, who heard all this, did not contradict it. But when I shewed a copy of this list to him, and mentioned the evidence for its exactness, he laughed, and said, "I was willing to let them go on as they pleased, and never interfered."
>
> *Boswell's Life*, 3:321

Boswell, then, was among the first to attempt to establish the Johnsonian canon, a task that may always remain incomplete owing to Johnson's anonymous writings in the periodical literature of his day. More to the point, the passage from Boswell suggests that an author may not always be taken at his word on the subject. Borneman lets stand without comment the statement by his interviewer, "You've done seven novels in English, some of which have been bestsellers, and ten works of non-fiction which have also sold well" (*FOCF*, 316). To establish a list of the seven novels is difficult. Here is one, based on statements by reviewers and critics and supplemented by WorldCat:

1. *Face on the Cutting-Room Floor* (1937)
2. *Love Story* (1941)
3. *Tremolo* (1948)
4. *Face the Music* (1953)
5. *Tomorrow Is Now* (1959)
6. *The Compromisers* (1962)
7. *The Man Who Loved Women: A Landscape with Nudes* (1968)

This seems to fit the "seven novels in English" of the interview, which may be based on a count that includes information from Brian Doyle's 1974 review of the Gollancz reprint: "'Cameron McCabe' was in fact a pen-name of Ernst Wilhelm Julius Bornemann, and he published at least two other books—*Face the Music* (for which I cannot trace a date) and *Tremolo* (published by Harper's, New York, 1948)" (*FOCF*, 305–6). Coe's *Guardian* review follows Doyle on this point almost verbatim. Nicole Brunnhuber, whose chapter on Borneman very usefully establishes the existence of the second novel, *Love Story*, and ties it to *The Compromisers*, repeats without evidence the seven-novels view.[11] I suggest, however, that the fourth item on this list, *Face the Music*, is most likely a bibliographical ghost. When the film *Face the Music* (American title *The Black Glove*) was released in 1954 by Hammer Studios, London, Borneman was credited as screenwriter and the film was said to be based on his novel of the same name. I have been unable to find evidence that the novel ever saw the light of day, if, indeed, it existed at all in that form. Borneman was working in the very popular genre of film noir and combined that with another of his dominant interests, jazz, to produce a film script about an American trumpeter falsely accused of murdering a Spanish singer. The film is said to be undistinguished. We are left (at least until further evidence appears) with a corpus of six novels written in English, and Borneman continues to display his tendency to include biographical interests with attempts to capitalize on the most popular trends of the day.

Before leaving this point about the canon, I should add that a physical examination of three of the novels in the list above supports the idea from the dust jacket of *Tomorrow Is Now* that Borneman was known as the author of *The Face on the Cutting-Room Floor* consistently throughout his novel-writing career. Opposite the title pages of *Tremolo* (Harper & Brothers, 1948), *The Compromisers* (Andre Deutsch, 1962), and *The Man Who Loved Women* (Coward-McCann, 1968), the listing of books by the same author includes *The Face on the Cutting-Room Floor* in each case. Such an examination also reveals continuing vagaries in Borneman's life story, and the difficulty of crediting completely information from publisher sources. Some vagaries are understandable, albeit duplicitous: whoever wrote the blurb for the dust jacket of *Tremolo* chose to describe Borneman's deportation from England and incarceration in Canada in this way—"He did post-graduate work at Cambridge, and then went to Canada to live." More troublesome on first glance is the appearance in the list of previous works of a title I had not seen before, *Something Wrong*: it is found in the front matter of both *The Compromisers* and *The Man Who Loved Women*, although the dust jacket of the latter does not include it among Borneman's "four previous novels." WorldCat shows a 1960 London publication by Four Square Books, with a German language version in 1968. I was about to tumble down yet another rabbit hole when I ran across an item in a bibliography of novels about popular music that indicated that *Something Wrong* was a reprint of *Tremolo*.[12] So at this point the corpus remains at six English novels.

## IV

> [*Helena* is] far the best book I have ever written or ever will write.
>
> Evelyn Waugh[13]

Encouraged by the literary playfulness of Borneman's first novel as well as the sheer pleasure of reading it, I decided to sample his other offerings. Rather than following him chronologically "book to book," however, I tried to stack the cards in his favor by moving to his fourth novel, *Tomorrow Is Now*, primarily because of what he said about it in a letter he wrote to Penguin in 1981 (*FOCF*, 332–34). The letter provides several valuable tidbits, among them that the ruthless director in *Face on the Cutting-Room Floor* took his name, Bloom, but only his name, from Joyce's main character in *Ulysses*, and that he had selected his first publisher, Victor Gollancz, because of shared political beliefs ("as a socialist I admired the orange-covered volumes of the Left Book Club which he had been publishing for some years"). Borneman states that his novels were well received except for

> the best of my books, *Tomorrow Is Now*, [which] came out during a newspaper strike and was lost—literally. Only years later, when the book had long gone out of print (only 500 copies had been found till then), we discovered the remaining 9500 copies in a deserted warehouse. They were never sent to the wholesalers and retailers. The book was dead.

Whether Borneman saw the irony—evident from a capitalist point of view—of the labor strike depriving the world of his "best" book—is unknown.[14]

Turning to the online used book market in January 2017, I found and purchased a copy for $25; another was listed for approximately $200. As I write this in July 2017, only two copies—at just under $200—are listed on Amazon. WorldCat shows a handful of library copies in the U.K., Ireland, and Australia; the only library copies listed in the Americas are four in Canada. The book indeed is lost or "dead." Whether it is worth resuscitation is the question. Was Borneman's evaluation anywhere close to accurate, or was it, as most agree Evelyn Waugh's evaluation of his novel *Helena* was, an exaggerated assessment based on polemical rather than aesthetic grounds? A closer look at the form and structure of the novel provides an answer.

## V

> Coffeehouse: A house of entertainment where coffee is sold, and the guests are supplied with news papers.
>
> Johnson's *Dictionary*

The second chapter of *Tomorrow Is Now* continues the modernist mode displayed in chapter one, as it introduces us to Sam Proctor, the seventeen-year-old son of Willy and Jean, during his lunch hour at the Eldorado, "a coffee bar frequented by teenagers, pansies, amateur guitar players, lesbians, unsuccessful painters and the so-called artistes from the nude revue round the corner" (15). (The name of the coffeehouse may remind some of us of the gentle irony Johnson used with "Happy Valley" in *Rasselas*.) Having failed miserably to follow his father's academic success, Sam has embraced the Teddy Boy culture and is now a very junior bank clerk whose physical description suggests the strength of his character— "weak brown eyes, the shade of thin tea" (14). The modernist mode I speak of is Borneman's way of representing conversation among people realistically overheard in a public place: out-of-context snatches here and there that the reader struggles to follow. This is far different from the way conversation is represented in the fiction of realism, where it is linear and, for the most part, two-sided. It is the mode of Ford Maddox Ford rather than Evelyn Waugh, to cite two near contemporaries among English writers. (In his depiction of conversation Waugh is a realist although in other ways perhaps a modernist.) And of course, it is the mode of James Joyce, in *A Portrait* and *Ulysses*, and earlier in *Dubliners*.

The influence of Joyce on Borneman is pervasive, if at times trivial. I spoke above about what I see as a parallel between the openings of *A Portrait* and *Tomorrow Is Now*. Just as Borneman borrowed a name from Joyce (Bloom) for one of the characters in his first novel, he works a Joycean connection, with a nod to metafiction, into the birth of the protagonist of *Tomorrow Is Now*: Willy's mother Maria remarks to his father Donald, "That must be the first compliment you've paid me since that day in Trieste when you kept congratulating me on renting James Joyce's old flat for Willy to be born in" (66). Borneman came to his appreciation of Joyce even before immigrating to England. He describes the cultural advantages of being a native Berliner: "Berlin between 1900 and 1930 was an education by itself ... . We had recognized Joyce as the greatest writer in the English tongue since Shakespeare at a time when the English still raved about Galsworthy and the Irish about Yeats" (*FOCF*, 319). It is no coincidence that the best parts of *Tomorrow Is Now* are the parts closest to Joyce's style.

The Eldorado forms a Bohemian melting pot that allows Borneman to touch on his lifelong intellectual interests—sex, music, and politics—often simultaneously. Consider the opening of the chapter, where we hear from a ranking member of the nude revue:

"To hell with Friday," said the Queen. "I want a small roast pig with an apple in the mouth." The Queen was naked. Oh, yes, she wore a coat, but everybody knew that she wore nothing underneath. She took off her crown and stared at the waitress ... . The waitress looked for help. She was a new waitress. There were always new waitresses and they were all pretty. This one was called Barbara and she was the niece of a real Duchess. The Queen, who was no real Queen, belched meditatively and said, "Tell Tony the Queen can't support fish. She wants her usual." The niece of the real Duchess departed worriedly in the general direction of the kitchen door. (14)

Whatever the Queen does onstage it is safe to assume some music is involved, but the music and sex are coarsened by their representative, and neither the British class system—with its false queens and "real" duchesses—nor British religious mores—a rejection of Friday dietary abstinence followed by a belch—come out any better.

Borneman undercuts his own wide-ranging satire of shallow characters with a bit of literary criticism, from a conversation between "two bearded men." Sounding a bit like Hemingway, another modernist influential on Borneman, cocoa beard comments to butter beard,

"Look at them from the outside ... . You'll never know what goes on inside. So be satisfied with what you can see ... . What I hate is novels where the writer pretends he's God ... . Most of us don't know why we're doing things ourselves—so why pretend we can read other people's motives?" (20–21)

Still, some people are rather easily read. When Sam hears the lyrics of an American pop song,

> *Do everything that*
> *They don't allow,*
> *For to-day is long past and*
> *To-morrow is now,*

he immediately determines to buy the recording, despite having no money—"I'm gonna borrow a quid off my old man"—and despite the pejorative reaction of his friend Wolf Tuvim—"City-bred white boy trying to make like a blues singer .... Compare this to the real country stuff and you'll see what's happened to American society" (22). Tuvim is a bright but cruelly cynical young man whose friendship with the much younger (five years), dumber Sam is inexplicable except perhaps as a ploy to curry favor with Sam's father, Tuvim's college instructor.

The world of the Eldorado is one where one's appearance matters disproportionately, something Borneman works with in his description of every patron. Tuvim habitually wears a scarf "in protest against the Establishment's demands for collars and ties" (14), so he too is rebelling— indeed, almost everyone in this novel is a rebel in one way or another. Tuvim is bumped twice provocatively by a young man in "a checked flannel shirt, a paisley cravat, cavalry twill slacks with 15-inch bottoms, and grey Italian suede shoes." Returning from a round trip to the juke box, the young man

> established gentle contact between his flank and Wolf Tuvim's shoulder. "Excuse me," he said in a voice like toffee .... Wolf Tuvim raised his thumb and pointed. "Up your brown, chum." "You don't have to bite my ear off, dearie," said the young man. "If you were a gent, chum, you'd cut it off yourself and send it to Gauguin by parcel post." ... He had nothing against queers but he disliked cavalry twill. "Where's Gauguin?" asked Sam Proctor. (16–17)

Sam's ignorance is hilarious, but we should not miss the larger point: Tuvim's acceptance of variations of sexual preference but not of fashion is of a piece with the free-floating intolerance exhibited by virtually all the characters of the novel.

## VI

> When in good humour [Johnson] would talk of his own writings with a wonderful frankness and candour, and would even criti- cise them with the closest severity .... [W]hen one was reading

his tragedy of "Irene," to a company at a house in the country, he left the room; and somebody having asked him the reason of this, he replied, "Sir, I thought it had been better."

*Boswell's Life*, 4:5

The setting for all but two of the remaining twenty chapters of *Tomorrow Is Now* is the home of Willy and Jean Proctor, occupied also by their son Sam and Willy's parents, Donald and Maria. (I treat the chapter about Donald and Maria Proctor's history, discussed in a moment, as within the Proctor home—it is a one-off, certainly, but gives no relief from the claustrophobic dominant setting.) Borneman's choice to limit himself to a quasi-theatrical setting while working in the novel genre is both curious and unfortunate. One problem immediately apparent is rendering the comings and goings of a small group of people without giving the impression of a French bedroom farce. Consider the events of fourteen pages, probably less than an hour of stage time. Sam enters his home after his stop at the record shop and calls for his grandmother, only to find his mother Jean home unexpectedly. She has been fired from "her latest job," and, when asked why, holds up a liquor bottle (29). After Jean and Sam hold a cross-purposes conversation, with Sam sitting part of the time on a "child's swing—a board suspended between two ropes—that hung in the staircase" (30), his favorite perch and a sign of his arrested development, she leaves hurriedly for a pub, avoiding her husband Willy, whom she hears returning from work. Sam and Willy converse combatively—"Don't let's always be quarrellin, Dad. I want to live cool, like. None of this frantic stuff like you an Mum and Grandad" (37)—until Monica shows up at the door for her surprise visit, the first in seven years. Sam and Monica are introduced and talk briefly before Sam is out the door, leaving Monica to seduce a willing Willy in the living room. They barely finish before Willy's parents come home.

After this hectic start, with no inkling that Borneman intended its frantic nature to be viewed humorously, he changes pace and mode with the most dreadfully bad section of the book, a chapter outlining the history of Willy's parents, who apparently participated in every act of militant socialism during the first half of the twentieth century. A few sentences will give the flavor:

> There [Donald] met Lenin and became a Bolshevik ... . [H]e escaped to England and got there just in time to map out the general strike on the Isle of Man ... . [H]e went on to Budapest to help Bela Kun lay the groundwork for the Hungarian Soviet Republic ... . [B]y a sheer freak of good luck [Maria] was sent to Austria ... to help run machine-guns across the Alps from Milan for the general strike ... . [W]hen the Prussian Government was dissolved and the Communists called for a general strike, Maria was caught by six S.A. men, raped, trussed up with her own belt and thrown into the river Spree. (55–59)

The chapter seems intended to illustrate the crushing struggle that the Left engaged in, at great personal loss—two of Maria and Donald's three children die very young as a direct result of opposition violence—but there are major problems both with tone and with credibility. The best light that can be cast on this section, aside from a wholly improbable notion that Borneman has adopted temporarily the style of Voltaire's *Candide*, is to see it as an anticipation of a technique that appeared later in two motion pictures, *Zelig* (1983) and *Forrest Gump* (1994), where the titular heroes witness or participate in defining historical events with a frequency that defies probability.

The impulse toward political propaganda present throughout the novel certainly weakens it (more about this later). An equally important weakness is Borneman's choice to structure most of the work as a stage play. We see a dysfunctional family whose repeated arguments quickly lose the interest of novelty. Depicting those arguments moves the writing away from the modernist technique exhibited in the coffee-house conversation, and far from the stream-of-consciousness that the novel's opening hints at and to which Borneman returns in a much later chapter. Contained as the family is in the house, the verbal conflicts seem inevitable and never-ending. The few major plot events—Sam is arrested for assaulting a policeman (which occurs "off-stage") and Willy finally decides to divorce Jean and marry Monica just as Monica decides not to accept him—pale in impact when compared with the constant bickering between Willy and everyone else. Borneman certainly could have found in his other works models for his novel that would have allowed him to range outside the living room—at the time he was writing screenplays for motion pictures and scripts for television series including one for *The Adventures of Robin Hood*, and he had previously written scripts for the radio program Orson Welles developed to capitalize on the success of *The Third Man*, *The Adventures of Harry Lime*—but he seems here rather to be trying to mimic the domestic drama of the Angry Young Men or Edward Albee. He indicates his awareness of the former in the words of a final argument between Willy and his father, who seems closer to the author's position here. To Willy's charge, "We've had our heroes, Father. Your kind of people don't have a monopoly on angry young men," Donald replies,

> "Oh, I've heard about them, your new English radicals with poison on their arrows and no targets to shoot them at, poor kids. I've read about them in novels, I've seen them on the stage … . The trouble with your generation is not that you're angry but that nothing can persuade you to turn your anger into action." (194–95)[15]

All this is not to deny Borneman's ability to write a powerful scene. The argument between Willy and Donald ends with Willy brutally battering him. The scene has been punctuated by Jean's appearance three times from upstairs in an increasingly dissociative state, so it is not totally surprising but shocking nonetheless when Willy runs

> blindly out of the room. In the staircase he knock[s] against something that hung from the swing … . There was a waxen quality to his wife's dead face, like a mask that settled into the mould of the past—a schoolgirl face, serene but empty … . The dead face of a witless child. (201)

She has hanged herself on the swing to which her son Sam customarily retreated.

So what connects Borneman's novel and Johnson's historical tragedy *Irene*? There are several related tangents, it seems to me, dealing with proper use of genre, the quest for popular success, the accuracy of authorial self-evaluation, and perhaps even the characteristics of literary movements. *Irene*, the least successful work Samuel Johnson ever wrote, was one that took him the most time and perhaps the most effort. He began it in 1736 but the play was not acted until 1749, and then only with the massive assistance of his friend David Garrick, who made changes in the script, put it on in the theater he managed, and took a leading role on stage. Why did it fail? Certainly not merely because of the ending: "In Johnson's drafts, the heroine … dies offstage … . Garrick changed this, creating the ill-advised onstage strangulation of Irene in act 5, a spectacle that audiences shouted down."[16] (The similarity of Irene's end and Jean's is, of course, nothing more than an unrelated coincidence.) *Irene's* failure lies much more in its being "misconceived in genre" (Belcher, 140) and in its having missed its moment. First, consider genre. The play's strengths lie in the arguments placed in the characters' mouths, but Johnson was far more successful, artistically, when he promulgated such arguments in essays, sermons, prose fiction, criticism, biographies, and even formal verse satire such as *London* and *The Vanity of Human Wishes*. In 1736 and to an only slightly lesser extent in 1749 he was attempting to make his mark on the English literary scene (as well as to make money), and he simply mismatched his talents with his medium.

Even if Johnson's skills had been more attuned to the stage, the type of play he chose to write had already seen its heyday. As Thomas Kaminski explains,

> historical tragedy, at least in its heroic form, was moribund in 1738. It managed to sustain itself only by entangling its plots in the rigging of contemporary politics. At least from the time of *Cato*, works in this genre achieved much of their success from their political associations … . But Johnson's play had no easily discernible political position … . Thus Johnson was working in an outmoded form and neglected to give his work the one quality that would have guaranteed it an audience—a specific political bias.[17]

Johnson, whether deliberately or not, chose aesthetic concerns over near-term political interests, hoping to achieve in *Irene* a lasting quality that he was later to argue Addison's *Cato* lacked, about which more in a minute.

At the risk of fumbling the slippery labels of literary movements, I would like to suggest a distinction between modernism and postmodernism more significant than most, at least when it comes to considering the modernism of Johnson and of Borneman. Although each literary movement simultaneously builds upon and rejects the one preceding, modernism more consciously embraces previous literary traditions, while postmodernism more deliberately rejects them. For Johnson the critic this is manifest in his middle ground, both accepting the consensus gentium—the judgment of history—and attempting to influence that judgment through tasteful distinctions, many based (in a circular fashion) on the previous judgments of history. His considered judgment of *Irene* is more "true" than Borneman's of *Tomorrow Is Now*, but both writers are making judgments within a literary continuum that postmodernism frequently denies.

## VII

How small of all that human hearts endure,
That part which laws or kings can cause or cure.
Oliver Goldsmith, *The Traveller* (1764)[18]

Over the past half century several books and many articles have been written about the politics of Samuel Johnson, indeed very contentious books and articles. But only recently, I believe, has a scholar highlighted the most important fact about Johnson and politics. As the above lines that Johnson contributed to Goldsmith's famous poem imply, politics pale in importance to other considerations when seeking for the causes of human happiness. Concomitantly, writes Nicholas Hudson, "Johnson came to see great literary art as deeper than politics, which helps to account for his increased concentration on literary criticism during the last decades of his life."[19] Johnson is perhaps the most opinionated major literary figure in history, and it certainly makes sense to examine what his opinions were regarding politics and the topic closely related to politics in the eighteenth century: religious affiliation. But, for Johnson, religious affiliation was not identical to religious beliefs, and aesthetics trumped partisan politics in the world of literature. We read Johnson, and have read him for over two hundred years, for *Rasselas*, *The Vanity of Human Wishes*, and his literary criticism, not for his contributions to the Parliamentary Debates or even for his four excellent political pamphlets.

Another statement by Nicholas Hudson on this topic resonates upon our reaction to the political message with which Borneman has imbued his novel:

> Voltaire wondered how the English could admire Shakespeare when they had *Cato*, but Johnson suggested that the popularity of Addison's play was transient precisely because it dramatized the writer's political opinions. "We pronounce the name of *Cato*, but we think on Addison." (135)

From the subtitle ("Welfare Willy") to the frequent arguments between Willy and his father, Borneman relentlessly enforces his political position, a somewhat impractical Marxist stance that finds fault with the younger generation's willingness to take advantage of the benefits accrued to them by previous socialists without continuing the movement. Overlaid is the domestic and sexual dysfunctionality of the Proctor family and of Monica, which leaves us finally with one of the most thorough depictions of absolute wretchedness in modern fiction.

The two chapters dealing with Willy's brawl with his father and Jean's suicide are bracketed by two chapters that escape from the Proctor house, very profitably in the first case. "The Versatile Girl from Radcliffe" shows Monica immediately after her return to the United States. Here Borneman turns again to the modernistic mode of his opening two chapters. We find Monica hung-over and in bed with a nineteen-year-old black prostitute named Lucy, a situation that reminds her of her life with Jean before Willy came into the picture. Borneman beautifully weaves language and memory together in the best passages since early in the novel. Monica recalls what a trendsetter Jean was in school ("At a bull session in the sorority house Jean one night coined the DDT phrase that spread to every campus in the nation: drop dead twice"). Lucy's "Doan gimme that Radcliffe stuff" brings to mind Willy's son ("*Gimme*. Who used to talk like that? My God, yes, Sam Proctor. October 18, this must be the day of the trial"). Lucy senses the reason for Monica's current sexual reluctance: "Yuh been shackin with uh man … . Thass whatcher lef behint. An doan snow me with that Radcliffe jive." This prompts a mental riff by Monica: "*The Radcliffe Jive*, what a lovely phrase. Like *The G.I. Jive* or *The Forsyte Saga* or *The Canterbury Tales*. To-night at 8:30, The Radcliffe Jive, played by The Versatile Girls from Radcliffe" (171–74). Monica and Jean's undergraduate college was mentioned much earlier in the book, but surely the renewed emphasis in this particular dramatic situation is meant to suggest, to some readers at least, the most publicized lesbian novelist of the century, Radclyffe Hall (1880–1943), the banning of whose novel *The Well of Loneliness* (1928) in Britain led to a famous obscenity trial. Borneman's allusion is teasing, much like Eliot's "Shakespeherian rag."

The stream-of-consciousness passage that accompanies Monica and Lucy's lovemaking at the chapter's end is filled with somewhat obscure literary allusions, as Borneman seems to be attempting to outstrip Eliot and Joyce. Here is the entire paragraph, Monica's interior monologue:

> Farewell, farewell, farewell. Willy, Jeannie, farewell. Child of mine, unborn, farewell to you. Time too swift, swiftness never ceasing. Reinhardt, Reinhardt, come soft rest of cares. Come, night, come naked virtue's only tire. And so Gertrude Stein, having been in Baltimore for a winter and having become more humanized and less adolescent and less lonesome, went to Radcliffe. And they saw neither sun nor moon but they heard the roaring of the sea. Stew bum, stew bum, sat on the road, along came a farmer with a beardless goat. For a' the blude that's shed on the earth rins through the springs o' that countrie. (177)

Monica's final failure with Willy sparks her farewells, which give way to a line from George Peele's sonnet from the end of *Polyhymnia* (1590), the context of which is a regret of loss of youth. The sonnet, sometimes titled "Farewell to Arms," begins with these two lines: "His golden locks time hath to silver turn'd; / O time too swift, O swiftness never ceasing!"[20] After the mysterious, repeated "Reinhardt" we find lines from George Chapman's "Epithalamion" (1598) in *Hero and Leander*: "O come, soft rest of cares! come, Night! / Come, naked Virtue's only tire."[21] Peele's sonnet and Chapman's wedding song provide a meaningful contrast with a brief exchange between Monica and Lucy only a few pages earlier: "'How old are you, Lucy?' ... 'I nineteen, gal. And I bin hustlin muh bustle since I twelve.' 'Nineteen, eh? Let's get married.' 'Reckon yuh too olt fuh me, sister,' the girl said scornfully" (172).

A sentence taken verbatim from the fourth chapter of Gertrude Stein's *Autobiography of Alice B. Tolklas* comes next into Monica's mind, both for the author's lesbianism and for her Radcliffe connection. The paragraph ends with lines from a medieval Scottish ballad, as rendered by Walter Scott, divided by a reminder of Monica's stew bum dream from the very beginning of the novel. Borneman includes four lines of a six-line section of Thomas the Rhymer's ballad:

> And they saw neither sun nor moon,
> But they heard the roaring of the sea.
> It was mirk mirk night, and there was nae stern light,
> And they waded thro' red blude to the knee;
> Fo a' the blude that's shed on earth,
> Rins thro' the springs o' that countrie.[22]

The ballad presents the ambiguous story of Thomas True, falling under the control of a Fairy Queen; whether for good or ill is debatable. The sexual enthrallment echoes Monica's in the arms of Lucy: "The girl's arms were around her, no way back, I am gone, I am gone, from this there is no return" (177).

Sorting through the crosscurrents of this chapter can tell us much, I think, about Borneman as a writer. First, he enjoyed being avant-garde in his depictions of human sexuality, especially lesbianism. This goes hand-in-glove with a desire to become notorious enough to be a popular success. The publisher's blurb of his next novel, for instance, described a main character as "one of the few convincing portraits of a lesbian ever painted by a male hand."[23] Apart from these commercial concerns, however, are Borneman's artistic aims, and, while Monica's final reverie is far from Molly Bloom's, it is not implausible, I think, to see one as a forerunner of the other. This does not mean that Monica has escaped the wretchedness of the rest of the characters in the novel, as her sexual excitement in tinged with loss, regret, and lack of freedom.

The final chapter in *Tomorrow Is Now*, the shortest in the book, is not an after-thought, but it does suggest that Borneman had trouble coming up with an ending. "The Jailbirds" shows Sam and his friend Wolf Tuvim separately incarcerated, the former for his assault on a policeman and the latter for a violation of the Official Secrets Act. Sam's situation is truly wretched, as he is injected with heroin forcibly by a prison gang in an attempt to habituate him and thus imprison his will along with his body. Tuvim, on the other hand, banters with his warder: he suggests that eventually the "two little rabbits, those agitator rabbits" will be more than a match for the "real powerful police fox," once they outnumber their government oppressors (202–203). The thud is audible as Borneman lapses into pedestrian prose and stale political theory.

## VIII

> Wo Freiheit ist und Recht, da ist das Vaterland.
> Dies ist uns aber nun und wir ihm unbekannt.
> Es streite, wer da will: es ist dahin gekommen,
> Der falsche Frieden hat das Land nun eingenommen,
> Die Faulheit aber uns.

> [Where freedom is and justice, there is the fatherland. But that is now for us and we for it unknown. Dispute it if you want. It has come to this. False peace has now taken over the country because of our sloth.][24]
>
> Daniel Von Czepko, 1605–1660

> The conclusion, in which nothing is concluded.
>
> Johnson, *The History of Rasselas*[25]

Samuel Johnson gave the final chapter of his prose apologue a seemingly facetious title. The work concludes, but the characters continue in what the previous forty-eight chapters suggest will be futile quests for happiness in this life. Yet few readers of *Rasselas* have been so misguided as to see the work as representative of an absurdist world. I argued forty years ago that a major reason for this is how Johnson shaped his narrative, ending his characters' quest for meaning with a philosophical discussion of the immortality of the soul in the penultimate chapter.[26] Among others, Boswell had anticipated me: In *Rasselas* "Johnson meant, by shewing the unsatisfactory nature of things temporal, to direct the hopes of man to things eternal" (*Life*, 1:342). Here, then, is an area of great divergence between Johnson and Borneman, it seems to me.

Borneman's subtitle, *The Adventures of Welfare Willy in Search of a Soul*, is sardonically facetious in a way that Johnson's final chapter title is not. Both writers saw clearly what Imlac says earlier in *Rasselas*, "Human life is every where a state in which much is to be endured, and little to be enjoyed" (50), but Borneman's secular socialism leaves him bound in miseries to the extent that, in this novel at least, he loses the ability to sustain the aesthetic facility that he occasionally shows. His politics, then, undercuts his art, and was one of the twin causes of the failure of what he considered, ironically because of its political message, I suspect, his best novel. He displayed the same type of bias that Evelyn Waugh showed when evaluating his most obviously Catholic novel, *Helena*, which Waugh's religious faith caused him greatly to over-estimate. Borneman's last word is a self-styled "Envoi," a poem from a German Lutheran writer that illustrates both his strength (the imaginative employment of a literary convention that originated in the fourteenth century with a quotation from a seventeenth-century poet) and his weakness (the tenacity with which he enforced his political views at the expense of his art).

The other main cause of the failure of *Tomorrow Is Now* is its genre confusion—not gender confusion—which I attribute to Borneman's allowing his desire for commercial success to prompt him to mix literary types inauspiciously. Johnson's oft-quoted sentiment, "No man but a blockhead ever wrote, except for money" (*Life*, 3:19) comes to mind. Borneman was certainly no blockhead and perhaps not until he attained an academic position in the 1970s in Austria was he somewhat financially established. As he cast about for literary work in the 1950s, novel-writing was certainly a continuing option. Moreover, Borneman demonstrates in several ways in *Tomorrow Is Now* his ability to write well in the modes and traditions of the modern novel. But the book turns out to be as misconceived in genre as Johnson's *Irene*: the plot may have worked on stage but not on the page and, like Evelyn Waugh, Borneman seems never to have recognized this particular failure. Recognizing and admitting one's own failures, of course, is difficult for us all, and the strength of Boswell's biography is never better illustrated than in the understated treatment of Johnson's assessment of *Irene*, "I thought it had been better."

# Notes

## Notes to Introduction: Modernity Johnson? *Anthony W. Lee*

1   For the old stereotype, see, e.g., Thomas Babington Macaulay, *Life of Samuel Johnson* (New York: Longmans, Green, and Co., 1896). For the twentieth-century recovery effort, see, e.g., James L. Clifford, *Young Sam Johnson* (New York: McGraw-Hill, 1955) and *Dictionary Johnson: Samuel Johnson's Middle Years* (New York: McGraw-Hill, 1979); Donald J. Greene, *The Politics of Samuel Johnson* (rev. ed. Athens, GA: University of Georgia Press, 1990).

2   The secondary literature on Modernism is vast. Here are a few studies I have found helpful: Douglas Mao and Rebecca L. Walkowitz, "The New Modernist Studies," *PMLA* 123, no. 3 (2008): 737–48 (see also their bibliography); David E. Chinitz, *T. S. Eliot and the Cultural Divide* (Chicago: University of Chicago Press, 2003); Gabriel Josipovici, *What Ever Happened to Modernism?* (New Haven, CT: Yale University Press, 2010); Genevieve Abravanel, *Americanizing Britain: The Rise of Modernism in the Age of the Entertainment Empire* (Oxford: Oxford University Press, 2012); Donald Pizer, *Toward a Modernist Style: John Dos Passos* (New York: Bloomsbury Academic, 2013).

3   <https://www.rem.routledge.com/>. See also Mark Wollaeger, ed., *The Oxford Handbook of Global Modernisms* (Oxford: Oxford University Press, 2012) and Howard Booth and Nigel Rigby, eds, *Modernism and Empire: Writing and British Coloniality, 1890–1940* (Manchester: Manchester University Press, 2000).

4   The three authors born outside the British Isles examined here, Borges, Nabokov, and Borneman, were all steeped in the Anglo-American

Modernist tradition, the last two spending significant portions of their lives in the United States and England, respectively.

5  "Modernism" is defined here as the artistic and cultural movement that peaked in the early to mid-twentieth century, while "modernity" is the European cultural shift from the medieval period that began to emerge most visibly in the seventeenth century.

6  *Natural History*, century 5:493.

7  *Essay on Criticism*, ll.324–25; see also this *Dictionary* entry:
> To MO'DERNISE. v.a. [from modern.]
> To adapt ancient compositions to modern persons or things; to change ancient to modern language.

8  For a full account of the quarrel in England, see Joseph M. Levine, *The Battle of the Books: History and Literature in the Augustan Age* (Ithaca, NY: Cornell University Press, 1991).

9  "Life of Swift," in *Lives*, 3:193. Johnson appears to have closely associated the notion of the modern with Swift; see this *Dictionary* entry:
> MO'DERNISM. n.s. [from modern.]
> Deviation from the ancient and classical manner. A word invented by *Swift*.
> Scribblers send us over their trash in prose and verse, with abominable curtailings and quaint *modernisms*.                    *Swift*.

10  See *Rasselas*, chap.10, Yale *Works*, 16:39–40; Preface to Shakespeare (Yale *Works*, 7:59–60, 89).

11  Yale *Works*, 2:406, 16:41; *Lives*, 1:294, 295.

12  "Johnson as Critic," in *Anna Karenina and Other Essays* (New York: Pantheon, 1967), 197–218 (197).

13  Other aspects of *Idler* 61 and its companion essay, No. 62—despite the satirical surface—are distinctly Johnsonian in theme. See, for example, his critical opinions upon Shakespeare as the poet of Nature, Denham and Waller as the initiators of correct English verse tradition, the assessment of Otway's powers of moving the passions, etc.

14  Numerous other instances might be cited: see, e.g., his running series of acute commentary upon the metaphysical poets in the "Life of Cowley," or his analysis of a famous pair of couplets from "Cooper's Hill" in the "Life of Denham," etc.

15  See James Basker, "Dancing Dogs, Women Preachers and the Myth of Johnson's Misogyny," *The Age of Johnson: A Scholarly Annual* 3 (1990): 63–90 and Eithne Henson, "Samuel Johnson and the Condition of Women," in *The Cambridge Companion to Samuel Johnson*, ed. Greg Clingham (New York: Cambridge University Press, 1997), 67–84.

16  See, e.g., Michael Bundock, "Johnson and Women in Boswell's *Life of Johnson*," *The Age of Johnson: A Scholarly Annual* 16 (2005): 81–109.

17 See James Basker, "'The Next Insurrection': Johnson, Race, and Rebellion," *AJ* 11 (2000): 37–51, and Elizabeth Lambert, "Johnson, Burke, Boswell, and the Slavery Debate," in *Community and Solitude: New Essays on Johnson's Circle*, ed. Anthony W. Lee (Lewisburg: Bucknell University Press, 2019), 167–90.

18 "Johnson and Imperialism," in Clingham, *Cambridge Companion to Samuel Johnson*, 114–26. See also Hawes, "Periodizing Johnson: Anti-Colonial Modernity as Crux and Critique," in *After the Imperial Turn: Thinking with and through the Nation*, ed. Antoinette Burton (Durham, NC: Duke University Press, 2003), 217–29.

19 See W. K. Wimsatt, *Philosophical Words: A Study of Style and Meaning in the Rambler and Dictionary of Samuel Johnson* (New Haven, CT: Yale University Press, 1948) and Richard B. Schwartz, *Samuel Johnson and the New Science* (Madison, WI: University of Wisconsin Press, 1971).

20 See his letters to Lewis Paul in *Letters*, 1:24–27, *passim*; *Boswell's Life*, 5:246.

21 See *Boswell's Life*, 1:444, 4:288, and 5:29 (Hume), and 2:348 and 447–48 (Gibbon).

22 Leslie Stephen, *Samuel Johnson* (New York: Harper and Brothers, n.d.), 10–11.

23 Charles Ryskamp and Frederick A. Pottle, eds, *Boswell: The Ominous Years, 1774–1776* (New York: McGraw-Hill, 1963), 93. A hygienically scrubbed version appears in *Boswell's Life*, 1:250.

24 See *Boswell's Life*, 3:6, 4:326–28, 348–50.

25 Yale *Works*, 3:79–80. See also *Rasselas*, chapter 16, Yale *Works*, 16:62. Another writer whose late work hovers upon the fringes of Modernism, Thomas Hardy, was probably influenced by the *Rambler* 14 description:

> Some way within the limits of the stretch of landscape, points of light like the topaz gleamed. The air increased in transparency with the lapse of minutes, till the topaz points showed themselves to be the vanes, windows, wet roof slates, and other shining spots upon the spires, domes, freestone-work, and varied outlines that were faintly revealed. It was Christminster, unquestionably; either directly seen, or miraged in the peculiar atmosphere. (*Jude the Obscure*, "At Marygreen")

26 For an additional example of Johnson's depiction of urban alienation, see *London*, ll.182–83, 190–93,

> But hark! Th' affrighted crowd's tumultuous cries
> Roll thro' the streets, and thunder to the skies: …
> Then thro' the world a wretched vagrant roam,
> For where can starving merit find a home?
> In vain your mournful narrative disclose,
> While all neglect, and most insult your woes. (Yale *Works*, 6:56–57)

27   Yale *Works*, 5:144. The term "penthouse" does not connote luxury in this period: see *Dictionary*, s.v. "penthouse," "A shed hanging out aslope from the main wall."

28   Nicholas Seager and Lance Wilcox, eds, *The Life of Mr. Richard Savage* (Peterborough, ON: Broadview, 2016), 110–11.

29   "Poetry in the Eighteenth Century," in *The New Penguin Companion to English Literature: From Dryden to Johnson*, ed. Boris Ford (Harmondsworth: Penguin, 1982), 276.

30   See, e.g., Valerie Eliot and John Haffenden, eds, *The Letters of T. S. Eliot: Volume 4: 1928–1929* (New Haven: Yale University Press, 2013), 486.

31   See Christopher Ricks and Jim McCue, eds, *The Poems of T. S. Eliot*, 2 vols (Baltimore, MD: Johns Hopkins University Press, 2015), 2:64–65.

32   From a note in Lucy Thayer's copy of *Ara Vos Prec*: see Ricks and McCue, 36, 500.

33   *Boswell's Life*, 4:4. See *Poems of T. S. Eliot*, 2:500, for the identification to which I am indebted.

34   Eliot, "The Love Song of J. Alfred Prufrock," ll.57, 56, 58; *Poems of T. S. Eliot*, 1:7.

35   *ABC of Reading* (New York: New Directions, 2010), 186.

36   *Guide to Kulchur* (New York: New Directions, 1970), 179, 180.

37   Stanza 12; Richard Sieburth, ed., *Ezra Pound: Poems and Translations* (New York: Library of America, 2003), 556.

38   *The Pound Era* (Berkeley and Los Angeles: University of California Press, 1971), 288. See also Leavis' observation, "The trade of writing could once support a Johnson. It is now commercial in senses and at levels inconceivable in Johnson's time," *New Bearings in English Poetry* (Ann Arbor: University of Michigan Press, 1960), 148.

39   Stanza 5; *Ezra Pound: Poems and Translations*, 552.

40   See C. J. Ackerley and S. E. Gontarski, *The Grove Companion to Samuel Beckett* (New York: Grove, 2004), 283–84:
     > Owned 1799 ed. of *Dictionary*: Cf. "tardigrade" and equidependency (*Watt*, 30–31); owned Hill's 1887 *Boswell's Life of Johnson*, *Johnsonian Miscellanies*, and *Rasselas*.

41   Ibid., 257.

42   Deidre Bair, *Samuel Beckett: A Biography* (London: Jonathan Cape, 1978), 257.

43   *A Portrait of the Artist as a Young Man* (New York: Penguin, 2016), 94.

44   Johnson's death-bed scene re-enacts that of Addison: see Stephan Miller, *Three Deaths and Enlightenment Thought: Hume, Johnson, Marat* (Lewisburg: Bucknell University Press, 2001), chapter three, "The Death of Johnson."

45   "A Sketch of the Past," in *Moments of Being*, ed. Jeanne Schulkind, 2nd ed. (San Diego: Harvest Books, 1984), 157.

46  *The Second Common Reader*, ed. Andrew McNeillie (San Diego: Harcourt, 1986), 118.
47  *The Essays of Virginia Woolf: Volume 4, 1925–1928*, ed. Andrew McNeillie (Orlando: Harvest Books, 1994), 309–13.
48  Woolf walked by Johnson's house at Gough Square—twice—the second time en route to visit T. S. Eliot for tea: see *The Diary of Virginia Woolf*, ed. Anne Olivier Bell, 5 vols (New York: Harcourt Brace Jovanovich, 1977), 1:56, 5:146.
49  *Orlando: A Biography*, ed. Maria DiBattista (San Diego: Harcourt, 2006), 162–63.
50  *To the Lighthouse*, ed. Margaret Drabble (Oxford: Oxford University Press), 50.
51  *The Second Common Reader*, 118. Further implications of this association will be explored in my chapter on Johnson and Woolf, below.
52  For Thrale, see James L. Clifford, *Hester Lynch Piozzi (Mrs. Thrale)*, 2nd ed. (New York: Columbia University Press, 1987), xxvi–xxvii; for Ramsay, see *To the Lighthouse*, 71, *passim*.
53  Ibid., 91, 140, *passim*.

## Notes to Chapter 1: Johnson, T. S. Eliot, and the City
### Melvyn New

1  "Proust's Influence on Sterne: A Remembrance of Things to Come," *MLN* 103 (1988): 1031–55; Tristram Shandy: *A Book for Free Spirits* (New York: Twayne-Macmillan, 1994); "Three Sentimental Journeys: Sterne, Shklovsky, Svevo," *The Shandean* 11 (1999): 126–34; "Reading Sterne through Proust and Levinas," *Age of Johnson* 12 (2001): 329–60; "Sterne and the Modernist Movement," in *Cambridge Companion to Laurence Sterne*, ed. Thomas Keymer (Cambridge: Cambridge University Press, 2009), 160–73.
2  Laurence Sterne, *A Sentimental Journey*, with an introduction by Virginia Woolf (London: Oxford University Press, 1928).
3  In postmodernism's philosophical and aesthetic devaluation of the author as creator and its consequent embrace of pastiche, leveling, and discontinuity, one might find some scattered seeds of the academic post-modernist's present ideologies, but thoughtful postmodernism remains in constant dialogue with the past, and especially with modernism, while its classroom "interpreters" have too often been in communication only with the cultural moment and no other time. The most characteristic sign defining this crude reading of postmodern theory is its instinctive flinching when the concept of literary genius or even "very best" authors is introduced into a discussion; "nonjudgmental evaluation" is the oxymoron within which these postmodernist academics wage their war with logic.

4   *Boswell's Life*, 2:449 (March 20, 1776); hereafter cited in text. Johnson's belief that literary worth has to do with endurance over time is worth noting.

5   "Ethics," in *A Cultural History of Comedy: The Age of Enlightenment*, ed. Elizabeth Kraft (forthcoming).

6   "Rasselas in an Eighteenth-Century Novels Course," in *Approaches to Teaching the Works of Samuel Johnson*, ed. David R. Anderson and Gwin J. Kolb (New York: Modern Language Association of America, 1993), 122; both Gide and Conrad are cited from this text.

7   David Perkins, "Johnson and Modern Poetry," *Harvard Library Bulletin* 33 (Summer 1985): 303–12 (307).

8   Perkins, 308; quoted from Samuel Johnson, *"London: A Poem" and "The Vanity of Human Wishes,"* with an Introductory Essay by T. S. Eliot (London: Frederick Etchells and Hugh Macdonald, 1930), 16.

9   *The Poems of T. S. Eliot*, vol. 1 (Baltimore, MD: Johns Hopkins University Press, 2015); if Christopher Ricks's exquisite ear failed to hear any verbal echoes, I doubt any will be found. All quotations from Eliot's poetry will be from this volume, cited as *Poems*.

10  Johnson had moved to London the year before his poem was published in 1738, when he was 28 years old. Eliot would not move to London until four years after he had in hand a fairly complete draft of the poem in 1911, but he had had some experience of city life in St. Louis, Boston, Paris, Oxford, and London; the poem, he said, was written primarily in Munich (*Poems*, 1:363). *Prufrock* was first published in 1915, when Eliot was 26.

11  Boswell records many such expressions of Johnson's love of London life, so many that the Index has a separate heading under "London" for "… loves it" with six separate entries; perhaps the one for September 30, 1769, best summarizes his attitude: "The happiness of London is not to be conceived but by those who have been in it. I will venture to say, there is more learning and science within the circumference of ten miles from where we now sit, than in all the rest of the kingdom" (*Boswell's Life*, 2:75).

12  Melvyn New, ed., *The Complete Novels and Selected Writings of Amy Levy, 1861–1889* (Gainesville: University Press of Florida, 1993), 385. Levy's poem has been enshrined in the Queen's Walk, South Bank, London, along with those of other "London" poets, including Johnson and Eliot.

13  Needless to say, Eliot turned as well to Dante's *Divine Comedy* for his epigraph (*Inferno*, XXVII, 61–62), and elsewhere in the poem. One measure of the historical distance between Johnson and Eliot, but not, I think, the spiritual distance, is Johnson's single mention of Dante recorded in Boswell's *Life*, in a comparison praising *Pilgrim's Progress*: "It is remarkable, that it begins very much like the poem of Dante; yet there was no translation of Dante when Bunyan wrote" (*Boswell's Life*, 2:238).

14  The lecture will appear in vol. 5 of Iman Javadi et al., eds, *The Complete Prose of T. S. Eliot: The Critical Edition* (Baltimore, MD: Johns Hopkins University Press, forthcoming); it is presently available online.

15  Significantly, in view of Johnson's political orientation in *London*, Eliot's lecture moves on specifically to the politics accompanying the secular faith in future perfection that he has been condemning, summarizing a condemnation of *realpolitik* with "a sentence attributed to Disraeli": "in order to get power and keep it a man must be prepared to do things which neither a punctilious country gentleman nor an honest trader could do in his private capacity without losing his self-respect." Although perhaps characteristic of Disraeli's thought, I have been unable to find evidence of his having spoken or written these words. It is noteworthy that the few mentions of Jews in this lecture (that Marx was a Jew, that one of the "limitations of Judaism" was that it believed in a secular perfection) point in a direction particularly pertinent to the present discussion: like Juvenal's Greek invaders and Johnson's French ones, the Jew could be rendered in caricature as embodying urban existence—the ultimate *cosmopolitan*. Needless to say, Amy Levy's short life gives a lie to the stereotype.

16  Anthony Lee has collected Johnson's thoughts on perfectibility in his *Annotated Rambler* (forthcoming), including several particularly pertinent to the present discussion. E.g., "the word *perfection* ... in its philosophical and exact sense ... can be of little use among human beings," *The Plan of a Dictionary of the English Language* (1747; Yale *Works*, 18:49); or again, in the advertisement to the fourth edition of the *Dictionary* (1773): "Perfection is unattainable, but nearer and nearer approaches may be made ..." (Yale *Works*, 18:375); and one further example, from *Adventurer* 85 (1753): "[I]t is, however, reasonable to have perfection in our eye; that we may always advance towards it, though we know it never can be reached" (Yale *Works*, 2:416–17). For Johnson's possible sympathy with the Armenian position on perfectibility, as preached by William Law and John Wesley, see Richard E. Brantley, "Johnson's Wesleyan Connection," *ECS* 10 (1976–1977), 143–68.

17  David F. Venturo, *Johnson the Poet: The Poetic Career of Samuel Johnson* (Newark: University of Delaware Press, 1999), 75–76. Venturo is quoting Eliot's "Johnson as Critic and Poet," in *On Poetry and Poets* (New York: Farrar, Straus and Cudahy, 1957), 205.

18  Howard D. Weinbrot, "Johnson's *London* and Juvenal's Third Satire: The Country as 'Ironic' Norm," *MP* 73, no. 4 (1976), S56–S65 ("A Supplement to Honor Arthur Friedman"). Weinbrot concludes that "we are to see Thales' departure as intelligent and thoughtful" (S64).

19  *Samuel Richardson, Sir Charles Grandison,* 6 vols (1753–1754), 2:398; John Milton, *Complete Poems and Major Prose*, ed. Merritt Y. Hughes

(New York: Odyssey Press, 1957), 209–12; hereafter cited in text. This passage begins the debate between Adam and Eve over whether they should separate and divide their labor, which is the immediate opportunity leading to their fall; separation and division of labor are, one might suggest, the essence of urban experience. Johnson, *Dictionary*, cites the Miltonic passage to illustrate "prune." See Milton's extensive description of Eden in 4:205ff.

20   Cf. Robert DeMaria's astute comments on the choice of "Thales" as his voice in the poem: "Thales is said to be the first philosopher to acknowledge the eternal God and his Providence in governing the world. As a character he is curiously like Demetrius in *Irene*, who goes off with Aspasia to instruct the West ... . Pious philosophers, combining fundamental Christian beliefs with ancient wisdom and natural science, Thales and Demetrius are embodiments of the Johnsonian hero" (*The Life of Samuel Johnson: A Critical Biography* [Oxford: Blackwell, 1993], 49–50); for another connection between *London* and *Irene*, see below, n.33. DeMaria reinforces the insights of Edward and Lillian Bloom, "The Rhetoric of 'London,'" in *Eighteenth-Century Studies in Honor of Donald F. Hyde*, ed. W. H. Bond (New York: The Grolier Club, 1970), 116–17; for example: "Thales, that is, acquires a religiosity lacking in Umbricius ... . Thales is ... fashioned after many early Christians; they, eager to flee the depravity of the large cities, set forth as lonely wanderers (eremites) through the countryside." I find this identification more convincing than Walter Jackson Bate's view that Thales is not the Greek philosopher but the lyric poet mentioned by Plutarch (*Samuel Johnson* [New York: Harcourt Brace Jovanovich, 1979], 172).

21   Venturo argues persuasively that Walpole is figured as Orgilio, and notes that "any reference in 1738 to an arrogant builder of palaces who traded in parliamentary seats and bishoprics (line 204) had to be directed at the prime minister" (74).

22   Cf. Johnson, *Dictionary*, s.v., "pastoral": 1. Rural; rustic; 2. Relating to the care of souls.

23   See Laurence Sterne's sermon "The case of Hezekiah and the messengers," preached at the resplendent new ambassador's chapel in 1764, a possible rebuke of the Earl of Hertford's pride in his possessions; see Melvyn New, ed., *Sermons*, Florida Edition of the Works of Laurence Sterne (Gainesville: University Press of Florida, 1996), 4:157–66.

24   *Hamlet*, III.i.78–79; we might recall Hamlet's remark that "Denmark is a prison," his own sense of urban imprisonment. Ricks and McCue finds additional scriptural echoes in this section of the poem—most interesting, perhaps, 2 Samuel 12:22, where David recounts his prayer for the unborn child of his adulterous union with the wife of Uriah: "And he said, While the child was yet alive, I fasted and wept: for I said, Who can tell

whether God will be gracious to me, that the child may live." It is a prayer that is not answered.

25  Andrew Varney, "Johnson's Juvenalian Satire on London: A Different Emphasis," *RES* 40 (1989): 202–14.

26  Varney, 213; he quotes a passage from Henry Sacheverell's "inflammatory sermon" *The Perils of False Brethren, Both in Church and State*, delivered November 5, 1709, and thus for a service that produced exceptionally rabid sermons recalling the Gunpowder Plot from Anglican pulpits throughout the century; the date itself should thus have warned Varney that it was hardly a representative statement of quotidian eighteenth-century Anglican belief.

27  Matthew Henry, *An Exposition of All the Books of the Old and New Testament* ... 3rd ed. (1721–1725), 5:24.

28  Luke 6:20 reads "blessed are the poor," without the addition of "in spirit," a curtailment that allows the passage to be read more simply in social or economic terms; Matthew's complication moves toward the reading I am suggesting, that Enlightenment faith in the capacity of human intellect and activity to envision and then bring into being a future perfection is in itself an heretical mindset: "'Tis to come off from all Confidence in our own Righteousness and Strength, that we may depend only upon the Merit of Christ for our Justification .... [T]he Philosophers did not reckon Humility among their moral Virtues, but Christ puts it first ... ." (Henry, 24). It is important to recognize the increasing importance in the century of Matthew 5:48 ("Be ye therefore perfect, even as your Father ..."), partly due to Methodism's influence, but primarily, it might be argued, because the verse embodies a theology seemingly in tune with undeniable economic and social progress. One might reconcile the several texts by placing individual perfection solely in the realm of the eternal, our existence in time rendering claims to perfection a false "Confidence" in one's own "Righteousness and Strength." This would not negate, then, the virtue of striving to perfect both oneself and one's society, but would keep in mind that earthly economic and social perfection is not the ethical perfection Matthew 5:48 has in view.

29  John Wain, *Samuel Johnson* (New York: Viking Press, 1974), 86. That the issue of Johnson's attitude toward London remains indeterminate is indicated by Aaron Santesso, "Johnson as Londoner": "Critics have tended to divide into those who see Johnson's attitude towards London as wholly admiring and those who perceive only stubborn disdain. Each position has its textual evidence" (Eric Rasmussen and Aaron Santesso, eds, *Comparative Excellence: New Essays on Shakespeare and Johnson* [New York: AMS Press, 2007], 161). Rather than resolving this debate, I hope putting Johnson into proximity with modernism helps explain why a "divided mind" is precisely what the urban Christian must live with.

Augustine recognized the dichotomy in his own day, of course, positioning the City of God against the City of Man; not the concept but its continuing relevance is what *London* and *Prufrock* struggle to represent.

30    Obviously Juvenal worships different gods, but my point is that Johnson cannot help but read his portrait of Rome within his own ethical framework, wherein the conflict between city vice and country virtue becomes the religious/secular struggle I am suggesting. Interestingly, one of Dryden's added lines in his translation of Satire 3 reads "Nor place, nor persons now are sacred held"; and in describing the physical destruction caused by a falling building, he speaks of "One vast destruction: not the soul alone / But bodies, like the soul, invisible are flown" (John Dryden, *The Poems*, ed. Paul Hammond and David Hopkins (London: Longman, 2000), 4:21, 38 (ll.27, 415–16); the latter translates "quis membra, quis ossa invenit? obtritum vulgi perit omne cadaver more animae" ("Who can identify the limbs, who the bones? The poor man's crushed corpse wholly disappears, just like his soul") (*Juvenal and Persius*, trans. G. G. Ramsay [Cambridge, MA: Loeb Classical Library, 1979], 50–53).

31    2 Peter 3:5–7. When in 1666 a special service was annexed to the *Book of Common Prayer* in response to the London fire, 2 Peter 3 was included in the Order for Evening Prayer. Obviously, many passages in scripture tell of divine wrath because of the corruption of the people; e.g., Isaiah 1:7: "Your country is desolate, your cites are burned with fire: your land, strangers devour it in your presence, and it is desolate, overthrown by strangers"; this passage, along with passages from Lamentations and Psalms, were part of the special service for September 2, which continued to be observed at St. Paul's until 1859. Most interesting, perhaps, in relation to Matthew's "poverty of spirit" are these passages from the Commination for the service: "abandon us not to our selves; but reduce us … by any the severest course [and] … subdue us unto thy self, and make us see the things belonging to our peace…" (*BCP*, 1681). See Jack Gilpin, "God's Terrible Voice: Liturgical Response to the Great Fire of London," *Anglican and Episcopal History* 82 (2013), 318–34.

32    The most obvious example in modernism is *Ulysses*, one foot anchored in Homer, the other in a seeming rejection of Christianity. A question we have yet to resolve concerning modernism is whether any thoughtful and literate mind has yet freed itself from the Christian inheritance, whether even the harshest attacks on the religious heritage are indications of the difficulty of separating from it. Especially for artists, inheriting a tradition steeped in Christian thought, this difficulty seems apparent. Whether whatever postmodernism turns out to be will have success in finally rejecting this inheritance remains to be seen, but for now, I suspect those women "talking of Michelangelo" (l.36), who might provoke disgust in any educated reader because they reduce the portrayer of the "Creation of Adam" and the

"Pieta" to cocktail-hour chitchat (not to mention Eliot's comical rhyme), are also possibly reflecting the poem's framework. In my deriving two of the artist's most famous works from his evocation, I anticipate what I hope to demonstrate, namely the centrality of Eden and crucifixion to the poem; the women are not, after all, discussing Ben and JLo.

33    Johnson seems to have had Babel in mind when he wrote these lines in *Irene*, perhaps even as he was also writing *London*:

> How Heav'n in Scorn of human Arrogance,
> Commits to trivial Chance the Fate of Nations!
> While with incessant Thought laborious Man
> Extends his mighty Schemes of Wealth and Pow'r,
> And tow'rs amid triumphs in ideal Greatness;
> Some accidental Gust of Opposition
> Blasts all the Beauties of his new Creation.
> O'erturns the Fabrick of presumptuous Reason,
> And whelms the swelling Architect beneath it (II.iii.1–9; I quote from the 1749 edition; Johnson is thought to have finished most of the play before he arrived in London in 1737.)

34    Nicholas Hudson, "Samuel Johnson, Urban Culture, and the Geography of Postfire London," *SEL* 42 (2002): 577–600 (582).

35    Hudson sees the situation differently:

> Here is where Johnson's urban reflections belong to a distinctly bygone era .... Since the Romantics, there has been a strong tendency in Western culture to view ... "urban man" [as] an alienated and troubled individual, shaped by an environment that overwhelms the senses, confuses traditional beliefs, and destroys communities .... 
> But the older Johnson ... clearly surmounted this alienation .... (596)

I would suggest, to the contrary, that this alienation was, in Johnson's happier moments, suppressed, but in a life where "much is to be endured and little to be enjoyed," I think his response to the city quite precisely foreshadowed that of the post-Romantic "urban man"; we might claim for him, then, the title of first urban modernist, except that it might better be awarded to Juvenal in Rome.

36    David Venturo has reminded me, most aptly, that Milton compares the serpent's first sighting of Eve with a simile indicating that Satan is now a city dweller: "As one who long in populous City pent, / Where Houses thick and Sewers annoy the Air, / Forth issuing on a Summer's Morn to breathe / Among the pleasant Villages and Farms ..." (*Paradise Lost*, 9:445–48).

37    Cf. Ricks and McCue, 398: "Like Eve's apple, the peach (*pêche*) tempts to sin (*péché*)."

38    "Life of Milton" in Samuel Johnson, *The Lives of the Poets*, ed. John H. Middendorf (New Haven: Yale University Press, 2010), 1:194 (vol. 21 of the Yale *Works*).

## Notes to Chapter 2: "Saint Samuel of Fleet Street": Johnson and Woolf   *Anthony W. Lee*

1   I wish to acknowledge Ellen Moody and Christine Holzberg-Jackson for their kind assistance with earlier drafts of this chapter.

2   See Elisa de Courcy, "The Dreadnought Hoax Portrait as an Affront to the Edwardian Age," *Early Popular Visual Culture* 3, no. 1 (May 2005) <https://doi.org/10.1080/17460654.2017.1379425>, accessed January 9, 2018; Jan Rüger, "The Symbolic Value of the Dreadnought," in *The Dreadnought and the Edwardian Age*, ed. Robert Blyth, Andrew Lambert and Jan Rüger (Farnham: Ashgate, 2011), 9–18; Quentin Bell, *Virginia Woolf* (London: Triad/Paladin, 1987), 1:157–61; and Hermione Lee, *Virginia Woolf* (New York: Alfred A. Knopf, 1997), 278–83 (cited hereafter as Lee, *Virginia Woolf*).

3   Virginia Woolf, *The Platform of Time: Memoirs of Family and Friends* (London: Hesperus Press, 2008), 159.

4   *The Times* (February 5, 1960): 12.

5   The phrase is found elsewhere in Woolf; see, e.g., the short story "The Man who Loved his Kind"; *To the Lighthouse*, ed. Margaret Drabble (Oxford: Oxford University Press, 1992), 265.

6   Andrew McNeillie, ed., *The Essays of Virginia Woolf: Volume 4, 1925–1928* (Orlando, FL: Harvest, 1994), 310–11.

7   *Essays of Virginia Woolf: Volume 4*, 311. For a recent critical appreciation of Johnson's "elegant" poise, see David Fairer, "The Agile Johnson," in *Samuel Johnson: New Contexts for a New Century*, ed. Howard D. Weinbrot (San Marino, CA: Huntington Library, 2013), 33–46.

8   *The Second Common Reader*, ed. Andrew McNeillie (San Diego, CA: Harcourt, 1986), 120.

9   *The Common Reader, First Series*, ed. Andrew McNeillie (Orlando, FL: Harcourt, 1984), 1. For the passage Woolf quotes, see Yale *Works*, 23:1470–71.

10   Johnson is mentioned, or alluded to, in *A Room of One's Own*, *To the Lighthouse*, and *Orlando*. He is referred to in the following essays: "Addison," "Coleridge as Critic," "Congreve's Comedies," "Dr. Burney's Evening Party," "A Friend of Johnson," "Genius of Boswell," "Gothic Romance," "How it Strikes a Contemporary II," "How Should One Read a Book?" "Indiscretions," "Maria Edgeworth," "Mrs. Thrale," "Patmore's Criticism," "Sheridan," "Sterne," and "Women and Fiction." I count mentions of him in Woolf's *Diaries* at least thirteen times. This list does not presume to be exhaustive but rather aspires merely toward suggestiveness.

11   See, e.g., Lytton Strachey's comment that Woolf was "the inventor of a new prose style," in *The Diary of Virginia Woolf Vol. One, 1915–1919*

(New York: Harcourt Brace Jovanovich, 1977), 277 (May 25, 1919); W. K. Wimsatt, Jr., *The Prose Style of Samuel Johnson* (New Haven, CT: Yale University Press 1941).

12   For Woolf's reading, see Lee, *Virginia Woolf*, 16; for Johnson's see Robert DeMaria, Jr., *Samuel Johnson and the Life of Reading* (Baltimore: Johns Hopkins University Press, 1997).

13   See Lee, *Virginia Woolf*, 6–7; Johnson's conversational prowess is legendary and is exhibited exhaustively in Boswell's *Life of Johnson*.

14   See J. K. Johnstone's remark about the Bloomsbury gatherings, where "conversation became an art in its midst and was more important than it had been, perhaps, since the days of Dr. Johnson," *The Bloomsbury Group* (New York: Noonday Press, 1963), 17.

15   See Lewis Perry Curtis and Herman W. Liebert, *Esto perpetua: The Club of Dr. Johnson and his Friends, 1764–1784* (North Haven, CT: Archon Books, 1963).

16   Victoria Rosner, ed., *The Cambridge Companion to the Bloomsbury Group* (Cambridge: Cambridge University Press, 2014), 2.

17   From an English translation of Johnson's Latin epitaph for Goldsmith see James Boswell, *Life of Johnson*, ed. R. W. Chapman (Oxford: Oxford University Press, 1980), 779n1.

18   *A Room of One's Own* (San Diego, CA: Harcourt Brace and Company), 18.

19   *Boswell's Life*, 1:467.

20   If one suspects Boswell of artfully polishing up the remark, compare it to the original, from his *London Journal*: "For my part I mind my belly very studiously and very carefully; for I look upon it that he who does not mind his belly will hardly mind anything else."

21   See James L. Clifford, *Young Sam Johnson* (New York: McGraw-Hill, 1955), 129.

22   See Walter Jackson Bate, *Samuel Johnson* (New York: Harcourt Brace Jovanovich, 1977), 371–79.

23   At least nine times in 1895, 1904, 1910, 1913, 1915, 1921, 1925, 1936, and 1941.

24   See, e.g., Walter Jackson Bate, *The Achievement of Samuel Johnson* (New York: Oxford University Press, 1955), 92–95.

25   See Lee, *Virginia Woolf*, 710–14.

26   From the Continental Congress's Address to the People of Great Britain, quoted in Yale *Works*, 10:453n8.

27   *Boswell's Life*, 3:200. For a fuller discussion of these issues, see Thomas E. Curley, "Samuel Johnson and *Taxation No Tyranny*: 'I am willing to love all mankind, *except an American*,'" in *New Essays on Samuel Johnson: Revaluation*, ed. Anthony W. Lee (Newark: University of Delaware Press, 2018), 87–110.

28  See, e.g., Anna Snaith, "Leonard and Virginia Woolf: Writing Against Empire," *The Journal of Commonwealth Literature* 50, no. 1 (2015): 19–32; Constance S. Richards, *On the Winds and Waves of Imagination: Transnational Feminism and Literature* (New York: Garland, 2000), 39–72. For a useful general study, see Kathy J. Phillips, *Virginia Woolf Against Empire* (Knoxville: University of Tennessee Press, 1994).

29  See Panthea Reid, "Virginia Woolf, Leslie Stephen, Julia Margaret Cameron, and the Prince of Abyssinia: An Inquiry into Certain Colonialist Representations," *Biography* 2, no. 3 (Summer 1999): 323–55.

30  *Three Guineas*, Jane Marcus, ed. (Orlando: Harcourt, 2006), 43.

31  These are some of the more important conflicts spanning Johnson's lifetime upon which the above calculation is based: the War of the Spanish Succession (1702–1713); the War of the Quadruple Alliance (1718–1720); the War of Jenkins's Ear (1739–1742); the War of the Austrian Succession (1742–1748); the Jacobite Risings of 1715–1716, 1719, and 1745–1746; the Seven Years' War (1756–1763); the American Revolutionary War (1775–1783); and the Fourth Anglo-Dutch War (1780–1784). See also chapter five, below, "Johnson Goes to War."

32  See Winston S. Churchill, *A History of the English-Speaking Peoples*, vol. 3, *The Age of Revolution* (New York and London: Cassell, 1957), chapter 5.

33  For the negative connotations in Johnson's writings, see *Rambler* 38, where, speaking of the indolent rich, Johnson observes:

> He will soon be involved in perplexities, which his inexperience will render insurmountable; he will fly for help to those whose interest it is that he should be more distressed, and will be at last torn to pieces by the vulturs that always hover over fortunes in decay. (Yale *Works*, 3:209)

In *Rambler* 59 he writes, "an extortioner gains the appellation of vulture" (Yale *Works*, 3:314).

34  See Paula Maggio, "Taking Up Her Pen for World Peace: Virginia Woolf, Feminist Pacifist. Or Not?" in *Virginia Woolf: Writing the World*, ed. Pamela L. Caughie and Diana L. Swanson (Liverpool: Liverpool University Press, 2015), 37–42; Grace Brockington, "'Tending the lamp' or 'minding their own business'? Bloomsbury Art and Pacifism during World War I," *Immediations* 1, no. 1 (2004): 7–19.

35  "Thoughts on Peace in an Air Raid," in *Virginia Woolf: Selected Essays*, ed. David Bradshaw (Oxford: Oxford University Press, 2008), 216–19 (216).

36  *The History of Rasselas, Prince of Abyssinia* (Yale *Works*, 16:27–28).

37  *A Writer's Diary: Being Extracts from the Diary of Virginia Woolf*, ed. Leonard Woolf (San Diego, CA: Harcourt Brace Jovanovich, 1982), 4, 5.

38  See my discussions of these three in "Who's Mentoring Whom? Alliance and Rivalry in the Johnson-Carter Relationship," in *Mentoring in*

*Eighteenth-Century British Literature and Culture*, ed. Anthony W. Lee (Burlington and Surrey: Ashgate, 2010), 191–210; *Dead Masters: Mentoring and Intertextuality in Samuel Johnson* (Bethlehem: Lehigh University Press, 2011), 110–17; and "Allegories of Mentoring: Frances Burney's *Cecilia* and Samuel Johnson," *The Eighteenth-Century Novel* 5 (2006): 249–76.

39  See James Basker, "Dancing Dogs, Women Preachers and the Myth of Johnson's Misogyny," *AJ* 3 (1990): 63–90; "Samuel Johnson as Patron of Women," *AJ* 1 (1987): 59–77; Eithne Henson, "Johnson and the Condition of Women," in *The Cambridge Companion to Samuel Johnson*, ed. Greg Clingham (New York: Cambridge University Press, 1997), 67–84.

40  "Swift's 'Journal to Stella,'" in *The Second Common Reader*, 71, 76–77.

41  See Steven Lynn, *Samuel Johnson after Deconstruction: Rhetoric and the Rambler* (Carbondale, IL: Southern Illinois University Press, 1992).

42  *The Common Reader, First Series*, 97. It should be noted that Woolf read Johnson's Life of Addison before writing her essay. She quotes directly from it once (103) and alludes indirectly to it at least twice (100, 102).

43  *An Essay on Criticism*, l.153; *The Poems of Alexander Pope*, ed. John Butt (New Haven, CT: Yale University Press, 1963), 149.

44  *Boswell's Life*, 1:210n1. Woolf recurs to the image in her essay on Addison: "A writer should give us direct certainty; explanations are so much water poured into the wine." (*The Common Reader, First Series*, 99).

45  For Johnson, see *Idler* 84, *Diaries, Prayers, Annals* (vol. 1 of Yale *Works*); for Woolf, see her collected diaries (five volumes; condensed in *A Writer's Diary*) and *Moments of Being*.

46  *Selected Essays*, 122–23. The open ellipse after "a Christian, or" is Woolf's, not mine. Perhaps not incidentally, Woolf's passage here alludes to Johnson's Life of Addison:

> Lord Warwick was a young man of very irregular life … . Addison, for whom he did not want respect, had very diligently endeavoured to reclaim him; but his arguments and expostulations had no effect. One experiment, however, remained to be tried: when he found his life near its end, he directed the young lord to be called; and when he desired, with great tenderness, to hear his last injunctions, told him, "I have sent for you that you may see how a Christian can die." (Yale *Works*, 22:638–39)

Woolf also alludes to this scene in her essay on Addison: see *The Common Reader, First Series*, 100. See also the discussion of Joyce's allusion to the passage in the Introduction, above.

47  "A Sketch of the Past," in *Moments of Being*, ed. Jeanne Schulkind, 2nd ed. (San Diego, CA: Harcourt Brace and Company, 1985), 69.

48  See, e.g., Norman O. Brown, *Life Against Death: The Psychoanalytic Meaning of History* (Hanover, NH: Wesleyan University Press, 1985),

179–201, and Donald T. Siebert, "Swift's Fiat Odor: The Excremental Re-Vision," *Eighteenth-Century Studies* 19, no. 1 (Autumn 1985): 21–38.

49    Friday, January 29; *The Diary of Virginia Woolf, Vol. 5, 1936–1941*, ed. Anne Olivier Bell, assisted Andrew McNeillie (San Diego, CA: Harcourt Brace Jovnavich, 1984), 52–53 (52).

50    See those of Thomas Hardy (*Diary*, July 25, 1926), Yeats (*Diary*, November 8, 1930), etc.

51    "Leslie Stephen," in *Selected Essays*, 115.

52    See *To the Lighthouse*, 64.

53    Yale *Works*, 3:319; Yale *Works*, 2:261.

54    "The Art of Biography," in *Selected Essays*, 122.

55    Arthur Murphy, *An Essay on the Life and Genius*, in *JM*, 1:459.

56    *Rambler* 60 (Yale *Works*, 3:318–19).

57    *Great Books* (New York: Touchstone, 1997), 432.

58    See the Introduction, above, page 68, for additional critical reflections upon the kicked stone passage.

59    For Johnson's intertextuality, see, e.g., my "'We make the music which we imagine ourselves to hear': Milton, Pope, Shakespeare, and the Poetics of Intertextuality in Johnson's *Dictionary* and *Rambler*," in *Reading the British Eighteenth Century: New Essays in Criticism*, ed. Jesse Swan (Lewisburg: Bucknell University Press, forthcoming, 2019), and "No Poem an Island: An Intertextual Reading of Samuel Johnson's *London*," in Lee, *New Essays on Samuel Johnson: Revaluation*, 153–66. For Woolf, see, e.g., Raphaël Ingelbien, "Intertextuality, Critical Politics and the Modernist Canon: The Case of Virginia Woolf," *Paragraph* 22, no. 3 (November 1999): 278–92, and Anne E. Fernald, "Woolf and Intertextuality," in *Virginia Woolf in Context*, ed. Bryony Randall (Cambridge: Cambridge University Press, 2012), 52–64.

## Notes to Chapter 3: "Intellectually 'Fuori del Mondo'": Pound's Johnson    *Joe Moffett*

1    David Perkins, "Johnson and Modern Poetry," *Harvard Library Bulletin* (1985), 308.

2    Piotr K. Gwiazda, for example, in his comparative study of influence (*James Merrill and W. H. Auden: Homosexuality and Poetic Influence* [New York: Palgrave, 2007]) demonstrates the need to alter Bloom's model when discussing gay writers. Even before him, Gilbert and Gubar posit the term "anxiety of authorship" to describe the more fundamental problems for women writers not considered by Bloom's study (Sandra Gilbert and Susan Gubar, *The Madwoman in the Attic: The Woman Writer and the Nineteenth-Century Literary Imagination* (New Haven, CT: Yale University Press, 1979).

3    Harold Bloom, *The Anxiety of Influence: A Theory of Poetry*, 2nd ed. (New York: Oxford University Press, 1997), xxiii. Bloom's emphasis.

4    *Anxiety*, xxiv.

5    *Anxiety*, xviii.

6    *Anxiety*, 14. Bloom explains his use of the term "antithetical" thus: "I am using 'antithetical' in its rhetorical meaning: the juxtaposition of contrasting ideas in balanced or parallel structures, phrases, words." *Anxiety*, 65.

7    *Anxiety*, 66.

8    Richard Sieburth charts the evolution of the representation of money in Pound's poetry from his early use of gold as a symbol to his later reliance on the concept of Social Credit. See "In Pound We Trust: The Economy of Poetry/The Poetry of Economics," *Critical Inquiry* 14, no. 1 (Autumn 1987): 142–72.

9    Alireza Farabakhsh points out that the grouping to which this canto belongs—the so-called *Fifth Decad of Cantos*—uniquely works in a didactic mode not commonly seen as central to Modernism: "The Anti-Modernist Quality of Ezra Pound's *The Fifth Decad of Cantos* (Cantos XLII–LI)," *War, Literature, and the Arts* 24 (2012): 1–15.

10   Ezra Pound, *The Cantos* (New York: New Directions, 1995), 230.

11   *The Cantos*, 229.

12   Pound's statement runs thus: "I suggest that finer and future critics of art will be able to tell from the quality of painting the degree of tolerance or intolerance of usury extant in the age and milieu that produced it" (Ezra Pound, *Guide to Kulchur* [New York: New Directions, 1938], 27).

13   *Cantos*, 230.

14   *Guide*, 180.

15   Hugh Kenner notes that, "If Pound's Enlightenment, with its stress on Bayle, Voltaire, and a few historians, and the antecedents of Revolutionary America, is not precisely that of an 18th century specialist, that is because of the sharp selection and reemphasis incident to solving a poetic problem two centuries later": "Ezra Pound and the Light of France," *Yale French Studies* 10, French-American Literary Relationships (1952): 55]. Robert Casillo shows that one of the more lamentable things Pound takes away from his affection for Voltaire is a virulent anti-Semitism: "The Desert and the Swamp: Enlightenment, Orientalism, and the Jews in Pound," *Modern Language Quarterly* 45, no. 3 (1984): 263–86.

16   *ABC of Reading* (New York: New Directions, 1934), 186.

17   *Personae: The Shorter Poems* (New York: New Directions, 1990), 188.

18   See John B. Vickery, *The Modern Elegiac Temper* (Baton Rouge: Louisiana State University Press, 2006).

19   *Personae*, 185.

20   *Personae*, 188.

21   *Personae*.

22   *Personae*, 60.

23   Kenner, *The Pound Era* (Berkeley: University of California Press, 1971), 151. For a more recent assessment of Pound's understanding of philology as seen in his evocation of Old English and other archaic languages, see J. Mark Smith, "The Energy of Language(s): What Pound Made of Philology," *ELH* 78, no. 4 (Winter 2011): 769–800. The reference also calls to mind the statement "Non Angli sed Angeli, si forent Christiani," attributed to Gregory in 573 when British slave children were presented to him.

24   For a general discussion of the literary appropriation of Anglo-Saxon origins, see Allen J. Frantzen, *Desire for Origins: New Language, Old English, and Teaching the Tradition* (New Brunswick: Rutgers University Press, 1990). For a discussion of Pound's use of Old English, see Chris Jones, *Strange Likeness: The Use of Old English in Twentieth-Century Poetry* (Oxford: Oxford University Press, 2006).

25   While there are exceptions, such as David Jones or T. S. Eliot, the Modernists generally cast a skeptical eye toward conventional religion. See Emily Griesinger, for example, for an analysis of Woolf and religion: "Religious Belief in a Secular Age: Literary Modernism and Virginia Woolf's *Mrs. Dalloway*," *Christianity & Literature* 64, no. 4 (2015) <https://doi.org/10.1177/0148333115585279>, accessed June 12, 2018. For an analysis of the role of religion in postwar literature, see Amy Hungerford, *Postmodern Belief: American Literature and Religion since 1960* (Princeton, NJ: Princeton University Press, 2010), as well as Norman Finkelstein, *On Mount Vision: Forms of the Sacred in Contemporary American Poetry* (Iowa City: University of Iowa Press, 2010).

26   *Guide*, 178.

27   *Guide*, 181.

28   *Guide*, 180; Pound's italics.

29   *Guide*.

30   *Guide*, 182.

31   *Guide*, 180.

32   *Guide*, 181. Pound's ellipses.

33   *Personae*, 90.

34   Pound argues that "Johnson's verse is not as good prose as that often found in Tom Jefferson's letters. There is probably no couplet in the two reprinted poems that has the quality of Jefferson's." *Guide*, 181.

35   Ezra Pound, "Mr. Hueffer and the Prose Tradition in Verse," *Poetry* 4, no. 3 (1914): 115.

36   "Mr. Hueffer and the Prose Tradition in Verse," 180.

37   "Mr. Hueffer and the Prose Tradition in Verse," 179.

38  Another way to read Pound's praise is, as Lawrence Lipking points out, in the context of his and Eliot's understanding of Johnson's diction as a result of his work as lexicographer: *Samuel Johnson* (Cambridge, MA: Harvard University Press, 2000), 91–92.

39  *Guide*, 180.

40  *Guide*, 179.

41  *Guide*, 177

42  *Anxiety*, xxiii.

43  *Anxiety*, 69. Bloom suggests, briefly and in passing, that the nation of one's origin may have an effect on how influence is handled: "It seems true that British poets swerve from their precursors, while American poets labor rather to 'complete' their fathers." Of course, the situation is even more complicated in Pound's case, where we find a poet who displays, early on, Anglophilia, but who is American in origin. *Anxiety*, 68.

44  *Guide*, 182.

45  *Guide*, 179. Pound's ellipses.

46  *Cantos*, 816.

47  *Personae*, 194.

48  Peter Makin memorably describes the emotional tenor of the poems thus: "we find that the form of the Pisan Cantos is, first, a simple cry of pain and, second, a naming-over of what has been known, sorrowing over the lost, and trying to find, in what is left, some hope-worthy meaning and reason to go on": *Pound's Cantos* (Baltimore, MD: Johns Hopkins University Press, 1985), 239.

49  See Michael O'Driscoll, "Ezra Pound's *Cantos*: 'A Memorial to Archivists and Librarians,'" *Studies in the Literary Imagination* 32, no. 1 (Spring 1999):173–189 for an account of Pound's deployment of sources and his examination of archivists themselves.

50  *Cantos*, 520.

51  See my "'A Coin for a Closed Eye': Pound's Influence on Wright's *Appalachian Book of the Dead*," *The Southern Literary Journal* 44, no. 1 (Fall 2011): 55–72.

52  *Cantos*, 517–18.

53  *Cantos*, 518–19.

54  *Cantos*.

55  *Cantos*, 513.

56  *Cantos*, 516.

57  *Cantos*, 513.

58  *Cantos*, 521.

59  *Cantos*, 523.

60  Pound meekly recalls, "Whitman liked Oysters / at least I think it was oysters." Gone is the strident rhetorical style that marked such work as the

"usury canto." Instead Pound's voice is intimate, self-doubting, grasping. *Cantos*, 515.

61   *Cantos*, 521.

62   *Cantos*.

63   *Cantos*, 436.

64   *Cantos*, 822.

65   *Cantos*, 823.

## Notes to Chapter 4: The Antinomies of Progress: Johnson, Conrad, Joyce    *Clement Hawes*

1   I am very grateful for the acute responses to an earlier draft of this essay by Ashby Bland Crowder, Karina Williamson, Amittai Aviram, and Mrinalini Sinha.

2   Thomas Babington Macaulay, "Samuel Johnson," in *Encyclopedia Britannica*, 8th ed. (Boston: Little, Brown, & Co., 1852).

3   See Clement Hawes, "Johnson and Empire," in *The Cambridge Companion to Samuel Johnson*, ed. Greg Clingham (Cambridge: Cambridge University Press, 1997), 114–15.

4   Clement Hawes, *The British Eighteenth Century and Global Critique* (New York: Palgrave, 2005), 169–70.

5   Johnson, *The Life of Gray*, in *The Lives of the Poets*, ed. Roger Lonsdale, 4 vols (Oxford: Clarendon Press, 2006), 4:184.

6   Fredric Jameson, "Modernism and Imperialism," in *Nationalism, Colonialism, and Literature*, ed. Terry Eagleton (Minneapolis: University of Minnesota Press, 1990), 44.

7   Stephen Kinzler, *The True Flag: Theodore Roosevelt, Mark Twain, and the Birth of American Empire* (New York: Henry Holt, 2017), 136.

8   J. G. A. Pocock, *The Machiavellian Moment: Florentine Political Thought and the Atlantic Republican Tradition* (Princeton, NJ: Princeton University Press, 1975), 540.

9   Eviatar Zerubavel, *Time Maps: Collective Memory and the Social Shape of the Past* (Chicago: University of Chicago Press, 2003), 14.

10   John Micklethwait and Adrian Woodbridge, *The Company: A Short History of a Revolutionary Idea* (New York: Modern Library Edition, 2003), 168.

11   Linda Gordon, *The Second Coming of the KKK: The Ku Klux Klan of the 1920s and the American Political Tradition* (New York: Liveright, 2017).

12   James Q. Whitman, *Hitler's American Model: The United States and the Making of Nazi Race Law* (Princeton, NJ: Princeton University Press, 2017), 116.

13   Stuart Hall, *The Fateful Triangle: Race, Ethnicity, Nation*, ed. Kobena Mercer (Cambridge, MA: Harvard University Press, 2017), 101.

14  John Richetti, *The English Novel in History, 1700–1780* (London: Routledge, 1999).

15  Steve Pincus, *1688: The First Modern Revolution* (New Haven, CT: Yale University Press, 2009).

16  P. J. Cain and A. G. Hopkins, *British Imperialism: Innovation and Expansion, 1688–1914* (London: Longman, 1993).

17  Albert O. Hirschman, *The Passions and the Interests: Political Arguments for Capitalism before Its Triumph* (Princeton, NJ: Princeton University Press, 1977).

18  *Boswell's Life*, 3:292.

19  Bill Goldstein, *The World Broke in Two: Virginia Woolf, T.S. Eliot, D. H. Lawrence, E.M. Forster, and the Year that Changed Literature* (New York: Henry Holt, 2017), 294.

20  Anthony Paul, "From Stasis to Ékstasis: Four Types of Chiasmus," in *Chiasmus and Culture*, ed. Boris Wiseman and Anthony Paul (New York: Berghahn Books, 2014), 19–44.

21  Henry Louis Gates, Jr. and Kwame Anthony Appiah, "Samuel Johnson," in *The Dictionary of Global Culture* (New York: Alfred E. Knopf, 2004), 344.

22  Ford Madox Ford, *The March of Literature from Confucius' Day to Our Own* (Normal, IL: Dalkey Archive Press, 1994), 614.

23  Teju Cole, "In Place of Thought," *The New Yorker* (August 27, 2013) <https://www.newyorker.com/books/page-turner/in-place-of-thought>, accessed November 8, 2018.

24  Harold Bloom, *The Anatomy of Influence: Literature as a Way of Life* (New Haven, CT: Yale University Press, 2011), 127.

25  Samuel Johnson, "Butler," *Lives*, 3:4–5.

26  Greg Clingham, *Johnson, Writing, and Memory* (Cambridge: Cambridge University Press, 2002), 162.

27  Samuel Johnson, *Rasselas and Other Tales*, Yale *Works*, 16:97.

28  Johnson, Preface to Shakespeare, Yale *Works*, 7:605.

29  Derek Attridge, "Unpacking the Portmanteau; or, Who's Afraid of Finnegans Wake," in *On Puns: The Foundation of Letters*, ed. Jonathan Culler (Oxford: Basil Blackwell, 1988), 140.

30  See, e.g., the "*Infantes barbati*" of *Rambler* 25 (¶ 11); *Boswell's Life*, 4:99; letter to Richard Brocklesby (1722–1797), August 19, 1784 (*Letters*, 4:372–73 and n4), and Hawkins, "Apothegms, Sentiments, and Occasional Reflections":

> He was no great friend to puns, though he once by accident made a singular one. A person who affected to live after the Greek manner, and to anoint himself with oil, was one day mentioned before him. Johnson, in the course of conversation on the singularity of his

> practice, gave him the denomination of, This man of *Greece*, or *grease*, as you please to take it. (*JM*, 2:18)

31  Johnson, "Pope," *Lives*, 4:79.

32  For "entrances," see George Kubler, *The Shape of Time: Remarks on the History of Things* (New Haven, CT: Yale University Press, 1962), 6–7.

33  Johnson, *The Life of Savage*, in *Lives* 3:146.

34  Ibid.

35  Ibid., 154.

36  Samuel Johnson, *The Rambler* 106, Yale *Works*, 4:200.

37  Samuel Johnson, "Taxation No Tyranny," Yale *Works*, 10:454.

38  Neil Lazarus, *Nationalism and Cultural Practice in the Postcolonial World* (Cambridge: Cambridge University Press, 1999), 1. His source is Theodor Adorno, who in 1951 writes in *Minima Moralia: Reflections from Damaged Life*, "One must have tradition in oneself, to hate it properly." Lazarus, 267.

39  Lazarus, 267.

40  Greg Clingham, "Resisting Johnson," in *Johnson Re-Visioned*, ed. Philip Smallwood (Lewisburg, PA: Bucknell University Press, 2001), 20.

41  Fredric Jameson, *The Political Unconscious: Narrative as a Socially Symbolic Act* (Ithaca, NY: Cornell University Press, 1981), 206–80.

42  Joseph Conrad, *The Nigger of the Narcissus* (1897; Garden City, NY: Doubleday, 1954), xiv.

43  Linda Dryden, "'The Difference between Us': Conrad, Wells, and the English Novel," *Studies in the Novel* 45, no. 2 (2013): 217.

44  Anthony Paul and Boris Wiseman, "Introduction," *Chiasmus and Culture*, 8.

45  Maya Jasanoff, *The Dawn Watch: Joseph Conrad in a Global World* (New York: Penguin, 2017), 232–33.

46  *Political Unconscious*, 279.

47  Alan Axelrod, *The Gilded Age, 1876–1912: Overture to the American Century* (New York: Sterling Publishing Co., 2017), 297.

48  *Political Unconscious*, 271.

49  Joshua Gooch, "'The Shape of Credit': Imagination, Speculation, and Language in *Nostromo*," in *Texas Studies in Language and Literature* 52, no. 3 (2010): 267.

50  Joseph Conrad, *Nostromo: A Tale of the Seaboard*, ed. Keith Carradine (Oxford: Oxford University Press, 1984), 84.

51  *Nostromo*, 520–21.

52  Ibid., 77.

53  Bloom, *Anatomy*, 112.

54  Richard Ellman, *James Joyce* (Oxford: Oxford University Press, 1959; New Haven, CT: Yale University Press, 1983), 5.

55   James Joyce, *A Portrait of the Artist as a Young Man*, ed. Hans Walter Gabler and Walter Hettche (New York: Garland, 1993), 275.

56   *James Joyce*, 351.

57   Roberto Harari, *How James Joyce Made His Name: A Reading of the Final Lacan*, trans. Luke Thurtson (1995; New York: Other Press, 2002), 49.

58   Lawrence Kramer, *Modern Opera: Wagner and Strauss* (Berkeley: The University of California Press, 2004), 5.

59   Franco Moretti, "Ulysses and the Twentieth Century," in *Close Reading: The Reader*, ed. Frank Lentricchia and Andrew DuBois (Durham, NC: Duke University Press, 2003), 324.

60   Ibid., 331.

61   James Joyce, *Ulysses*, ed. Hans Walter Gabler (New York: Random House, 1986), 239.

62   Ellman, *James Joyce*, 360.

63   Ibid., 300.

64   Kubler, *Shape of Time*, 55–56.

65   Vincent Sherry, *James Joyce: Ulysses* (Cambridge: Cambridge University Press, 1994), 104–13.

66   *Finnegans Wake*, ed. Robbert-Jan Henkes, Erik Bindervoet, and Finn Fordham (Oxford: Oxford University Press, 2012), 308.

67   Shelly Brivic, *Joyce through Lacan and Žižek* (New York: Palgrave Macmillian, 2008), 194–216.

68   For a well-considered negative answer to this question, see Leonard B. Meyer, "Innovation, Choice, and the History of Music," *Critical Inquiry* 9, no. 3 (1983): 517–44.

69   A. Alvarez, *Samuel Beckett* (New York: Viking, 1973), 46.

70   Attridge, "Unpacking the Portmanteau," 149.

71   Ibid., 145.

72   Geoff Boucher, "Joyce: Lacan's Sphinx," in *The Literary Lacan: From Literature to Lituraterre*, ed. Santanu Biswas (London: Seagull Books, 2012), 153.

73   Chinua Achebe, "An Image of Africa," *Research in African Literatures* 9, no. 1 (1978): 1–15.

74   Clement Hawes, "Johnson and Imperialism," in *The Cambridge Companion to Samuel Johnson*, ed. Greg Clingham (Cambridge: Cambridge University Press, 1997), 97.

75   Viktor Shklovsky, *Theory of Prose*, trans. Benjamin Sher (Elmwood Park, IL: Dalkey Archive Press, 1990).

## Notes to Chapter 5: Johnson Goes to War    *Jack Lynch*

1   *Boswell's Life*, 4:319.

2   J. L. Ward, "Dr Johnson, the Jacobite," *Chambers's Journal* 8th series, 1 (May 1932): 372–74 (372).

3   *Boswell's Journal of a Tour to the Hebrides with Samuel Johnson, LL.D., 1773*, ed. Frederick A. Pottle and Charles H. Bennett (New York: Heinemann, 1963), 163.

4   Ward, "Dr Johnson, the Jacobite," 372.

5   Johnson, *The Bravery of the Common English Soldiers*, Yale Works, 10:281–84.

6   See Brian Hanley, *Samuel Johnson as Book Reviewer: A Duty to Examine the Labours of the Learned* (Newark: University of Delaware Press, 2001), 183–87. J. D. Fleeman supports the attribution in *A Bibliography of the Works of Samuel Johnson*, 2 vols (Oxford: Clarendon Press, 2000), 1:687.

7   See Paul Tankard, "'That Great Literary Projector': Samuel Johnson's Designs, or Projected Works," *The Age of Johnson: A Scholarly Annual* 13 (2002): 103–80 (152).

8   Winston S. Churchill, *A History of the English-Speaking Peoples*, vol. 3, *The Age of Revolution* (New York and London: Cassell, 1957), chapter 5.

9   *The Poems of Samuel Johnson*, ed. David Nichol Smith and Edward L. McAdam (Oxford: Clarendon Press, 1941), v.

10  George Whale, *The Forty Years of the Johnson Club, 1884–1924: A Paper by George Whale (Member and Former Prior) Read at a Meeting of the Club on 13th December, 1924, in the "Upper Room," Johnson House, Gough Square, Fleet Street, London* (London: privately printed, 1925), 18.

11  See also H. V. Morton, *In Search of London* (New York: Dodd, Mead, 1951), 121–22, on the damage sustained by the house in World War II.

12  John McLure Hamilton, *Men I Have Painted* (London: Fisher, Unwin, 1921), 163–64.

13  Whale, *Forty Years*, 18.

14  H. H. Asquith, *Occasional Addresses, 1893–1916* (London: Macmillan, 1918), vii.

15  Asquith, "Dr. Johnson and Fanny Burney," in *Studies and Sketches* (London: Hutchinson & Co., 1924), 80.

16  Margot Asquith, *Margot Asquith's Great War Diary, 1914–1916: The View from Downing Street*, ed. Michael and Elanor Brock (Oxford: Oxford University Press, 2014), 296.

17  See, for instance, "Dr. Johnson's House, Gough Square," *Old London* 1 (Christmas 1948): 8–10.

18  Max Egremont, *Siegfried Sassoon: A Life* (New York: Farrar, Straus and Giroux, 2005), 27; Jean Moorcroft Wilson, *Siegfried Sassoon: The Journey from the Trenches: A Biography (1918–1967)* (London: Gerald Duckworth and Co., 2003), 114.

19  Edward Howard Marsh, *Rupert Brooke: A Memoir* (New York: John Lane, 1918), 141 n.1. See also Walter de la Mare, *Rupert Brooke and the Intellectual Imagination: A Lecture* (New York: Harcourt, Brace and Howe, 1920), 4, 5, 15.

20  On Tietjens as an eighteenth-century figure, see Philip Davis, *In Mind of Johnson: A Study of Johnson the Rambler* (Athens: University of Georgia Press, 1989), 47, and Ashley Chantler and Rob Hawkes, eds, *An Introduction to Ford Madox Ford* (Farnham: Ashgate, 2015), 142.

21  Robert Graves, *Good-Bye to All That: An Autobiography*, ed. Richard Perceval Graves (Providence, RI: Berghahn Books, 1995), 6–7.

22  Asquith, "Some Popular Frenzies in the Eighteenth Century," in *Sketches and Studies*, 51.

23  Paul Fussell, *The Great War and Modern Memory* (New York: Oxford University Press, 1975), 162.

24  George Saintsbury, *The Peace of the Augustans: A Survey of Eighteenth Century Literature as a Place of Rest and Refreshment* (London: G. Bell and Sons, 1916), 177.

25  *Boswell's Life of Johnson*, abr. and ed. Gerard Edward Jensen (Boston: Houghton Mifflin, 1917); *Boswell's Life of Johnson*, abr. and ed. Charles Grosvenor Osgood (New York: Charles Scribner's Sons, 1917); R. W. Chapman, ed., *Selections from Boswell's Life of Johnson* (Oxford: Clarendon Press, 1919); and S. C. Roberts, *The Story of Dr. Johnson, Being an Introduction to Boswell's "Life"* (Cambridge: Cambridge University Press, 1919).

26  S. C. Roberts, *The Story of Doctor Johnson; Being an Introduction to Boswell's Life* (Cambridge: Cambridge University Press, 1919), 1.

27  Fussell, *The Great War and Modern Memory*, 162.

28  R. W. Chapman, *Two Centuries of Johnsonian Scholarship: Being the Twelfth Lecture on the David Murray Foundation in the University of Glasgow Delivered on May 3rd, 1945* (Glasgow: Jackson, Son and Co., 1945), 29.

29  *Johnson's Journey to the Western Islands and Boswell's Journal of a Tour to the Hebrides with Samuel Johnson, LL.D.*, ed. R. W. Chapman (London: Oxford University Press, 1924), vii–viii.

30  Chapman, *The Portrait of a Scholar and Other Essays Written in Macedonia, 1916–18* (Oxford: Oxford University Press, 1920), 5.

31  Chapman, *Portrait of a Scholar*, 22.

32  Kathryn Sutherland, *Jane Austen's Textual Lives: From Aeschylus to Bollywood* (Oxford: Oxford University Press, 2005), 24.

33  *Boswell's Life*, 3:266. See also H. R. Kilbourne, "Dr. Johnson and War," *ELH* 12, no. 2 (June 1945): 130–43 (138).

34  *Saturday Review* 130 (1920): 392.

35  *The Johnson Calendar; or, Samuel Johnson for Every Day in the Year: Being a Series of Sayings and Tales, Collected from His Life and Writings, ος και θνητος εων επετ αθανατοισι θεοισι*, ed. Alexander Montgomerie Bell (Oxford: Clarendon Press, 1916), 15.

36  Ibid., 16–18.

37   Roberts, *The Story of Doctor Johnson*, 150.

38   "Dr. Johnson as John Bull," *Evening Post* 78.104 (October 29, 1909): 9.

39   Quoted in Kevin Hart, *Samuel Johnson and the Culture of Property* (Cambridge: Cambridge University Press, 1999), 67–68.

40   *Johnson Club Papers by Various Hands* (London: T. Fisher Unwin, 1920), 57.

41   Archibald Rutledge, "Dr. Johnson on the Great War," *The [New] Outlook* 111 (September 22, 1915): 230–32 (230).

42   Rutledge, "Dr. Johnson on the Great War," 232.

43   John Richardson, "War," in *Samuel Johnson in Context*, ed. Jack Lynch (Cambridge: Cambridge University Press, 2012), 393–99 (394).

44   Donald Greene, *The Politics of Samuel Johnson*, 2nd ed. (Athens: University of Georgia Press), 241.

45   See Peter Brock, *Pacifism in Europe to 1914* (Princeton, NJ: Princeton University Press, 1972), 321–22.

46   Greene, *Politics*, 175.

47   Richardson, "War," 397.

48   Richardson, "War," 398–99.

49   Fussell, *The Great War and Modern Memory*, 139.

50   *Adventurer* 99, in Yale *Works*, 2:433.

51   Yale *Works*, 10:370, quoted in *Advocate of Peace* 10, no. 1 (July 1879): 7.

52   James Brown Scott, "Public Opinion versus Force," *Advocate of Peace* 77, no. 9 (October 1915): 217–18 (217).

53   W. Kent, "Dr. Johnson," *Socialist Review* 17 (October–December 1920): 345–52.

54   Frank Crane, "Septic Patriotism," *The State* (Columbia, SC; April 14, 1919), 4. Crane had, in the first few months of the war, published an essay on "Patriotism and Idiotism," in *War and World Government* (New York: John Lane, 1915), 77–80. Not everyone bought it. "The hackneyed phrase of Dr. Johnson, 'Patriotism is the last refuge of a scoundrel,' is invariably misapplied and therefore perverted," wrote the editorial team on *The Christian Register* 94 (November 25, 1915): 1. See also Frederick Page, *An Anthology of Patriotic Prose* (London: Oxford University Press, 1915), 192.

55   David Hannay, "Waftage," *Blackwood's Magazine* 198 (1915): 541–50 (545–46).

56   David Starr Jordan, "The Last Cost of War," *Advocate of Peace through Justice* 86, no. 2 (February 1924): 110–14 (111).

57   Hugh Kingsmill, *Samuel Johnson* (New York: Viking, 1934), 53.

58   E. S. Roscoe, *Aspects of Doctor Johnson* (Cambridge: Cambridge University Press, 1928), 15.

59   Christopher Morley, "Two Days We Celebrate," in *Mince Pie: Adventures on the Sunny Side of Grub Street* (New York: George H. Doran Company, 1919), 124.

60   Winston Churchill, *The Second World War: The Gathering Storm* (Boston: Houghton Mifflin, 1948), 3.
61   Kilbourne, "Johnson and War," 130, 143.

### Notes to Chapter 6: Samuel Beckett and Samuel Johnson: Like-minded Masters of Life's Limitations    *Thomas M. Curley*

For the grandchildren who give meaning to life: Anna Marie, Maeve Elizabeth, Rowan Thomas, and Ariana Beckett.

1   I am deeply grateful to Carolyn Morwick, Myron Yeager, and my son, Jon Curley, for generously proofreading this essay. The authoritative text is *Samuel Johnson: Rasselas and Other Tales*, ed. Gwin J. Kolb, vol. 16 of Yale *Works*, 112. For Johnson's phobias, see *JM*. A typical entry in *Prayers and Meditations* read "I am now to review the last year, and find little but dismal vacuity … much intended and little done" (1:88), and in Hester Thrale's *Anecdotes*: "The vacuity of life had at some early period of his life struck so forcibly on the mind of Johnson, that it became … his favourite hypothesis" (1:251). Charles Hinnant, in *Samuel Johnson: An Analysis* (New York: St. Martin Press, 1988), focused on Johnson's existential anxieties: the "present becomes not the moment of presence, but that which is no longer or not yet," and the consequence is a "profound feeling of ontological insecurity" (9). A succession of Johnsonians, including Walter Jackson Bate, Robert Voitle, Arieh Sachs, Fredric Bogel, and Greg Clingham, shares, without stressing, this insight.
2   Samuel Beckett to Lawrence Shainberg, July 15, 1979, UOR MS JEK A/2/268, cited by Ulrika Maude, "Beckett, Body and Mind," *The New Cambridge Companion to Samuel Beckett* (New York: Cambridge University Press, 2015), 182.
3   *Samuel Johnson: The Complete English Poems*, ed. J. D. Fleeman (New Haven: Yale University Press, 1971), 83.
4   Beckett's statement about *Rasselas*, as noted on September 30, 1953 by Patrick Bowles, "How to Fail: Notes on Talks with Samuel Beckett," *PN Review* 20 (1994): 24.
5   Johnson, Review of Soame Jenyns's *A Free Enquiry into the Nature and Origin of Evil*, Yale *Works*, 17:413.
6   Johnson, "Life of Browne," Yale *Works*, 19:318–19. Johnson quotes from the conclusion to chapter four of Browne's *Hydriotaphia*.
7   2:149–51. For an analysis of Johnson's muttering quotation habit, see Anthony W. Lee, *Dead Masters: Mentoring and Intertextuality in Samuel Johnson* (Bethlehem: Lehigh University Press, 2011), 106–10.
8   *Boswell's Life*, 3:153.
9   Seamus Heaney, *Crediting Poetry: The Nobel Lecture* (Dublin: Gallery Press, 1996), 13.

10  John Pilling in *Beckett Before Godot* (Cambridge: Cambridge University Press, 1997), 6, 54–55, asserts that between 1937 and 1946 Beckett was "least certain as to how best to proceed as a writer," and John Dilks' fine "Samuel Beckett's Samuel Johnson," *Modern Language Review* 98 (2003): 285–98, argues persuasively that, early on, during this formative period of time, Beckett's transformed image of Johnson allowed the Irishman aesthetic and emotional space to distance himself from James Joyce.

11  For Beckett researching Thomas Carlyle, see *Beckett's Dream Notebook*, ed. John Pilling (Reading: Beckett International Foundation, 1999), 40 [item 287], and for Beckett's other early reading of Johnsoniana, see James Knowlson (who calls his subject a "soul-mate" of Johnson), *Damned to Fame: The Life of Samuel Beckett* (New York: Simon and Shuster, 1996), 249–50 and n.35.

12  Beckett to Thomas MacGreevy, July 7, 1936, *Letters of Samuel Beckett*, ed. Martha Dow Fehsenfeld et al., 4 vols (Cambridge: Cambridge University Press, 2009–2016), 1:352. (Henceforth, *LSB*.) The four volumes of Becket's correspondence are comprehensive but not complete. John Calder, in *The Philosophy of Samuel Beckett* (Edison, NJ: Riverrun Press, 2001), calls attention to Beckett's habit of turning to literary authorities, such as Johnson, whom he viewed in his own distinctive nihilistic image: "Beckett took what he needed wherever he found it and was fascinated every time he discovered that his own preoccupations, general frame of thinking and *penchant* for a pessimistic outlook on the world were not peculiar to himself" (9).

13  For a detailed overview of the Notebooks with additional manuscripts, including a handwritten and a typescript draft of *Human Wishes* personally handed over to Cohn, see her *Just Play: Beckett's Theater* (Princeton, NJ: Princeton University Press, 1980), 149–59, and Dilks, "Samuel Beckett's Samuel Johnson".

14  Dilks, "Samuel Beckett's Samuel Johnson," 292, is the indispensable source for most of Beckett's background research for *Human Wishes*.

15  Cohn, *Just Play*, 145.

16  Thomas Seccombe, "Introductory Essay," in *Doctor Johnson and Mrs Thrale: Including Mrs Thrale's Journal of the Welsh Tour Made in 1774 and Much Hitherto Unpublished Correspondence of the Streatham Coterie*, ed. A. M. Broadley (London: John Lane, 1910), 3–77.

17  C. E. Vulliamy, *Mrs. Thrale of Streatham: Her Place in the Life of Dr. Samuel Johnson and in the Society of Her Time, Her Character and Family Affairs, Reviewed in the Light of Newly Assembled Evidence* (London: Jonathan Cape, 1936).

18  Cited by Cohn, *Just Play*, 150.

19  Cited by Linda Ben-Zvi, *Samuel Beckett* (Boston, MA, Twayne Publishers, 1986), 53.

20  Beckett to Mary Manning Howe, July 11, 1937, Harry Ransom Humanities Research Center, University of Texas at Austin, and cited by Knowlson, *Damned to Fame*, 250 and 671 n.43.

21  For Beckett's fondness for variations on the Johnsonian usage of "panted on" in his writings and for his reliance on Vulliamy on the supposed relationship between Johnson and Mrs. Thrale, see Fredrik N. Smith, *Beckett's Eighteenth Century* (New York: Palgrave, 2002), 120–21 and 112–13 respectively.

22  Beckett to George Reavey, July 27, 1737, in *Letters of Samuel Beckett*, 1:522. Not in *Letters* is another letter of July 23, 1937 to MacGreevy (the beginning of which is missing), confirming Beckett's lingering desire for a plot centered on a troubled romance between old Johnson and Mrs. Thrale. This incomplete letter is cited by N. F. Lowe, "Sam's Love for Sam: Samuel Beckett, Dr. Johnson and *Human Wishes*," in *Poetry and Other Prose / Poesies et Autre Proses* (Atlanta, GA: Rodopi, 1999), 8:123:

> Thrale's death anyway is the causa irritans. It really is clear enough now, my particular special plea anyway, but I keep pushing it back, like material into a dye. With good effect, I think. For example, it only occurred to me yesterday, when mending a puncture in the middle of night on the Bray road, that Thrale must have been syphilitic. No negligible accretion to the theme.

23  Thomas Carlyle, *On Heroes, Hero-Worship, and the Heroic in History* (1840) (New York: Doubleday & Company, n.d.), 166.

24  Cited by Cohn, *Just Play*, 158.

25  Beckett to Cohn, November 21, 1972, *Letters of Samuel Beckett*, 4:315: "Seem to remember I had in mind 4 acts, one for each year between Thrale's death & widow['s] remarriage. Johnson was planned to appear towards end of Act 1."

26  Beckett to Reavey, August 4, 1737, in *LSB*, 1:533.

27  Beckett to Thomas MacGreevy, August 14, 1937, Harry Ransom Humanities Research Center, and cited by Pilling, *Beckett Before Godot*, 163.

28  Beckett to Reavey, April 21, 1940, Harry Ransom Humanities Research Center, and cited by Pilling, *Beckett Before Godot*, 151. As cited by Lowe, "Sam's Love for Sam," 8:193, the message was reiterated to Reavey on May 21, 1940: "And I wrote half of a first act of Johnson."

29  Beckett to Cohn, June 27, 1965, *LSB*, 3:668.

30  Leslie Stephen, *Samuel Johnson* (New York: Harper & Brothers, 1878). In support of Stephen's seminal impact on *Human Wishes*, Cohn mentions that Beckett's third Notebook "leaps to Chapter V of Leslie Stephen's 1878 *Samuel Johnson*, for information on the several inhabitants of Johnson's London house at Bolt Court" (157). Lowe, "Sam's Love for Sam," 8:192–93, also corroborates Beckett's reliance on Stephen.

31  Beckett, *Human Wishes*, in *Disjecta: Miscellaneous Writings and a Dramatic Fragment*, ed. Cohn (London: John Calder, 1983), 155–66.

32  Mary Bryden reproduces the doodle, which may very well indicate "a channeling of energy away from a troublesome play development and towards absorption" into a more hospitable scenario, in "Figures of Golgatha: Beckett's Pinioned People," in *The Ideal Core of the Onion: Reading Beckett Archives*, ed. John Pilling and Mary Bryden (Reading: Beckett International Foundation, 1992), 55–56. Cohn notes this doodle in *Just Play*, 160, and Smith identifies the male figure as Johnson next to a woman in a wedding gown (*Beckett's Eighteenth Century*, 114).

33  Beckett, *Waiting for Godot* (New York, Grove Press, 1954), 8b–9b. Lowe, "Sam's Love for Sam," 8:195–96 and especially 199, stresses the looming influence of Jeremy Taylor's *Holy Living and Holy Dying* (1650–1651) on *Human Wishes* and *Waiting for Godot*, including on Pozzo's comment, "They give birth astride of a grave," and on Vladimir's comparable remark, "Astride of a grave and a difficult birth." For Beckett's fascination with the crucifixion throughout his writings, see C. J. Ackerly and S. E. Gontarski, *The Grove Companion to Samuel Beckett: A Reader's Guide to His Works, Life, and Thought* (New York: Grove Press, 2004), 592–93.

34  Yale *Works*, 2:180–81. Lionel Kelly notes Beckett's citing of the first sentence in this quotation from *Idler* 58 in his Notebooks, in "Beckett's *Human Wishes*," in *The Ideal Core of the Onion*, ed. Pilling and Bryden, 31. See also *Rambler* 101 for a similar theme.

35  Beckett to MacCreevy, December 6, 1933, about reading Jeremy Taylor, in *LSB*, 1:172, and Pilling, *Beckett Before Godot*, 165.

36  Beckett to Maria Peron, August 17, 1951, *LSB*, 2:282.

37  Beckett to Alan Schneider, December 29, 1957, *LSB*, 3:83.

38  Beckett to Barbara Bray, *circa* late 1958, Trinity College, Dublin MS10948/1/35.

39  Beckett to Bray, March 26, 1959, *LSB*, 3:204. Beckett's next letter to Bray, commenting on his delight in reading the recent authoritative Yale edition of *Diaries, Prayers, and Annals*, is dated June 9, 1959.

40  My sense of the seminal connection of *Human Wishes* with *Waiting for Godot* and *Krapp's Last Tape* was an independent discovery, but many Beckett scholars have happily affirmed the literary relationship of the three plays, especially Lionel Kelly: "I shall claim that the Prayers and Meditations are certainly called on in *Krapp's Last Tapes*, where Beckett employs the strategies of introspection found in Johnson's text, from which he also takes the notion of the anniversary, and the act of self-inspection that goes with it in Johnson" ("Beckett's *Human Wishes*," 22).

41  Beckett, *Krapp's Last Tape and Other Dramatic Pieces* (New York: Grove Press, 1960), 18.

42  See the entry for *Krapp's Last Tape* in Ackerly and Gontarski, *The Grove Companion to Samuel Beckett*, 305.

43  Beckett to Schneider, December 29, 1957 and September 12, 1960, respectively, in *LSB*, 3:83, and *No Other Better Served: The Correspondence of Samuel Beckett and Alan Schneider*, ed. Maurice Harmon (Cambridge, MA: Harvard University Press, 1998), 77.

44  Beckett scholars have long suspected that the Johnson project of the latter 1930s and *Human Wishes* influenced many later novels and plays. For example, Dilks, "Samuel Beckett's Samuel Johnson," 296, and Smith, *Beckett's Eighteenth Century*, 111, see a Johnson signature in *Watt*, *Molloy*, *Malone Dies*, and *The Unnamable*. Knowlson, *Damned to Fame*, 250, and Ben-Zvi, *Samuel Beckett*, 53–55, agree, and add to this list *Come and Go*, *Endgame*, *Not I*, *Footfalls*, *Theater I*, and *Company*. Ulrika Maude, in her fine "Beckett, Body and Mind," in *The New Cambridge Companion to Samuel Beckett* (Cambridge: Cambridge University Press, 2015), 170–84, goes so far as to consider Johnson virtually omnipresent in Beckett's canon: "Even though Beckett never managed to finish his play about Johnson, the man can be seen everywhere in Beckett's writing, which repeatedly dramatizes the habit-ridden, eccentric, ageing, decaying and often suffering body" (182).

45  Beckett to Richard Roud, April 7, 1958, *LSB*, 3:125.

46  Cohn, "Growing (Up?) with Godot," in *Beckett at 80: Beckett in Context*, ed. Enoch Brater (New York: Oxford University Press, 1986), 7, as well as Sophie Vassett, "An Introduction to *Human Wishes*" and Stephanie Chapman, "Theater Review," in *Johnsonian News Letter* 62, no. 2 (September 2011): 43–47 and 48–50, respectively.

47  See "A Catalogue of Samuel Beckett's Library," in *Samuel Beckett's Library*, ed. Dirk Van Hulle and Mark Nixon (Cambridge: Cambridge University Press, 2013), 261–87.

48  Beckett to Deidre Bair in Paris, April 13, 1972, *Samuel Beckett: A Biography* (New York: Simon & Schuster, 1978; rpt. 1990), 257 and n.73.

## Notes to Chapter 7: The "Plexed Artistry" of Nabokov and Johnson    *Carrie D. Shanafelt*

1  Jeffrey Meyers, "Shade's Shadow," *The New Criterion* 24, no. 9 (May 2006): 31.

2  Nabokov obviously split his time working in literary criticism, translation, poetry, memoir, and novels, but also in lepidoptery. The vast extent of his butterfly collections and scientific attentions have only recently begun to be appreciated. See Kurt Johnson and Steve Coates, *Nabokov's Blues: The Scientific Odyssey of a Literary Genius* (Cambridge, MA: Zoland Books, 1999).

3    In his memoir *Speak, Memory*, Nabokov repeatedly describes the sensation he has of not existing in linear time. "I confess I do not believe in time. I like to fold my magic carpet, after use, in such a way as to superimpose one part of the pattern upon another." Vladimir Nabokov, *Speak, Memory: An Autobiography Revisited* (New York: Vintage, 1989), 139.

4    Vladimir Nabokov, *Pale Fire* (New York: Vintage, 1988), 7.

5    Vladimir Alexandrov describes this theory at length in his book *Nabokov's Otherworld*, in which he is careful not to pin down precisely what *is* the transcendental secret of Nabokov's subjective literary art, which Nabokov himself refused to do and only hinted at; rather, he points out that there is a common otherworldly, semi-divine absence that unites and organizes Nabokov's later fictional works. Vladimir E. Alexandrov, *Nabokov's Otherworld* (Princeton, NJ: Princeton University Press, 1991).

6    Vladimir Nabokov, *Lolita* (New York: Vintage, 1997), 32. This quotation appears in the context of Boswell's longer comments on Johnson's affinity for cats, especially Hodge. *Boswell's Life*, 4:197.

7    Samuel Johnson, *Rasselas*, in *Yale* Works, 16:46.

8    Charles Taylor, "The Politics of Recognition," in *Multiculturalism*, ed. Amy Gutman (Princeton, NJ: Princeton University Press, 1994), 29.

9    Adam Potkay, *The Passion for Happiness: Samuel Johnson and David Hume* (Ithaca, NY: Cornell University Press, 2000).

10   Regarding a conversation with Johnson about Berkeley, Boswell reports, "I observed, that though we are satisfied his doctrine is not true, it is impossible to refute it. I never shall forget the alacrity with which Johnson answered, striking his foot with mighty force against a large stone, till he rebounded from it, 'I refute it *thus*.'" *Boswell's Life* 1:471.

11   "Fielding being mentioned, Johnson exclaimed, 'he was a blockhead;' and upon my expressing my astonishment at so strange an assertion, he said, 'What I mean by his being a blockhead is that he was a barren rascal.'" *Boswell's Life* 2:173–74.

12   David Hume, *A Treatise of Human Nature* (Oxford: Oxford University Press, 2000), 201.

13   *Treatise*, 165.

14   David Hume, *An Enquiry Concerning the Principles of Morals* (Oxford: Oxford University Press, 1998), 76.

15   *Enquiry*, 115–16.

16   On this point of female chastity, Johnson is fully in agreement with Hume. Boswell reports Johnson's opinion of the importance of female chastity on a few occasions. In the *Journal of a Tour to the Hebrides*: "Consider, of what importance to society the chastity of women is. Upon that all the property in the world depends" (*Boswell's Life*, 5:209).

17   It is worth noting that Adam Smith strongly disagreed with his colleague Hume on the function of objective or communal judgment. He writes,

"I judge of your sight by my sight, of your ear by my ear, of your reason by my reason, of your resentment by my resentment, of your love by my love. I neither have, nor can have, any other way of judging about them." Adam Smith, *The Theory of Moral Sentiments* (New York: Penguin, 1989), 25.

18  Nabokov, *Pale Fire*, 130.

19  Ian Donaldson, "Samuel Johnson and the Art of Observation," *ELH* 53, no. 4 (1986): 779–99 (794).

20  Samuel Johnson, *The Lives of the Most Eminent English Poets: With Critical Observations on Their Works*, ed. Roger Lonsdale, 4 vols (Oxford: Oxford University Press, 2006), 4:103.

21  Alvin Kernan, *Samuel Johnson and the Impact of Print* (Princeton, NJ: Princeton University Press, 1987), 234.

22  Vladimir Nabokov, "The Servile Path," in *On Translation*, ed. Reuben Arthur Brower (Cambridge, MA: Harvard University Press, 1959), 97–110.

23  Alexander Pushkin, *Eugene Onegin*, trans. Vladimir Nabokov (Princeton, NJ: Princeton University Press, 1981), 9.

24  Edmund Wilson, "The Strange Case of Pushkin and Nabokov," *The New York Review of Books* 4, no. 12 (July 15, 1965), 3–6 (3).

25  Willard Van Orman Quine, "Meaning and Translation," in *On Translation*, ed. Brower, 148–72.

26  Ludwig Wittgenstein, *Tractatus Logico-Philosophicus*, trans. David Pears and Brian McGuinness, 2nd ed. (Abingdon: Routledge, 2001), 3.

27  Willard Van Orman Quine, *Word and Object* (Cambridge, MA: Massachusetts Institute of Technology University Press, 1960), 3.

28  Vladimir Nabokov, *Ada, or Ardor* (New York: Vintage, 1969, 1990), 94–95.

29  Wilson, "Strange Case," 3.

30  Brian Boyd, Pale Fire: *The Magic of Artistic Discovery* (Princeton, NJ: Princeton University Press, 2001).

31  Paul J. Thibault, *Social Semiotics as Praxis: Text, Social Meaning-Making, and Nabokov's* Ada (Minneapolis: University of Minnesota Press, 1991).

32  Alexander Pope, "An Essay on Criticism," in *The Poems of Alexander Pope*, ed. John Butt (New Haven, CT: Yale University Press, 1963), 153.

33  Martine Hennard, "Playing a Game of Worlds," *Modern Fiction Studies* 40, no. 2 (Summer 1994): 314.

34  A. E. Housman, frequently cited by Kinbote, describes the sublime in terms of shaving as well: "Experience has taught me, when I am shaving of a morning, to keep watch over my thoughts, because, if a line of poetry strays into my memory, my skin bristles so that the razor ceases to act." A. E. Housman, *The Name and Nature of Poetry* (Cambridge: Cambridge University Press, 1933), 47.

35  Immanuel Kant, *Prolegomena to Any Future Metaphysics*, trans. Gary Hatfield (Cambridge: Cambridge University Press, 1997), 34.

36  Charles Taylor, *Sources of the Self: The Making of the Modern Identity* (Cambridge, MA: Harvard University Press, 1989), 390.

## Notes to Chapter 8: Johnson and Borges: Some Reflections
### Greg Clingham

I am grateful to my colleague and friend Manuel Delgado Morales, emeritus Presidential Professor of Spanish at Bucknell University, for providing the translations from the Bioy Casares-Borges conversations that stimulated this essay, and also for twenty-five years of excellent conversation about literatures, languages, cultures, family, and life in general (including football).

1   Adolfo Bioy Casares, *Borges*, ed. Daniel Martino (Barcelona: Ediciones Destino, 2006), 187. Cited hereafter as Casares.

2   Norman Thomas Di Giovanni, *The Lesson of the Master: On Borges and His Work* (New York: Continuum, 2003), 173. Cited hereafter as *Lesson*.

3   Willis Barnstone, "With Borges in Buenos Aires," in *Jorge Luis Borges: Conversations*, ed. Richard Burgin (Jackson: University Press of Mississippi, 1998), 138–39. Cited as Burgin *Conversations* hereafter.

4   *Borges profesor: curso de literatura inglesa en la Universidad de Buenos Aires*, edición, investigación y notas de Martín Arias y Martín Hadis (Buenos Aires: Emecé, 2010). The English edition is *Professor Borges: A Course on English Literature*, ed. Martín Arias and Martín Hadis, trans. Katherine Silver (New York: New Directions, 2013), cited as *Professor Borges*.

5   Jorge Luis Borges, "The Art of Verbal Abuse," in *On Writing*, ed. Suzanne Jill Levine (New York: Penguin Books, 2010), 37. This volume cited hereafter as *On Writing*.

6   Yale *Works*, 17:421.

7   *Borges at Eighty: Conversations*, ed. Willis Barnstone (Bloomington: Indiana University Press, 1982), and Willis Barnstone, *With Borges on an Ordinary Evening in Buenos Aires* (Urbana: University of Illinois Press, 1993).

8   Jorge Luis Borges, "An Autobiographical Essay," in *The Aleph and Other Stories 1933–1969*, ed. and trans. Norman Thomas Di Giovanni (New York: E. P. Dutton, 1970), 203–60. This essay cited hereafter as "Autobiographical Essay."

9   See note 1.

10  Casares, 109. Emecé, an eminent Argentine publishing house, founded in 1939 by Mariano Medina del Rio, is still operating. Emecé published the work of Borges, Bioy, and many other twentieth-century Latin American, Spanish, and American writers.

11 To date I have been unable to visit the Mariano Moreno Library to see these manuscripts. Some Borges documents pertaining to Johnson are owned by the Argentinean art collector Jorge Helft (b. 1934), which, he tells me, are located at his homes in Paris and Buenos Aires <http://cimam.org/jorge-helft/>. Other manuscripts pertaining to Borges' interest in Johnson may be in the possession of Maria Kodama (b. 1937), whom Borges married in 1986.

12 *Boswell's Life*, 3:250–51.

13 Mathew Arnold, Preface, *The Six Chief Lives from Johnson's "Lives of the Poets" with Macaulay's "Life of Johnson"* (London, 1878), ix.

14 *The Idea of Disability in the Eighteenth Century*, ed. Chris Mounsey (Lewisburg, PA: Bucknell University Press, 2014), 18.

15 Lennard J. Davis, "Dr. Johnson, *Amelia*, and the Discourse of Disability in the Eighteenth Century," in *"Defects": Engendering the Modern Body*, ed. Helen Deutsch and Felicity Nussbaum (Ann Arbor: University of Michigan Press, 2000), 61–62.

16 For the ophthalmological account of Johnson's eyes, see L. C. McHenry, Jr. and R. MacKeith, "Samuel Johnson's Childhood Illnesses and the King's Evil," *Medical History* 10 (1966): 386–99, especially 394–95, elaborated on by John Wiltshire, *Samuel Johnson in the Medical World* (Cambridge: Cambridge University Press, 1991), 17–20. Helen Deutsch does not mention Johnson's blindness in *Loving Dr. Johnson* (Chicago, IL: University of Chicago Press, 2005). There are no references to blindness in the cumulative index to volumes 1–20 of the *Age of Johnson*.

17 In an interview with Rita Guibert, Borges explicitly links his blindness, inwardness, a deeper sense of time, and a significant development of auditory memory (Burgin *Conversations*, 42–44).

18 A discourse enlarged on by Chris Rojek, *Celebrity* (London: Reaktion Books, 2001).

19 Daniel Waissbein, *TLS* (July 27, 2007), 6.

20 James Woodall, *Borges: A Life* (New York: Basic Books, 1996), 88.

21 For di Giovanni's account of the contentious, litigious, dispute that arose between him and E. P. Dutton, his former publisher, and Borges' widow, Maria Kodama, see "The Borges Papers" <http://www.digiovanni.co.uk/borges.htm>, accessed November 8, 2018.

22 For Boswell and Eckermann, see Greg Clingham, *Boswell: The Life of Johnson* (Cambridge: Cambridge University Press, 1992), 121–23.

23 Alvin Kernan, *Samuel Johnson and the Impact of Print* (Princeton, NJ: Princeton University Press, 1987), 110.

24 John Radner, *Johnson and Boswell: A Biography of Friendship* (New Haven, CT, Yale University Press, 2012).

25 For the intimate link between Johnson's writing and his voice, see, for example, Sir John Hawkins' remark: "His discourse, which through life

was of the didactic kind, was replete with original sentiments expressed in the strongest and most correct terms, and in such language, that whoever could have heard and not seen him, would have thought him reading." Sir John Hawkins, *The Life of Samuel Johnson, LL.D.*, ed. O M Brack, Jr. (Athens, GA: University of Georgia Press, 2009), 102.

26    Stephen Miller, *Conversation: A History of a Declining Art* (New Haven, CT: Yale University Press, 2006).

27    *Lives*, 1:200.

28    For Borges' evolving relationship with the baroque style of Browne, from early emulation to late repudiation via intertextuality and translation, see Christopher Johnson, "Intertextuality and Translation: Borges, Browne, and Quevedo," *Translation and Literature* 11, no. 2 (Autumn 2002): 174–94.

29    ll.297–300; Alexander Pope, *Poetical Works*, ed. Herbert Davis (London: Oxford University Press, 1967), 72.

30    Jorge Luis Borges, "Literary Pleasure," in *The Total Library: Non-Fiction 1922–1986*, ed. Eliot Weinberger, trans. Esther Allen, Suzanne Jill Levine, and Eliot Weinberger (London: Penguin Books, 1999), 29. This volume cited hereafter as *Total Library*.

31    V. S. Naipaul, "Comprehending Borges," *The New York Review of Books* (October 19, 1972), 4.

32    Paul de Man, "A Modern Master," *The New York Review of Books* (November 19, 1964), 4, 3.

33    Paul Fussell, *Samuel Johnson and the Life of Writing* (London: Chatto & Windus, 1972), chapter 3, "The Force of Genre."

34    Kernan, *Samuel Johnson*, 108.

35    See Greg Clingham, *Johnson, Writing, and Memory* (Cambridge: Cambridge University Press, 2002), 124–27.

36    Jacques Derrida, *Memoirs of the Blind: The Self-Portrait and Other Ruins*, trans. Pascale-Anne Brault and Michael Naas (Chicago: University of Chicago Press, 1993), 33–34.

37    See Clingham, *Johnson, Writing, and Memory*, 113–14.

38    For a fuller discussion of these propositions, see Greg Clingham, "Johnson, Ends, and the Possibility of Happiness," in *Samuel Johnson After 300 Years*, ed. Greg Clingham and Philip Smallwood (Cambridge: Cambridge University Press, 2009), 33–54.

39    Woodall, *Borges: A Life*, xxix.

40    Lawrence Venuti, *The Translator's Invisibility: A History of Translation* (London: Routledge, 1995), especially chapter 1, "Invisibility."

41    "Homeric Versions," *On Writing*, 57. For a fuller account of Borges and translation, see Suzanne Jill Levine, "Borges on Translation," in *The Cambridge Companion to Jorge Luis Borges*, ed. Edwin Williamson (Cambridge: Cambridge University Press, 2013), 43–55, and Sergio

Waisman, *Borges and Translation: The Irreverence of the Periphery* (Lewisburg, PA: Bucknell University Press, 2005), 48–49.

42   *Lives*, 2:125, 147. For a fuller account of the centrality of translation in the *Lives*, see Clingham, *Johnson, Writing, and Memory*, chapter 5, "Translation and Memory in the *Lives of the Poets*."

43   Michel Foucault, *The Order of Things: An Archaeology of the Human Sciences* (New York: Vintage Books, 1973), 47–48.

44   The place of Cervantes in Johnson's thought remains largely unexplored, but see Eithne Henson, *"The Fictions of Romantick Chivalry": Samuel Johnson and Romance* (Madison, NJ: Fairleigh Dickinson University Press, 1992), chapter 4, "Johnson and *Don Quixote*."

## Notes to Chapter 9: Ernest Borneman's *Tomorrow Is Now* (1959): Thoughts about a Lost Novel, with Glances toward Samuel Johnson and other Modernists   *Robert G. Walker*

1   *The Lives of the Poets*, ed. John H. Middendorf, 3 vols (New Haven, CT: Yale University Press, 2010), 1:270; vol. 21 of Yale *Works*.

2   Ernest Borneman, *Tomorrow Is Now: The Adventures of Welfare Willy in Search of a Soul* (London: Neville Spearman, 1959), 9; hereafter cited in the text.

3   James Joyce, *A Portrait of the Artist as a Young Man*, quoted from *The Portable James Joyce* (New York: Viking, 1966), 245.

4   *The Idler and The Adventurer*, ed. W. J. Bate, John M. Bullitt, and L. F. Powell (New Haven, CT: Yale University Press, 1963), 312; vol. 2 of Yale *Works*.

5   Tim Parks, *The Novel: A Survival Skill* (Oxford: Oxford University Press, 2015), 13. I owe the linking of Parks with Johnson to Jack Lynch's recent talk, "Johnson's Lives," printed in *JNL* 68 (March 2017): 6–15; hereafter cited in the text.

6   *Boswell's Life*, 1:425; hereafter cited in the text by volume and page number.

7   Cameron McCabe, *The Face on the Cutting-Room Floor*, with an introduction by Jonathan Coe (London: Picador Classic, 2016). As well as all quotations from this novel, all references to front matter and back matter are to this edition (hereafter *FOCF*). David Collard's review "Murder Who Wrote" appeared in *TLS* (December 21, 2015). I will refer also to a review by Coe, "Whodunnit and Whowroteit," in *The Guardian* (September 2, 2016).

8   Collard, "Murder Who Wrote."

9   Collard, "Murder Who Wrote."

10   A related issue, raised recently, is how much misinformation about Borneman was deliberately produced by the author himself. Dagmar

Herzog describes him as a "gifted and hardworking con artist ... who fled Nazi Berlin a few weeks before he was able to finish *Gymnasium* and spent the rest of his life inventing educational degrees he had never earned, while becoming spectacularly successful in the literary, music, and film worlds, ultimately also acquiring an academic post in Salzburg and in 1991 the Honor Cross First Class of the Republic of Austria," "Sexuality in Austria: An Update," in *Austrian Studies Today*, ed. Gunter Bischot and Ferdinand Karlhofer (New Orleans: University of New Orleans Press, 2016), 161–69 (167). Herzog follows Detlef Siegfried's *Moderne Lüste: Ernest Borneman–Jazzkritiker, Filmemacher, Sexforscher* (Wallstein: Göttingen, 2015), a work I have not seen.

11   "Borneman wrote seven novels, five plays, six movie scripts": Nicole Brunnhuber, *The Faces of Janus: English-Language Fiction by German-Speaking Exiles in Great Britain, 1933–45* (Oxford: Peter Lang, 2005), 50.

12   Roman Iwaschkin, *Popular Music: A Reference Guide* (1986; London: Routledge, 2016), 574.

13   Douglas Lane Patey, *The Life of Evelyn Waugh: A Critical Biography* (1998; repr., Oxford: Blackwell, 2001), 289. For this remark Patey relies on an earlier biographer (and friend of Waugh's), Christopher Sykes, *Evelyn Waugh: A Biography* (1975; repr., Harmondsworth: Penguin, 1977), 451.

14   Borneman seemed to have remarkably bad luck with strikes. In his interview with Reinhold Aman in 1979 he was asked about his massive history of pre-patriarchic societies in Europe: "[Aman]: You've written a famous book of nearly a thousand pages that bears the title *Patriarchy* and for some mysterious reason has never been translated into English ... . [Borneman]: Actually I wrote it in English, but the manuscript got lost during a postal strike in England on the way to my typist. By then I had moved to Germany, so I had to reconstruct it all in German. The most horrible job I ever did in my life. Took nearly ten years" (*FOCF*, 309).

15   See Brunnhuber's *The Faces of Janus* for a discussion of the way in which Borneman's second novel, *Love Story* (1942), at least anticipates the movement: the protagonist's "treatment of women, disillusionment and contempt for socio-political engagement provide him with some characteristics of the figure to emerge in British post-war literature, the 'Angry Young Man.' ... [T]he exiled author seems to have had his finger on the pulse of innovations in English literature" (76, 77).

16   Wendy Laura Belcher, *Abyssinia's Samuel Johnson: Ethiopian Thought in the Making of an English Author* (Oxford: Oxford University Press, 2012), 156; hereafter cited in the text. One need not accept Belcher's argument that "*Irene* was not well received by contemporary audiences partly because it did not meet their expectations of an English oriental drama" (140) in order to find very valuable her discussion and her summaries of the previous criticism.

17  Thomas Kaminski, *The Early Career of Samuel Johnson* (New York: Oxford University Press, 1987), 13–14.

18  Samuel Johnson, *Poems*, ed. E. L. McAdam, Jr., with George Milne (New Haven, CT: Yale University Press, 1964), 356; vol. 6 of Yale *Works*.

19  Nicholas Hudson, *A Political Biography of Samuel Johnson* (London: Pickering & Chatto, 2013), 135; hereafter cited in the text.

20  *The Works of George Peele*, ed. A. H. Bullen (Boston, MA: Houghton, Mifflin, 1888), 2:302.

21  *The Book of Elizabethan Verse*, ed. W. S. Braithwaite (Boston, MA, H. B. Turner & Co., 1906), 373. Regarding "Reinhardt," in personal correspondence Melvyn New has suggested a possible reference to Max Reinhardt (1873–1943), the Austrian theater and film director. He and Borneman have in common residence in Berlin in the early 1930s, an interest in Brecht, who worked in Reinhardt's theater and about whom Borneman later wrote, and a love of film work. Reinhardt famously specified, among reasons for moving from actor to director, his distaste for having to stick on a beard nightly. But I have not been able to find any personal connection between them, and the allusion would be out of sorts with the others in the paragraph.

22  "Thomas the Rhymer, Part I," in *Minstrelsy of the Scottish Border*, 2nd ed., 2 vols. (Kelso: J. Ballantyne, 1802), 2:254.

23  Ernest Borneman, *The Compromisers* (London: Andre Deutsch, 1962), front matter.

24  *Tomorrow Is Now*, 205; translation assistance provided by Michael Shaughnessey and an anonymous reader. The poem is even more anti-establishment in the next few (and final) lines: "Shutter all the churches. And chase God himself out. He'll be in our conscience."

25  Samuel Johnson, *Rasselas and Other Tales*, ed. Gwin J. Kolb (New Haven, CT: Yale University Press, 1990), 175; vol. 16 of Yale *Works*; hereafter cited in the text.

26  Robert G. Walker, *Eighteenth-Century Arguments for Immortality and Johnson's "Rasselas,"* ELS Monograph Series 9 (Victoria, BC: University of Victoria, BC, 1977).

# Contributors

**Greg Clingham** is the Director of the University Press and Professor of English at Bucknell University. He is the author of *Johnson, Writing, and Memory* (Cambridge: Cambridge University Press, 2002), the editor of *The Cambridge Companion to Samuel Johnson* (Cambridge: Cambridge University Press, 1997), and the co-editor of *Johnson After 300 Hundred Years* (Cambridge: Cambridge University Press, 2009), among many other publications on Johnson and his circle. He is presently preparing a volume of his unpublished essays on Johnson—"Dr. Johnson's Enlightenment"— and also writing on both Sir George Macartney's unpublished diplomatic papers from Russia, China, and the Cape of Good Hope and Lady Anne Barnard's archive and her depiction of life at the Cape c. 1800.

**Thomas M. Curley** is professor emeritus of English at Bridgewater State University and the author of several articles and books on the Age of Johnson. His biography, *Sir Robert Chambers: Law, Literature, and Empire in the Age of Johnson* (Madison, WI: University of Wisconsin Press) won the Choice Outstanding Academic Book Award in 1998. His most recent book, *Samuel Johnson, the Ossian Fraud, and the Celtic Revival in Great Britain*, was published by Cambridge University Press in 2009.

**Clement Hawes** holds a joint position at the University of Michigan in History and English. He specializes in British literature and history

1660–1800, writing broadly about the problematic of periodizing the Enlightenment. One of his consistent interests has been with the cultural dynamics of early empire. Recently he has expanded on a personal liking for travel by studying early modern travelogues. His publications include the two monographs *Mania and Literary Style: The Rhetoric of Enthusiasm from the Ranters to Christopher Smart* (Cambridge: Cambridge University Press, 1996) and *The British Eighteenth Century and Global Critique* (New York: Palgrave MacMillan, 2005); and the three edited volumes *Christopher Smart and the Enlightenment* (New York: St. Martin's, 1999), *Gulliver's Travels and Other Writings* (New York: Houghton Mifflin, 2003), and *Europe Observed: Multiple Gazes in Early Modern Encounters* (Lewisburg, PA: Bucknell University Press, 2008), coedited with Kumkum Chatterjee. He also coedited, along with Robert Caserio, *The Cambridge History of the English Novel* (Cambridge: Cambridge University Press, 2012). Among his works in progress is a monograph about geographical scale as a mode of inquiry and self-legitimation in the long eighteenth century.

**Anthony W. Lee** is currently Visiting Lecturer at Arkansas Tech University. His research interests center upon Samuel Johnson and his circle, mentoring, and intertextuality. He has published more than forty essays on Johnson and eighteenth-century literature and culture. He has also published five books, most recently *Community and Solitude: New Essays on Johnson's Circle* (Lewisburg, PA: Bucknell University Press, 2018) and *New Essays on Samuel Johnson: Revaluation* (Newark, DE: University of Delaware Press, 2018). Anthony has taught at a number of colleges and universities, including the University of Arkansas, Kentucky Wesleyan College, the University of the District of Columbia, and the University of Maryland University College, where he also served as Director of the English and Humanities Program.

**Jack Lynch** is Professor of English and chair of the Department of English at Rutgers University–Newark. He is the author or editor of nineteen books to date, including *The Age of Elizabeth in the Age of Johnson* (Cambridge: Cambridge University Press, 2003), *Anniversary Essays on Johnson's "Dictionary"* with Anne McDermott (Cambridge: Cambridge University Press, 2005), and *Deception and Detection in Eighteenth-Century Britain*

(Aldershot: Ashgate, 2008). With John T. Scanlan he edits *The Age of Johnson*. He is now at work on a life of the Shakespeare forger William Henry Ireland and a study of Samuel Johnson and literary biography.

**Joe Moffett**, a former Fulbright Scholar, is Associate Professor of English at Kentucky State University. He is the author of *Mysticism in Postmodernist Long Poems* (Bethlehem, PA: Lehigh University Press, 2014), *Understanding Charles Wright* (Columbia, SC: University of South Carolina Press, 2008), and *The Search for Origins in the Twentieth-Century Long Poem* (Morgantown, WV: West Virginia University Press, 2007), as well as articles in journals such as *ANQ*, *The Explicator*, *The Southern Literary Journal*, *Genre*, *Notes on Contemporary Literature*, *The Journal of the Midwest Modern Language Association*, and *Literature Interpretation Theory*.

**Melvyn New**, Professor Emeritus at the University of Florida, has been publishing on eighteenth-century literature for fifty years. He served as General Editor of the University of Florida Edition of the Works of Sterne, the ninth and final volume of which was published in 2014. Recent essays include "Richardson's *Sir Charles Grandison* and Sterne: A Study in Influence," *Modern Philology* 115, no. 2 (November 2017): 213–43; and, with M-C. Newbould, "Reconsidering a Sternean Attribution: Cambridge University Library's 'Sterne Volume,'" *The Library* 18, no. 4 (December 2017), 478–86. He has been the Book Review Editor for *The Scriblerian* for the past fifteen years.

**Carrie Shanafelt** is an assistant professor at Fairleigh Dickinson University in Teaneck, New Jersey. Her articles on popular literature, sexuality, and philosophy appear in *Literature Interpretation Theory* and in *The College English Association Forum*. She is currently writing a book about Jeremy Bentham's writings on pleasure and sexual diversity.

**Robert G. Walker** is a Senior Research Fellow at Washington & Jefferson College. He is the author of *Eighteenth-Century Arguments for Immortality and Johnson's "Rasselas"* (Victoria, B.C.: University of Victoria Press, 1977) and the co-editor of *Swiftly Sterneward: Essays on Laurence Sterne* *and His Times* (Newark, DE: University of Delaware Press, 2011), and has published essays and notes on various eighteenth-century and modern figures, including Johnson, Boswell, Richardson, Sterne, Hemingway, Ford, Koestler, Malaparte, and Waugh, in over twenty different journals, most recently *Modern Philology, Scottish Literary Review, Sewanee Review, 1650–1850,* and *Age of Johnson.* A frequent reviewer, he is a contributing editor of *The Scriblerian.*

# Index

Addison, Joseph 4, 14, 57–60, 61–62, 192
 works:
  "Battle of the Pygmies and Cranes" 10
  *Cato* 230
  *Works of Addison* 62
Adès, Thomas 2
Adorno, Theodor 99
Africa 87, 88
Africans
 enslaved 91–92
  *see also* John Locke
 termed "savages" 85
Albee, Edward 229
Aman, Reinhold 219, 276
America
 North 87, 92, 103, 110
 South and Central 59–60, 69–70, 120,
  179
Angry Young Men 229
Argentina 195
 National Library of 194
Arias, Martín 190
Arnold, Matthew 195, 209
Asquith, Herbert 118, 123
Attridge, Derek 110
Augustanism 3, 24–25, 59–60, 69
Austen, Jane 99, 213

authorial identity 202–3
 and eudamonia 196
 and invisibility 197, 204, 208

Bacon, Sir Francis 2, 6
Barnstone, Willis 192–93, 197, 198
the battle of the books
 *see Querelle des Anciens et des*
  *Modernes*
Baumann, Arthur 117
Bayle, Pierre 217
Beach, Sylvia 104–5
Beckett, Samuel 1, 12–13, 15, 18–19, 86,
 99, 133–63, 216
 works:
  *Human Wishes* 134, 135, 139, 149,
   150, 151–58
  *Krapp's Last Tape* 134, 158–62
  *Murphy* 151
  *The Unnameable* 109
  *Waiting for Godot* 134, 139, 157
Belcher, Wendy Laura 230
Bell, Alexander Montgomerie
 *Johnson Calendar* 123–24
Bentley, Richard 3
Berkeley, George 15–16, 68, 87, 101, 170,
 182

Bertrand Library, Bucknell University
    193
Bible 137, 153
    Amos 7:14  31
    Isaiah 38:15  31
    John 12:27  31
    Luke 6:20  33
    Matthew 5:3  33
    Matthew 14:6–11  31
    2 Peter 3:10  35
Bierce, Ambrose 92
*Bildungsroman* 90
biography 17, 44, 61–67, 96, 98, 99, 136,
    184, 191, 197–99, 216–17
Birrell, Augustine 118
Bloom, Harold 93, 104
    *The Anxiety of Influence* 70, 75, 78,
    79
Borges, Juan Luis
    blindness 195–96, 204–5, 207–8
    edition of Sir Thomas Browne 193
    English grandmother (Frances Anne
        Haslam) 190
    feeling for English prose 190
    Samuel Johnson 189–211
    love of Old Norse and Celtic 190
    "purity of language" 192
    translation 208–11
    translation of Johnson 193
Borneman, Ernest 19, 213–37
    discussion of corpus 220–22
    *Face on the Cutting Room Floor*
        217–20
Boswell, James 5, 7, 18, 45, 61, 67, 68, 95,
    115, 116, 130, 137, 166–67, 170, 190,
    196, 197–99, 216–17, 220, 226–27,
    236, 237
    works:
    *Journal of a Tour to the Hebrides* 121
    *Life of Johnson* 11, 12, 13, 15–16,
        44–45, 119, 120, 122, 124,
        125–26, 138, 139, 146, 157–58,
        160–61, 166, 170, 190, 194–95,
        199, 206
    *London Journal* 158–59, 162

Boucher, Geoff 111
Brooke, Rupert 119
Browne, Sir Thomas 42, 193–94,
    200
Brunnhuber, Nicole 221
Buenos Aires, University of 190,
    192–93
Burgess, Anthony
    *A Clockwork Orange* 109
Burgin, Richard 197, 200
Burroughs, William S. 2
Butler, Samuel 4, 192

the can-can 2
capitalism 80, 86–87, 89, 90, 93, 100,
    101, 103, 105, 110
Carlyle, Thomas 138, 140, 148
Casares, Adolfo Bioy 189, 192, 193,
    194, 195, 197–98, 199, 201
Cervantes, Miguel de 93, 94, 99, 102,
    107, 190
    *Don Quixote* 190, 191, 204,
        210–11
Chambers, Sir Robert 203
Chapman, George 233
Chapman, R. W. 121–22
Chaucer, Geoffrey 215
Chesterfield, Fourth Earl of 93
Chesterton, G. K. 190
chiasmus 90–91, 94, 100, 105
Christ 42
Christ, Ronald 197
Christianity 16–17, 23, 26–40
    Coptic Christians 94
    the Fall 27–29, 32
    Redemption 27–29, 33–34
Churchill, Charles 143
Churchill, Winston 116, 130
circularity 95, 97, 102, 111
clichés 110, 112
Clifford, James 117, 162
Clingham, Greg 94, 99
Cole, Teju 92
Coleman, Alexander 197, 200
Congreve, William 42

Conrad, Joseph 17, 22, 85–88, 91, 92,
    99–104, 111–13
    works:
    *Heart of Darkness* 100
    *Lord Jim* 22–23, 90
    *Nostromo* 101–4
conversation (and conversational style)
    193, 199, 200, 210–11
Cooke, William 197
creole 101
Croce, Benedetto 202

Dante, Alighieri 190
Davis, Lennard 196
de León, Fray Luis 208
de Man, Paul 203
de Panonia, Jan (aka Janus Vitalis) 194,
    195
de Quevedo, Francisco Gómez 194,
    195
defamiliarization 112
    *see also* Viktor Shklovsky
Defoe, Daniel 213
Delany, Patrick 64
Dembo, L. S. 197
Dennis, John 4
dependency theory 103
depression 90
Derrida, Jacques 110–11, 204–5
Destino (publisher) 193
di Giovanni, Norman 190, 192, 193,
    197, 198, 202
*Dictionary of Global Culture* 91
Dodd, Rev. William 203
Donne, John 190
Dos Passos, John 218
Doyle, Brian 221
Dreadnought Hoax 41, 47
Dryden, John 4, 10, 24–25, 51, 96, 206
    works:
    *Fables* 206
    translations 201, 204, 210
Dryden, Linda 100
du Bellay, Joachim 194
Dublin 14, 104, 107, 139

Eckermann, Johann 198–99
elegiac poetry 80
Eliot, T. S. 1, 10–11, 15, 16–17, 21–40,
    65, 69, 75, 78, 82, 215, 216, 228–29
    works:
    "The Christian in the Modern World"
        28–31
    *Little Gidding* 24
    *Love Song of J. Alfred Prufrock* 25–40
    "Milton" 21
    *Old Possum's Book of Practical Cats*
        10
    *The Wasteland* 16, 24–25, 69, 215,
        233
Ellman, Richard 104, 106
Emecé (publisher) 194
Emerson, Ralph Waldo 81, 190
Empson, William 4
Enguídanos, Miguel 197
the Enlightenment 6–7, 17, 19, 22–23,
    30, 36, 39–40, 70, 72, 86, 90, 92, 95,
    165–66, 187
epiphany, epiphanies 93, 105, 107, 113
epistemology 169, 180, 186
Eurocentrism 98

Falstaff 67
Faulkner, William 104
    *The Sound and the Fury* 109
Fielding, Henry 163, 170
film (motion pictures) 220, 221, 228–29
Fitzgerald, F. Scott 104
Flaubert, Gustave 92
Ford, Ford Maddox 77, 119, 224
Foucault, Michel 196, 210–11
Fussell, Paul 121, 127, 204

Gandhi, Mohandas K. 88
Garrick, David 126, 230
generational antagonism 94, 110
George III 98
Gidé, Andre 22
    *The Counterfeiters* 22–23
Goldsmith, Oliver 24, 44, 157, 231
Gollancz, Victor 222

Graves, Robert
  *Goodbye to All That* 119
Gray, Thomas 86, 96
the Great War for Empire
  *see* Seven Years' War
Greene, Donald 104, 125, 126
Greene, Graham 104
Guibert, Rita 197

Hadis, Martín 190, 191
Hall, Joseph 63
Hall, Radclyffe 233
Hammett, Dashiell 218
Harmsworth, Cecil 119
Hawkins, Sir John 197
Haynes, E. S. P. 124–25
hegemony, U.S. 87, 101, 103
Hemingway, Ernest 104, 218, 225
Henry, Matthew 33–34, 37
Herzog, Dagmar 275–76
historical sequences 96, 99, 103, 104, 109
Hitler, Adolf 88
Hogarth Press 86
Homer 80, 83, 200–201, 205, 209
  *Odyssey* 80, 107–8
Honorio Bustos Domecq 202
Horace 25, 122
Howe, Mary Manning 142, 147, 150
Hudson, Nicolas 36–37, 231–32
Hugo, Victor 190
humanism 195
  Christian humanism 60
Hume, David 167, 169–73, 175–76,
  179, 187
Huxley, Aldous 218

Ibarra, Néstor 198
imagination 99, 107, 108
imitation vs. originality 3
imperialism
  Belgian 100–101
  racism and 111
  U.S., settler colonialism in 87, 91, 92,
    101, 103
  *see also* dependency theory

interior monologue 108–9
Ireland 107
  independence of 88
  Irish language 112
  nationalism in 106
  oppressed by Anti-Catholicism 89

James, Henry 99
Jameson, Fredric 87, 99
Japan
  imperial conquest of Korea by 87
  invasion of Manchuria by 88
  rising of at end of *Finnegans Wake*
    110
  victory by over Russia 86
Jefferson, Thomas 77, 88, 98
Jim Crow laws 8
Johnson Club of London 117, 124
Johnson, Samuel
  American settler colonialism 103
  blindness 195–96, 200–201, 204–6
  body 95, 96
  Borges 189–211
  Dick Minim 4–5
  "Englishness" 192, 211
  ghost writing 203–4
  Johnson Studies 85, 113
  Lichfield 193
  living on Fleet Street 81
  moral essays 207
  nationalism, loathing of 106
  pacifism 49–50, 125–28
  progress 98
  puns 95–96
  science and technology 5–6
  slavery 5
  translation 208–11
  true wit 199–200, 201
  women 5, 54–55
  works:
  *Adventurer* 3, 8
  *Dictionary of the English Language*
    2–3, 10–11, 57–58, 63, 72, 92, 93,
    95, 117, 138, 147, 160, 162, 172–73,
    189, 192–93, 196, 197, 201–2, 223

*The Idler* 4, 48–49, 79, 92, 93, 116, 126, 131, 156, 174, 216
*Irene* 226–27, 229–30, 231, 236–37
*Journey to the Western Islands* 6, 121
Life of Addison 14, 57–60
Life of Ascham 138
Life of Browne 200
Life of Cowley 199–200
Life of Dryden 99, 138, 200–201, 204, 209–10
Life of Gray 43
Life of King 3
Life of Milton 3, 40, 51–54, 96, 201, 205–6
Life of Pope 96, 208, 209
Life of Savage 9, 96, 98
Life of Swift 3, 55–56, 63–65, 203–4
Life of Waller 214
*Literary Magazine* 5, 46, 116
*Lives of the Poets* 19, 59, 63, 93, 96, 189, 195, 201, 207, 209, 217
*London* 16, 24–40, 75, 118, 230
"Observations on the Present State of Affairs, 1756" 46
*Prayers and Meditations* 137, 145, 147, 159, 206
Preface to the *Dictionary* 189
*The Rambler* 8, 57, 60, 61, 85, 93, 95, 98, 112, 134–35, 173, 116
*Rasselas* 4, 14, 22, 41–42, 85, 90, 93, 94–95, 98, 106–7, 128, 131, 133, 135–36, 138, 168, 191, 206–7, 217, 224, 232, 235–36
Review of Samuel Bever's *The Cadet: A Military Treatise* 136, 192
Review of Soame Jenyns' *A Free Inquiry into the Nature and Origin of Evil* 136, 192
Shakespeare Edition 83, 92, 162, 207
Preface to Shakespeare 189, 207
*Taxation No Tyranny* 47, 98
*Thoughts on Falkland's Islands* 48, 126

*Vanity of Human Wishes* 10, 11, 24–25, 34, 72–80, 84, 127, 128, 130–31, 135, 160, 173–74, 230, 232
*Vision of Theodore* 135
*Johnsonian News Letter* 117, 131
Jordan, David Starr 129
Joyce, James 1, 15, 17, 86, 88, 91, 96, 138, 150, 153, 190, 215, 216, 218, 222, 224, 233, 234
body in 107–9
evasion by of "nets" 104, 106
puns in 109–11
quark 112
works:
*Dubliners* 105
"The Dead" 105
*Finnegans Wake* 107, 109
*A Portrait of the Artist as a Young Man* 13–14, 90, 105–6
*Ulysses* 4, 91, 107
Jewishness of Leopold Bloom in 107
Juvenal 26, 38, 72, 80, 93
*Satire 3* 24, 27, 29, 31, 34–35, 37
*Satire 10* 72, 74

Kafka, Franz 190
Kaminski, Thomas 230
Kant, Immanuel 151, 186–87
Kent, William 128
Kernan, Alvin 178–79, 199, 204
Keynes, Geoffrey 120–21
Kilbourne, H. R. 131
Kingsmill, Hugh 129–30
Kipling, Rudyard 87
Korea, annexed by Japan 88
Kramer, Lawrence 106–7
Kubler, George 109
*Kunstlerroman* 106

Lazarus, Neil 99
Leavis, F. R. 4
Levy, Amy 26–27
"London Plane-Tree" 26–27

lexicography 99, 201–2
literary pleasure 201–2, 209–11
Little Englandism 111
Locke, John 89
London 7–8, 12, 21–40, 49, 50, 81,
   96, 115, 117, 124, 139, 141, 169,
   216, 218, 221
   London fire 35–36
Lynch, Jack 217

Macaulay, Thomas Babington 85
mandate, symbolic 106
Mandeville, Bernard 85
Manguel, Alberto 194
"manifest destiny" 87
Maritain, Jacques 30–31
Martino, Daniel 193
McCue, Jim 25, 32
Mencken, H. L. 90
Mexico 87
Miller, Stephen 199
Milton, John 28, 40, 42, 56, 93, 190,
   191, 200–201, 205–7
   works:
   Paradise Lost 13–14, 28, 30,
      38–40, 51–52, 205
   Samson Agonistes 205
Mingus, Charles 2
Montaigne, Michel Eyquem de 42
Moretti, Franco 107
Morley, Christopher 130
Mounsey, Chris 196
Murphy, Arthur 197
Mussolini, Benito 17, 82

Nabokov, Vladimir Vladimirovich
   18–19, 165–87
Naipaul, V. S. 104, 202–3
national horizons 93, 94, 104,
   106
Native Americans 91, 92, 103
Nazis and Nazism 49, 50, 88, 152
Newman, John Henry 209
New York University 192, 200
the novel 88, 95, 107

O'Brien, Flann 218
Overbury, Thomas 63
Oxford English Dictionary 92

Panama Canal 101, 103
Parks, Tim 216–17
Pascal, Blaise 27–28, 39
pastoral 24, 29–31, 38
Pater, Walter
   "Notes on Leonardo da Vinci" 60
patronage 12, 93, 104–5, 110
   see also Chesterfield, Beach, and
      Weaver
Peele, George 233
perfectibility 28–29
Perkins, David 24
Perón, Juan 195
Philippines 87
Piozzi, Hester
   see Hester Thrale
Pocock, J. G. A. 87
Pope, Alexander 3, 10, 24–25, 42, 69, 77,
   78, 93, 110, 184, 200, 201, 209
   works:
   Essay on Criticism 58
   Homer translation 209
   Rape of the Lock 24
portmanteau words 110
postcolonial 17, 104
Postmodernism 22–23, 113
Pound, Ezra 2, 4, 11–12, 13, 15, 17,
   89–90, 104–5
   the Enlightenment 70, 76
   usury 70–71
   and The Vanity of Human Wishes
      75–80
   works:
   ABC of Reading 17, 69, 71, 83
   The Cantos 70, 80, 81–84
   The Guide to Kulchur 17, 69, 71, 75,
      78, 83
   Hugh Selwyn Mauberley 73, 81
   "Human Wishes" 75–80
   "The Seafarer" 74, 80
   The Spirit of Romance 17, 69

pragmatism 167, 182, 185, 187
prejudice 124, 125, 169, 171, 174, 217
Primrose, Archibald 124
progress 27–28, 85–113
Proust, Marcel 21, 137, 153, 217
puns 95, 109–10
Pushkin, Alexander Sergeyevich 179–81, 183

Querelle des Anciens et des Modernes 3
Quine, Willard Van Orman 167, 181–82, 186, 187

Radner, John 199
Raphael, Frederic 219
Ray, John
    The Wisdom of God Manifested in the Works of Creation 11
Realism 89, 90, 99, 101
Reed, Isaac 197
Reid, Alastair 197
Richards, I. A. 4
Richardson, John 125
Richardson, Jonathan 53
Richardson, Samuel 30, 213
    Sir Charles Grandison 30
Ricks, Christopher 25, 32
Roberts, S. C.
    Story of Doctor Johnson 120, 124
Rodman, Selden 197
romance 89, 90, 176
Romanticism 3, 23, 59–60, 69, 77
Rome 194
Roosevelt, Theodore 101
Routledge Encyclopedia of Modernism 2
Rowe, Nicholas 119
Rushdie, Salman 99–100
Rymer, Thomas 4

Sacheverell, Henry 32–33
Saintsbury, George
    The Peace of the Augustans 120
Sallust
    De conjuratione Catilinae 62
satyragraha campaign 88

Savage, Richard 97
Schulz, Bruno 21–22
science 27
Scott, Walter 234
The Seven Years' War 5, 92, 116
sexual double standard 109
Shakespeare 11, 15, 19, 42, 51, 54, 67, 68, 92, 93, 95, 96, 104, 110, 153, 180, 189, 190, 192, 206, 207, 210, 211, 224, 232
    works:
        Hamlet 32
        Twelfth Night 83
Shaw, William 197
Shklovsky, Viktor 21, 112
Smith, David Nichol 117
Smollett, Tobias 37
Society for the Abolition of the Slave Trade 91
Socrates 42, 201
The Spectator 57
Spenser, Edmund 194
Steevens, George 197
Stein, Gertrude 234
Stephen, Leslie 6–7, 61, 66, 154
Stern, Richard 197
Sterne, Laurence 21–24, 163, 180
    works:
        A Sentimental Journey 22
        Life and Opinions of Tristram Shandy 22–23
Stevenson, Robert Louis 190
Stravinski, Igor
    Petrushka 2
stream of consciousness
    see interior monologue
subjectivity 168–69, 173–74, 176, 179–80, 183–87
Suckling, Sir John 95
Sutherland, Kathryn 122
Svevo, Italo 21
Swift, Jonathan 3, 42, 91, 66, 78, 91, 96, 203–4
    and the excremental vision 64
    and "oriental scrupulosity" 63–64

works:
  *Journal to Stella* 55–56
Symons, Julian 219

Taylor, Charles 169, 187
Taylor, Jeremy
  *Holy Living and Holy Dying* 158
Taylor, Rev. John 158, 203
Temple, Sir William 3
Theophrastus 63
Thomson, James 174–75
Thrale, Henry 13, 143, 149
Thrale, Hester 15–16, 45, 136, 138,
  140–53, 197
*Times Literary Supplement* 28, 197,
  217
Towers, Joseph, 197
*translatio imperii* 87, 101
translation 80, 119, 139, 151, 179–81,
  192, 183, 204, 208–11
Tyers, Thomas 197

urbanism 21–40

Varney, Andrew 32–34, 36
Venturo, David 29–31, 38
Venuti, Lawrence 208
Viconian 111
Victorian Age 87
vision problems 90
Voltaire 11, 22, 71, 75, 232
  *Candide* 22–23, 228
Von Czepko, Daniel 235–36

Wain, John 34
Waissbein, Daniel 197
Walpole, Robert 31, 35, 122
Ward, H. Gordon 195
Ward, J. L. 115–16
Waugh, Evelyn 222–24, 236
Weaver, Harriet 105
Weinbrot, Howard 29, 31
Wells, H. G. 65, 190
West, Benjamin 92

"White Man's Burden" 87
Whitman, Walt 76–77, 190
Wilson, Edmund 181, 183–84
Wilson, Woodrow 88
Wittgenstein, Ludwig 182, 187
Woodall, James 198, 207
Woolf, Virginia 1, 14–15, 17, 21–22, 24,
  41–68, 86, 104
  Hogarth Press 86
  works:
  "Addison" 58–60
  *A Room of One's Own* 53
  *A Writer's Diary* 41
  *Between the Acts* 47
  *The Common Reader* 43, 57, 58, 59,
    60, 86
  "Dr. Burney's Evening Party" 15
  *Flush: A Biography* 61
  "The Modern Essay" 58
  *Moments of Being* 53
  *Mrs. Dalloway* 22, 109
  *Orlando* 15, 61, 86
  *Roger Fry* 61
  "Saint Samuel of Fleet Street" 17, 42,
    52
  "Sketch of the Past" 67
  *The Voyage Out* 47
  *Three Guineas* 47–48, 49
  *To the Lighthouse* 15, 66, 67
Wordsworth, William 25, 76, 192
World War One 28, 49, 73, 94, 116–17,
  127–28, 129
World War Two 1, 18, 28, 49, 87, 117,
  152, 153
  Battle of Britain 49–50
Wotton, William 3
Wright, Charles 82
Wycherley, William 42

Yale University 191
Yates, Donald 197
Yeats, William Butler 83, 104

Zerubavel, Eviatar 87